The
Sound
the
Stars
Make
Rushing
Through
the
Sky

The Sound

the

Stars

Make

Rushing

Through

the

Sky

The Writings of Jane Johnston Schoolcraft

Edited by Robert Dale Parker

University of Pennsylvania Press • Philadelphia

10 9 8 7 6 5 4 3 2 1

Published by
University of Pennsylvania Press
Philadelphia, Pennsylvania 19104-4112

A Cataloging-in-Publication record is available from the Library of Congress

ISBN-13: 978-0-8122-3981-2
ISBN-10: 0-8122-3981-4

Contents

Preface

This book began as a reaction against the routine underestimation of American Indian literacy both for historical times and for our own time. American Indian people left a much larger written record than historians usually realize, and early Indian writers left far more writing than literary historians imagine. If we look enough, we will find it. So far, we simply have not looked enough. Fortunately, that is changing, and I hope that this book will contribute to the change.

I also felt troubled by the near absence of knowledge or discussion about one particular area of literacy: early Indian poetry. That troubled me not simply because I care about poetry but also because I saw a connection between ideologies of poetry and broader ideologies of literacy. Most people, even people who do not care about poetry, still concede it a special status as a marker of high literacy. While I do not believe that it necessarily deserves that status, or that we should necessarily rank one kind of literacy over another, my skepticism will not change that deeply ingrained cultural bias. Moreover, as I discussed in an earlier book, *The Invention of Native American Literature* (2003), I felt troubled by the way that the cultural inflation of poetry into an epitome of high literacy often goes hand in hand with the stereotypical romanticizing of Indian oral culture. The romanticizing of Indian oral culture can have a condescending effect. After Native rituals, songs, and stories get transcribed and translated (usually with little or no credit to the Indian people who worked on the transcriptions and translations), they often get rewritten as poetry by well-meaning whites. Together, these habits reinforce the underestimation of Indian literacy, and for many years they cut actual Indian poets and poetry out of the literary, cultural, and historical conversation because that conversation was already filled to the brim with other texts masquerading as Indian poetry. (They are often fascinating texts, but they are not Indian poetry.)

All these concerns together provoked me to dig into the archives, find early Indian poetry—which I trusted would be there, though for the most part no one was paying attention to it—and edit an anthology of it. That project is now well under way. While working on the anthology, I returned to the poetry of Jane Johnston Schoolcraft, which I had earlier read casually, probably after seeing it mentioned in one of the standard reference books on Native American literature. Schoolcraft's writing, world, and life started to seem more interesting than I had realized, and I found myself with a hunch that she must have written more than people knew, and that manuscripts of her unknown writing must have survived. So I started looking.

Astonished by the scale and the earliness of the Schoolcraft manuscripts, people often ask how I found them, expecting some fascinating tale of lucky coincidence and scholarly derring-do. Lucky coincidence enters the story at one point, but dashing though I am, I cannot emphasize enough that this sort of scholarly magic, such as it is, comes simply from the decision to look for manuscripts, in combination with determined library work and patient follow-through, which I mention simply to encourage future scholars to take a similar path.

Except for a few translations from Ojibwe into English published in her husband's works, Jane Johnston Schoolcraft did not publish her own writings. This book relies mainly on her surviving manuscripts. In the winter of 1826–27, her husband, Henry Rowe Schoolcraft, put together a handwritten magazine that included a potpourri of items, mostly his own writings along with the writings of friends and neighbors, including some by Jane Schoolcraft. Henry, a saver, kept an incomplete copy of the magazine—so far as we know at present, the only copy that has survived—and for over a hundred years scholars paid it little attention. Then, in 1962, a transcribed edition of the magazine appeared, edited by Philip P. Mason. Mason's extensive annotations focused on Henry but also introduced readers to Jane Johnston Schoolcraft and her parents and siblings. It is a fascinating edition, but because the magazine is such a jumble of disconnected materials and does not clearly identify who wrote the various contributions, readers have a tough time finding their way through it. For another thirty years or so, it received little attention. Then gradually, scholars interested in Indian literature started to notice the contributions that Mason attributed to Jane Johnston Schoolcraft, and she began to receive increasingly frequent, if brief, notice in scholarly discussions of early Indian writing and in reference books about Indian writers.

When I returned to read Schoolcraft's poetry in 2002, and when I read Mason's notes and other scholars' references to his edition, several things stuck out, besides the fascinating story of the Johnston and Schoolcraft families. I saw that scholars had often been casual in their reading of the admittedly tangled tale told by the notes, for they attributed items to Jane Schoolcraft that I suspected—or sometimes could tell—that she did not write, and sometimes they included those items in the anthologies that reprinted work from Mason's edition. (See the section in this book on misattributions.) Far more provocatively, though, it sounded as if there were more poems by Jane Schoolcraft surviving in Henry's papers in the Library of Congress, so I looked into Henry's papers. They were hard to get hold of, even on microfilm, but sure enough, a section of the papers was devoted to Jane's poetry. Still, like Henry's various magazines, his papers are a stew of randomness and confusion. There were a group of poems in what I came to recognize as Jane's hand, but not everything in Jane's hand, it turned out, was by her, and not everything by her was in her hand. On top of that, she had other writings scattered here and there across the enormous collection of papers. Things got complicated. Meanwhile, as I began to work through the thicket of Henry's papers in the Library of Congress, receiving only two or three reels of microfilm at a time through interlibrary loan, which cramped my ability to cross-reference different parts of the collection, I started to look for more materials in other places. When I checked the WorldCat database, which gathers together the catalogs of a huge number of libraries, it turned out that only a week before I plugged in Jane Schoolcraft's name, someone had cataloged an entire collection of her poetry that was now suddenly available in, of all places, the Illinois State Historical Library in Springfield, Illinois. To this day I have never connected Springfield with any of the Johnstons or Schoolcrafts, but it was not hard to travel to Springfield from my home in Champaign, Illinois. It turned out that the Illinois State Historical Library was moving (to be absorbed into the new Abraham Lincoln Presidential Library), and as the librarians prepared for the move, they decided that they might as well catalog a bunch of old stuff that had been sitting in boxes for as long as anybody knew. In one of those boxes, they found the hand-bound manuscript of Schoolcraft's poetry. That is where lucky coincidence came in. According to the librarians, I was the first scholar to look at their Schoolcraft manuscript.

By this point, I was hooked. I came to identify with the impassioned scholar-researchers in A. S. Biatt's novel *Possession* (and the movie made from the novel), who obsessively track down a trail of manuscripts that record the writings and lives of two fictional nineteenth-century poets. (Though unlike the fictional scholars, I did not steal any manuscripts!) I followed every trail I could think of, contacted every library I thought might have relevant materials, and traveled to a good many libraries and collections, aided by generous research funding from the University of Illinois at Urbana-Champaign. (At a late stage in the project—though not nearly so late as I naively supposed—the University of Illinois Library purchased the microfilms of Henry Schoolcraft's papers in the Library of Congress, which helped the completion of this project, and which I am deeply grateful for.) If readers find these materials a tenth as interesting as they have become to me, then they are in for a most welcome and pleasing addition to American literary and cultural history.

One of the largest American Indian peoples, the Ojibwe are also known as the Chippewa but increasingly refer to themselves by the more traditional name Anishinaabe. I use another common term, Ojibwe (which itself has a variety of spellings), rather than Anishinaabe, partly because it is Schoolcraft's term.

Typically, I use the English names Jane Schoolcraft or Jane Johnston Schoolcraft, because that is how Schoolcraft signed her name. I have not seen any document that she signed with her Ojibwe name, Bamewawagezhikaquay, though in her home, depending on who spoke or listened and in what language, she was probably used to being called both Bamewawagezhikaquay and Jane. Perhaps, if she had written for Ojibwe speakers who did not speak English, or for people who attributed the same prestige and power to Ojibwe that they did to English, she would have signed her name Bamewawagezhikaquay, but she did not. Many in her small circle of readers were native speakers of Ojibwe, and many of the rest knew some Ojibwe, but all of them were native speakers of English. When I use the name "Schoolcraft" by itself, I refer to Jane Johnston Schoolcraft, rather than to Henry Rowe Schoolcraft (though until now Henry has been the famous "Schoolcraft"). Yet consistency in the use of names is not practical here because context calls for variation and because Jane Johnston lived over half her life before she took the name Schoolcraft. Often, when describing her youth or distinguishing between her and her husband, I use full or first and last names or first names only. For Ojibwe names and other words, I follow the spelling in the source documents, which varies because the Ojibwe language varies and because Ojibwe spelling was not yet standardized, so that the spellings in this book differ from modern Ojibwe spelling.

For biographical information on Jane Johnston Schoolcraft, Henry Rowe Schoolcraft, and the Johnston family I have drawn on many sources, including Chase S. Osborn and Stellanova Osborn, Richard G. Bremer, Elizabeth Hambleton and Elizabeth Warren Stoutamire, and Marjorie Cahn Brazer. But mostly I rely on the primary documents cited throughout the introduction and annotations. These are often unpublished letters and other manuscripts, including many letters between Jane and Henry. They exchanged notes during their courtship, and they wrote each other often during their marriage, because Henry often traveled away from home. Except for the work by Tammrah Stone-Gordon, the extensive historical writing on the Johnston family and on Henry—while impressively researched—remains minimally interpretive, yet sometimes it inclines toward unwitting interpretation directed by unreflective assumptions about white superiority and about how to write history. The work of Johnston family descendents in Hambleton and Stoutamire comes across best, in part because they tend to be more respectful of Indian people. Having searched for and read much of the same material, much of it in manuscript, I greatly admire the dogged research of Bremer and Brazer. Still, while Bremer tries to concentrate on what he calls "facts," he irrepressibly dislikes the people he writes about and describes Jane Johnston Schoolcraft (and Henry's second wife) in dismissively misogynist terms. Brazer says that she will make "no attempt to draw moral conclusions or make value judgments" (xv), implying that facts—and the selection and arrangement of facts—speak for themselves. Yet throughout her study she says things like (speaking of Jane's brother George) "He also continued to spend in a princely fashion. Perhaps the Indian in him could not adhere to the white man's 'pay up or do without'" (209). By contrast with these predecessors, my account of Schoolcraft draws on many different resources, including the heritage of feminism, the perspective of an American Indian studies scholar, the postcolonial rethinking of cultural relations, an engagement with critical race studies, and the background of a literary critic who sees the story of the Johnston and Schoolcraft families through the lens of an interest in Jane Johnston Schoolcraft's writing. Her literary achievement has held no interest for any of the historical writers except Stone-Gordon (see the introduction to this volume). Though the historians and antiquarians have seen a good deal of her writing (albeit not as much as I have), they ignore it, apart from the rare and brief quotation understood as a mere curiosity or, in misogynist terms, as the silly habit of a foolish woman. Instead, they concentrate on the history of the Johnston family. By contrast, I have left out most of the fascinating story of the Johnston family (though I still tell the story, interpreting it differently from my predecessors) so that I can focus on what will prove interesting in relation to Jane Johnston Schoolcraft's writing.

The available biographical information leaves as many questions as answers, which is hardly surprising, for lives are mysterious. Coincidences of motive and chance sort out what gets recorded, and which records survive, and which surviving records are accessible. Previous accounts have sometimes expressed a greater degree of certainty than I claim, even though they often rely on less evidence. I have tried to let the mysteries and uncertainties remain mysterious and uncertain rather than impose a false assurance. When I do not know and the records do not tell us, then I have acknowledged that plainly, whether about things such as Schoolcraft's schooling or marriage or her attitudes towards race. The last is an especially tricky question, since ideas of race in her time and place changed dramatically over her lifetime, and they also differed so vastly from such ideas today that we usually do not even ask the questions in terms that might seem recognizable from her perspective.

In reading the many eyewitness reports and later accounts of Schoolcraft, published and unpublished, I have been struck by how almost every account includes serious inaccuracies. That has proved a lesson about many things. For one, it is a lesson about modesty. It makes me wonder what inaccuracies I may repeat or may add to the story. Over the course of my work on this project, I have corrected many mistaken impressions of my own, which reminds me, as well, that I have surely continued to make errors. The proliferation of inaccurate accounts, especially as the inaccuracies get repeated or even magnified from one account to another, also makes me wonder about the almost inherent tendency for histories to evolve or devolve into versions, and about the odd way historians and critics, writing about Schoolcraft or anything else, often rely on each other without questioning, and without checking the sources to make sure. With that in mind, and with a scholarly disposition to see accounts as versions (for I am, after all, also a scholar and critic of the version-saturated fiction of William Faulkner), I have tried to check original sources as much as possible. I have also checked and rechecked my transcriptions, and in most cases I have had other eyes check them as well. One cannot document everything, but I have tried to leave the trail of sources visible so that future readers and researchers may pursue directions I have not considered or been able to include, and so that they may question my conclusions.

Henry Schoolcraft wrote an enormous amount, indeed, to my mind, an unimaginable amount, such that I wonder if his problems with paralysis owed partly to something like what we now call carpel tunnel syndrome. Readers of Jane Schoolcraft owe a good deal to Henry's facility at writing, whether it was fueled by pleasure or compulsion. He copied out many of her writings, and he saved as obsessively as he wrote. Many libraries have holdings of his correspondence and papers, which are the main source of her writings. The largest collection is the set of Henry Rowe Schoolcraft Papers in the Library of Congress, which take up twenty-eight feet of shelf space and include approximately 25,000 items. One could spend a lifetime reading carefully through his papers, especially as the documents often come in difficult-to-read handwriting, his own and other people's. Although I have spent many hours searching through his publications, papers, and manuscripts from many libraries, human fallibility and the mind-boggling quantity of documents make it likely that I have missed something relevant to Jane Schoolcraft's writing. I hope that others will continue the search.

Readers will see that this book is sometimes critical of Henry School-craft's appropriation or theft of American Indian stories for his own purposes, and yet they may suspect that my work in this volume is much the same. I acknowledge that by thinking otherwise, I may deceive myself. To my thinking, Henry Schoolcraft proceeded very differently from the way that I proceed here. He obscured the identities of the Indian people whose words he presented. He rewrote their stories, and he framed their work and his presentation of it exclusively for colonialist audiences. By contrast, I see my task principally as helping readers, not least Indian readers, to reach Jane Schoolcraft's writing, and I look forward to seeing how new readers, including Ojibwe and Indian readers, will make different things of Schoolcraft's writing and life from what I have made of them.

I have tried to put together an edition that pays full respect to the legacy of Jane Schoolcraft and the cultural world she grew out of. I have tried as well to put together a readers' edition, with accessible texts and a readable set of contextualizing materials and annotations, not weighed down by abstruse academic language. To some scholars' minds, that may mean dumbing down, but to me it means just the opposite. That is, I try to bring scholarly questions out toward the larger audience that makes such questions meaningful in the first place, and I also try to bring that larger audience's practicality and directness into the fusty corners of scholarly arcana. Last, and least, and yet still decidedly, I have tried to produce a scholarly edition. Some might say that a lesser-known writer like Schoolcraft does not deserve such a comprehensive or fully annotated treatment, but it seems to me a given that School-craft deserves the right to sit at last, so to speak, at the front of the bus.

Introduction:
The World and Writings of
Jane Johnston Schoolcraft

By the premature death of Mrs. Schoolcraft was lost a mine of poesy.
—Margaret Fuller

Who was Jane Johnston Schoolcraft, whose writings this book gathers for the first time? At the home where she was born and where she lived for most of her life, outside the surviving wing built for her and her husband, a historical marker stands in memory of her father. It mentions his daughter briefly, apparently as a curiosity, because she married a famous man. Next door, a similar marker at her own home tells about her husband, not mentioning her at all. Little known though she is, she often gets mentioned in the course of comments about her husband, her father, or her much-admired mother, but not mentioned as a writer. In recent years, a small number of Jane Schoolcraft's manuscripts have been published and reprinted, sometimes attracting as many as two or three pages of comment from literary critics, generally limited by minimal or inaccurate information and always pursued with no awareness of her larger body of writing. Thus Jane Johnston Schoolcraft remains a largely forgotten figure, sentenced to the dust heap that until recent decades was reserved for women's writing, women's history, and the history of early American Indian literacy. This book sets out to change that. It brings before the public for the first time Schoolcraft's remarkable body of writing and the fascinating story of her life and work, including her position as the first known American Indian literary writer.

The recovery of the poetry and other writings of Jane Johnston Schoolcraft (her English name) or Bamewawagezhikaquay (her Ojibwe name), Woman of the Sound the Stars Make Rushing Through the Sky, opens a new chapter in American Indian literary history and in American literary history. Beginning as early as 1815, Schoolcraft (1800–1842) wrote about fifty poems (depending on how you count multiple versions) in English and Ojibwe that have survived in manuscript. She also wrote out in English at least eight

traditional, previously oral Ojibwe stories; transcribed and translated an assortment of Ojibwe oral texts, including at least ten songs, sometimes in both
Ojibwe and English; and wrote or translated a handful of additional pieces
of nonfiction prose. Taken together, her extensive body of writing invites
readers to reconsider the role of Indian imagination in American literary
history and to consider an achievement on the order of Anne Bradstreet, the
first known American poet, or Phillis Wheatley, the first well known African
American poet. But unlike Bradstreet and Wheatley, she did not publish
(except for a few translations included with her husband's writings), and
though her friends admired her poetry, today she is almost unknown.
Eclipsed from the historical record by her famous husband, Henry Rowe
Schoolcraft (1793–1864), Jane Johnston Schoolcraft was nevertheless among
the first American Indian writers. She was also the first known American
Indian literary writer, the first known Indian woman writer, by some measures the first known Indian poet, the first known poet to write poems in a
Native American language, and the first known American Indian to write
out traditional Indian stories (as opposed to transcribing and translating
from someone else's oral delivery, which she did also).[1] Her stories became
a key source for Henry Wadsworth Longfellow's sensational bestseller *The
Song of Hiawatha*. Even so, her small body of posthumously published work
has barely started to receive notice, and this volume, which finally makes her
writing available—most of it from manuscripts and appearing here in print
for the first time—will show that what little has been known about her work
only scratches the surface of her legacy.

There is no space in the worn yet stubborn stereotypes of Indian people
to imagine a twenty-year-old Indian woman, fluent in Ojibwe language and
culture, writing the following lines of poetry in English in 1820, but she did:

> The sun had sunk like a glowing ball,
> As lonely I sat in my father's hall;
> I walk'd to the window, and musing awhile,
> The still, pensive moments I sought to beguile:
> Just by me, ran smoothly the dark deep stream,
> And bright silver rays on its breast did beam;—
> And as with mild luster the vestal orb rose,
> All nature betokened a holy repose,
> Save the Sound of St. Mary's—that softly and clear
> Still fell in sweet murmurs upon my pleas'd ear
> Like the murmur of voices we know to be kind,
> Or war's silken banners unfurled to the wind,

Now rising, like shouts of the proud daring foe,
Now falling, like whispers congenial and low. ("Pensive Hours")

Growing up on the St. Mary's River in the northern Great Lakes country, the
pensive young Jane Johnston lived a mostly peaceful, contemplative life, but
she also saw the War of 1812. What brought her to write poetry like this?
How does her writing range and vary, and how do her world and her writing
illuminate each other? With such questions in mind, this introduction describes the world that Jane Johnston Schoolcraft lived in, a world now mostly
lost to non-Native cultural memory. Then, building on that historical landscape, I describe Schoolcraft's poetry, stories, and translations, and consider
the ongoing conversation between her writing and her personal and cultural
histories, including the literary role of her writing, its contribution to the
history of anthropology, and its legacy for American literary history. I thus
offer a cultural history, a literary and cultural biography, and a literary-
critical introduction.

Schoolcraft's life and writings present a remarkable story historically,
culturally, anthropologically, and—far from least—literarily and aestheti-
cally. While across much of Indian America there were other Indian people
like Schoolcraft, they did not leave the store of written records that she left,
or their records have not survived or been noticed, or they expressed their
aesthetic imagination in forms other than literary writing. Nothing like the
story that Schoolcraft provides has reached literary history or found a place
in the dominant American culture's knowledge of its own history. Schoolcraft left a body of literary writing that presents itself both as special, in
writings marked out as literary or as culturally representative, and as routine,
through poems integrated into letters and letters integrated into poems.
Along the way, she left a picture of an Indian world that was part of the
American culture's mainstream, that joined in national and international
reading, thinking, and writing about the cultural, political, and domestic
concerns energizing the broader populace, and that at the same time remained deeply engaged in Native language and story. She brought her
Ojibwe and American worlds together by the unprecedented acts of writing
poetry in an Indian language, writing out English-language versions of Indian oral stories and songs on a large scale, and knowledgeably integrating
Indian language into English-language literary writing. She thus left a written
record that at one moment looks like something produced by a mainstream
American writer and at another moment, whether in a different work or in
the same work, looks like nothing ever seen before in the American literary

imagination or in the broader nation's understanding of its own Indian history.

The Cultural World of Jane Johnston Schoolcraft

Jane Johnston Schoolcraft lived across a wide range of intellectual and cultural worlds—riverside, lakeside, and oceanside; village, small western city, and big eastern city; Ojibwe, French-Canadian, American, Irish, and English—and her poetry, prose, and translations show a corresponding variety of forms and topics. While some of her writings are ephemeral or pedestrian, others are eloquent, lyrical, and emotionally stirring, recording an intensely lived personal life and the perspective of an Ojibwe and American woman caught up in the onrushing disruptions and changes of American colonialism. She was born and grew up in Sault Ste. Marie, in the upper peninsula of the Michigan Territory, where she was also one of the lights of a remarkable family. The Johnstons figured centrally in what by the early nineteenth century was well established as a so-called mixed-blood or métis (French for mixed) culture in the vast American Northwest, now the upper and eastern Midwest. Though the métis culture of the American Northwest was later mostly forgotten from the conquering culture's memory, recent historians have sought to recover it under the name of "the middle ground."[2] Holding oversimplified assumptions about racial categories and manifest destiny, Americans have tended to see themselves as belonging to separate races, imagining crisp boundaries between races and viewing whiteness as the natural, dominating center, the maker and bearer of the future. But from the late seventeenth century until well into the nineteenth century, there emerged in the old Northwest a métis world, "the middle ground," that was neither red nor white in the way those concepts later came to be understood. Instead, it was both red and white at once. It was not so much half-and-half or bicultural as it was its own evolving and mobile space in the cultural landscape.

Jane Johnston Schoolcraft and, each in their different ways, her Ojibwe mother Ozhaguscodaywayquay (Susan Johnston), her Irish-born father John Johnston, and her four brothers and three sisters were all contributors to that Midwest métis world. Bamewawagezhikaquay (Jane) and her sisters and brothers spoke Ojibwe fluently and routinely. In their lifetimes, the Johnston family saw their world shift not only from Ojibwe and French-Canadian cultural dominance to the dominance of the encroaching United States, but also from British rule to U.S. federal rule, with the accompanying changes in language and religion as well as shifts in the sense of centering cultural identity from Ojibwe and French to English and from Montreal to Washington

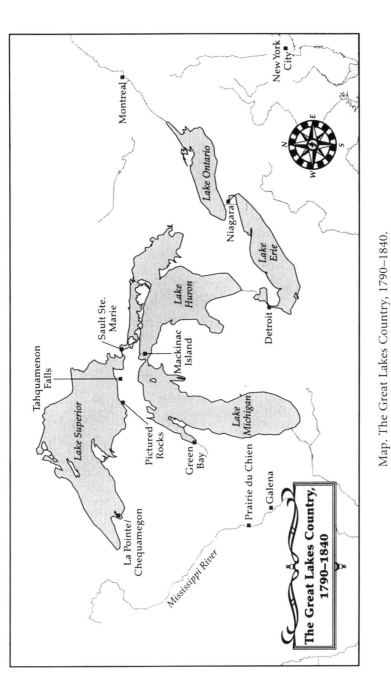

Map. The Great Lakes Country, 1790–1840.

and New York City. In these ways, Bamewawagezhikaquay was both Ojibwe and a United States citizen; she was Ojibwe and métis and white in her sense of cultural identity, a combination that allows her to anticipate the shape and range of many current Native American identities.

Schoolcraft's siblings were Lewis Saurin Johnston (1793–1825, Ojibwe name unknown), George Johnston or Kahmentayha (1796–1861), Eliza Johnston or Wahbunungoquay (1802–1883), Charlotte Johnston McMurray or Ogenebugoquay (1806–1878), William Miengun (Wolf) Johnston (1811–1863), Anna Maria Johnston Schoolcraft or Omiskabugoquay (1814–1856—Anna Maria married Henry's brother James), and John McDougall Johnston or Waubequon (1816–95). The family has already been the subject of a novel (Lewis, *Invasion*), an opera (Lewis and Murray, *Legend*), a children's book about Ozhaguscodaywayquay (Soetebier), three histories (Hambleton and Stoutamire, Brazer, Tomaszewski), and many memoirs and articles. The Johnston family were at once extraordinary and typical. They were extraordinary for their political and social influence in Ojibwe, British, American, and métis cultures; for the records they kept (George may have produced as much surviving writing as any American Indian up to his time—mostly letters, reports, and journals); and for their range of movement, and for their range of movement from everyday to elite cultures, from woodlands and waterways to literary salons and treaty negotiations, from Ojibwe elites to a frontier version of predominantly white high society, from British military service to U.S. officialdom, from menial labor and public disgrace to scholarly investigation into natural history and Ojibwe language, and from British poetry to Native storytelling. Though the Johnstons were extraordinary, I am also arguing that in another sense they were a special case of what may now seem like cross-cultural fluency but in its own time and place was itself as culturally central as it was culturally hybrid. Their trilingual Ojibwe, French, and English world of commerce, cultural exchange, government, and daily life stretched across an enormous expanse of what is now the United States and Canada, an area about a third the size of the mainland forty-eight states. Their stories have been told many times and deserve larger treatment than they can receive here, where the focus rests on bringing Schoolcraft and her writing into American and American Indian literary history. But the Johnston family's story is also partly the story of Jane Johnston Schoolcraft and her cultural and literary world, and so it must be told here as well, however briefly.

Ozhaguscodaywayquay was born in Chequamegon in the mid 1770s, near the present Chequamegon Bay and La Pointe in the northernmost part of what is now Wisconsin. Her father was Waubojeeg, a war chief famed for leadership in war and civil life as well as for eloquence in story and song (including what many accounts refer to as poems, meaning oral ritual and song, not written poetry).[3] John Johnston was born into a Scotch-Irish family in the north of Ireland in 1762. Despite irregular schooling, he was an avid reader. He took great pride in his status as a gentleman, and through that pride he would later come to identify with Ozhaguscodaywayquay's distinguished family and with his own first cousins James and William Saurin (Jane Schoolcraft's second cousins). James became the bishop of Dromore and William a member of parliament and then attorney general of Ireland from 1807 to 1822 (Huddleston). Johnston sought his fortune by another route, embarking for the United States and Canada in 1790 and eventually setting out as a fur trader, traveling by canoe to Mackinac Island and the Chequamegon area. When all but one of his voyageurs—French-Canadian men who hired out as guides and canoeists, and who often spoke Indian languages (more or less) and married (also more or less) Indian women— deserted him, he drew on his reading by comparing his plight to the fate of Robinson Crusoe (Johnston, "Autobiographical" 341). Bored and lonely, he also took up his pen:

> At Lapointe, a poor wand'rer had nothing to do,
> But to think of past pleasures, and mark how they flew,
> His pen he essay'd as a means of relief,
> And thus, in a transport, he vented his grief. ("The Wanderer," *Poetic Remains*)

It seems that his fancy turned to his future, as well as his past, for soon Johnston asked Waubojeeg for the hand of his youngest daughter. But Waubojeeg demurred. He had seen what often happened when white men married Indian women, after the custom of the country, as the whites put it (or in French, *à la façon du pays*). But the white men's typically casual approach to marriage with Indian women was not the custom of Ojibwe country. Rather, it was a custom that colonialist white men imposed on the country, rationalizing their racial double standard by seizing on that phrase to say, in effect, that Indian marriages were not serious marriages, and that since other white men married Indian women and then deserted their wives and children, so they could too. Indeed, it appears that Waubojeeg's sister, Obemaunoquay, married a prominent trader, John Sayer, in about 1780, but when Johnston mentions meeting her, in a letter, he refers to her as "Mrs. Sayer" yet makes no mention of her husband, suggesting that their marriage may have come apart.[4] It hardly seems surprising, then, that Waubojeeg told Johnston to go back to Montreal, which meant traveling about as far as from New York City to present-day Miami, Florida, and mostly by canoe. He

Figure 1. John Johnston. Oil painting by Joseph Wilson, Belfast, 1789.
Restored in 2006 by the Detroit Institute of the Arts. Chippewa County
Historical Society, Sault Ste. Marie, Michigan.

added, however, that if Johnston returned from Montreal in the spring and
still wanted to marry Ozhaguscodaywayquay, then he could. Waubojeeg
must have expected that that would be the end of it, but Johnston returned
to Montreal and then repeated the long trip back to Chequamegon, and
Waubojeeg kept his end of the deal.[5]

Indeed, it may have been a deal between men. Ozhaguscodaywayquay

had no say in the decision about her fate and was horrified to marry Johnston, who gave her the English name Susan. After the marriage, she ran off
to her grandfather, but her father beat her with a stick, threatened to cut her
ears off, and brought her back to Johnston (Jameson 3: 213–15). Neither the
compelled marriage nor the violence enforcing it seems typical of Ojibwe
marriages or Ojibwe fur-trade marriages.[6] We can only speculate about Waubojeeg's motives: perhaps he acted out of respect for Johnston's loyalty, personal friendship with him, or gratitude to Johnston for sharing his dwindling
food supplies the previous winter with the starving family of Waubojeeg's
father, Ma Mongazida, after unscrupulous traders conned Ma Mongazida
out of his supplies. Perhaps Waubojeeg sensed a greater reliability or higher
social status in Johnston, compared to other traders, or perhaps he deferred
to encroaching white authority. Most likely he acted from some combination
of these and other motives. Despite this disturbing start, however, by all
accounts the marriage grew into a happy match between partners devoted to
each other.[7] They moved to Sault Ste. Marie in 1793, where they built a log
cabin that was the largest home in the region, setting up what passed on the
frontier for something like baronial splendor. Though Ozhaguscodaywayquay learned to understand English, and Johnston learned Ojibwe, Ozhaguscodaywayquay spoke only Ojibwe. Even as she adapted to métis life, she held
onto Indian ways, raised her children to respect Indian people and traditions,
and grew into a figure of considerable influence in the Ojibwe world around
Lake Superior.

The success that John Johnston is credited with as a trader owed much
to Ozhaguscodaywayquay's skills and kinship networks. The typical version
of the story proceeds mainly from white, masculine, and capitalist angles
(even in accounts written by women) and so credits Johnston's success as a
trader to his own talents, but that success must have owed a great deal as
well to Ozhaguscodaywayquay's talents, influence, and connections. Over the
years, she also developed skills recognized by white men, for when John died
in 1828 (from multiple illnesses), she took over the business. The Ojibwes
were practiced traders and learned the ways of white traders, but they did
not see trade only in the white traders' capitalist terms. Instead, they also saw
trade as a blend of gift giving and kinship. It seems unlikely that John Johnston would have found much success as a trader without Ozhaguscodaywayquay's kinship network and ability to use that network, and he would have
realized that marrying her would aid his business. The historian Wilcomb E.
Washburn has provocatively suggested that to understand the history of the
fur trade we need to move away from capitalist-based assumptions and to
focus instead on noneconomic or indirectly economic means of exchange,

Figure 2. Ozhaguscodaywayquay. 1826 watercolor copy by Fielding Lucas of an 1826 sketch by James Otto Lewis. American Philosophical Society, Philadelphia, Pennsylvania.

on gifts and on symbolic and aesthetic exchange. To those dimensions, we also need to add the role of kinship.

The fur-trade historian Bruce M. White has argued that gift giving and kinship, reinforcing each other, structured Ojibwe social relations and relations with fur traders (*Significance of Gift Giving*, "Trade Patterns and Gender Roles"). Because they thought in kinship terms, White notes, Ojibwe people from the fur trade era referred to the president, king, and large trading companies as fathers (a usage encouraged by paternalistic whites, I would add) and referred to individual traders as brothers. When they traded or negotiated treaties to get rum, they described the rum as "milk," hence connecting it to the maternal. According to White:

> Frequently, the influence and success that a trader had with Indians corresponded to the strength and renown of his father-in-law. Leading traders often married the daughters of leading Ojibway; in marrying a chief's daughter, the trader gained a powerful ally among his Indian customers. Since the authority of a chief was generally the result of extended kinship ties, the trader may have formed actual ties with a larger number of people. . . . [T]he chief would often distribute the gifts that his son-in-law brought each year to trade. In so doing, the leader gave material demonstration of concern for the welfare of the other Indians within his family or within the larger group, showing that he was worthy, generous, and unselfish. These attributes might strengthen his ties to nonkin.
>
> In any case, gift giving was of continuing importance to the fur trader. Marrying into an Indian family did not lessen his obligation to give gifts; it simply provided him with a previously defined kinship network in which to carry on his gift giving. (195)

White's argument would apply to Waubojeeg, Ozhaguscodaywayquay, and John Johnston even though Waubojeeg died soon after his daughter's marriage. For a trader could gain influence not only through his father-in-law but also through his wife (as White notes in "Trade Patterns and Gender Roles"). Johnston needed kinship relations all the more because unlike most fur traders, who worked for powerful trading companies, he usually worked independently.[8] Given the centrality of kinship, an Ojibwe leader's children might inherit his or her influence, especially if they had the skill to sustain and use it, as Waubojeeg's children apparently did. Ozhaguscodaywayquay, her half-brother Waishkey, and her brother Keewyzi, who both followed her to Sault Ste. Marie, all wielded great authority (Cleland, *Place* 14–27). (Waishkey was close to Ozhaguscodaywayquay's children; this volume includes Schoolcraft's biography of Waishkey and Anna Jameson's sketch of his lodge.) In line with White's model, after John and Susan Johnston (Ozha-guscodaywayquay) moved to Sault Ste. Marie, he "sent her, with a retinue of his clerks and retainers, and in such state as became the wife of the 'great Englishman,' to her home at La Pointe, loaded with magnificent presents for all her family" (Jameson 3: 215). As Susan Sleeper-Smith describes it, "Marital and kinship strategies transformed trade into a social process and mediated the disruptions inherent in disparate and competing economic systems" (4). When European market capitalism met Indian gift-giving and kinship to build the fur trade, Indian kinship and marriage customs could not replace the market (any more than the market could replace Indian kinship systems), but they conditioned it. Moreover, as Indian women inserted white traders into a network of kinship relations, the Indian women also contributed their cultural, linguistic, and technological knowledge, all three central to fur traders, who in most cases depended on—and would have starved without—the Indian women they married.[9] In these contexts, the respect that Jane—and her family and Henry—held for Susan/Ozhaguscodaywayquay would be conditioned by their seeing her central role in the Johnston family's prominence and prosperity.

She and her family were ideally positioned to attract and wield influence, for La Pointe and Sault Ste. Marie were the cultural capitals of Lake Superior Ojibwe culture. If Sault Ste. Marie was the frontier to white people, for the Ojibwes it was a fabled center of lore, trade, and travel. Perched on the border between the United States and British Canada, it lay in the midst of traditionally British and Canadian influence, far from the centers of United States federal activity. Even on the American side of the St. Mary's River, where the Johnstons built their home, the British held sway among the largely French-speaking white people. During Jane Johnston's youth at Sault Ste. Marie, she may almost never have encountered non-métis white women, and her family, like the whites, Indians, and métis around them, identified with the British, not the Americans. It might seem remarkable that the Johnston children could grow up in a place where the only Christians were a few French-speaking Catholics and yet remain decidedly British and Protestant, but coming from Ireland, John Johnston would have found something familiar in being decidedly British and Protestant while living among Catholics.

When the War of 1812 came, John, as a captain, joined the British forces that surprised the Americans and took Mackinac Island in 1812. Though loyal to the British and close to his Indian allies, he also took pride in preventing Indian fighters from attacking American captives. Later, he brought Jane with him back to Mackinac where he helped defend Fort Mackinac—today a state park—against the American attack in 1814, briefly taking command of the fort himself. Young Jane made linen shirts for two Americans captured when American forces tried to advance through woods defended by Indian warriors. Jane's brother Lewis fought on the British side as well and was severely wounded. Meanwhile, American troops ransacked and burned the Johnstons' business and home in 1814, and the Johnstons never recovered financially (and for many years kept trying to win financial claims from both the British and the Americans), though they rebuilt their house and kept living like the local royalty that, on the Indian side, they were.[10]

Throughout, John retained his status as a British subject, even though he continued to live in the United States. From 1814 to 1816 he served as a British civil magistrate and justice of the peace for the Indian Territories (Prevost, Sherbrooke), but in 1817, he wrote his son George: "The Americans are going to pass a bill that will entirely exclude all British subjects from the Indian Trade so that what is to come of us in future—God only knows. I fear there is no other alternative, but to become American citizens" (Letter to George Johnston). But instead of becoming an American citizen, he continued in the fur trade by using his sons' American citizenship, since they were born within American borders.[11]

In a place where newspapers were scarce and books scarcer, John—no ordinary fur trader—built a large library. "I was surprised," wrote one traveler, "at the value and extent of this gentleman's library; a thousand well-bound and well-selected volumes, French and English, evidently much in use, in winter especially" (Bigsby 2: 127; see also Cox 303). As Ozhaguscodaywayquay educated her children into the Ojibwe world, so John taught them to read and write, drawing on his library. According to Henry, John took care "to teach [his daughters] the observance of many of those delacacies [sic] in word and action, and proprieties in taste; which constitute so essential a part of female education" ("Memoir" 64). All the children except Jane left the Sault for up to a few years of schooling in Canada or—for the two youngest—elsewhere in the United States, but mostly they received their English and literary education at home. John Johnston continued to write poetry, and Henry Schoolcraft transcribed his father-in-law's poems into a bound volume (Johnston, *Poetic Remains* LC70).[12] John "never came across good lines in the newspapers, or magazines, without calling attention to them, and reading them out" (H. R. Schoolcraft, "Memoir" 81–82). George, remembered as "a great reader" (Gilbert, "Memories" 631), copied favorite bits of poetry into his notebooks, including passages from Horace and Virgil (in English translation), *Hamlet*, *Romeo and Juliet*, and late eighteenth-century British poetry by Edward Young, Thomas Gray, and Ossian (James Macpherson) (G. Johnston, Notebooks). In letters he mentions Milton, and even Shakespeare's *Timon of Athens* (26 Sept. 1826 to H. R. Schoolcraft, LC6). After Jane's death, George published a book of Episcopal prayers and hymns that he translated into Ojibwe and Ottawa. Charlotte, too, filled note-books with hymns (in English and Ojibwe), songs, and a motley assortment of poems, some attributed to friends, one by Jane and in Jane's hand, but most of them unattributed. Among the unattributed pieces, those poems and snippets of poems that I have managed to identify come from such once more or less famous figures as Lucretia Davidson, James Montgomery, Sam-uel Speed, and Charles Sprague, as well as from Thomas Moore and Byron. This list gives a picture of the poems circulating through Sault Ste. Marie in the 1830s.[13] By then, however, it was easier to gain access to newspapers, magazines, and books than it was in Jane's formative years of reading, when she depended on her father's improbably large library. Henry's memoir of John Johnston and his notes for a memoir of Jane give a picture of the literary and educational world that she grew up in and that shaped her as a poet:

> Mr. Johnston possessed a small, but select library of history, divinity and classics, which furnished a pleasing resource during the many years of solitude, and particularly, the long winter evenings. . . . It was his custom on these occasions, to gather his family around the table, and while his daughters were employed at their needlework, he either read himself, or listened to one of his sons, adding his comments upon any passages that required it, or upon any improprieties or deficiencies in emphasis, punctuation, or personal manners. . . . His knowledge of English history, poetry and bellettres [sic], at least up to the time of Johnson and Goldsmith, was accurate and discriminating. . . . He had read the Tatler, Spectator, etc. with delight in his youth, and thought they could not be too often read. Of the great number of modern candidates for fame . . . he had read comparatively little beyond the works of Scott and Moore and Byron, and some pieces of Southey and Campbell. . . . [O]n this side of the Atlantic, he thought the claims of Irving most undisputed, and read the novels of Cooper with avidity. . . . [T]here are few authors of Great Britian [sic] or America, of whose works . . . I have not heard his judgment. ("Memoir" 63–64)

> Her father . . . directed her reading, and from him she derived, that purity of language, correct pronunciation, and propriety of taste and manners, which distinguished her. Under his direction she perused some of the best historians, the lives of Plutrarch [sic] the spectator and British essayists generally with the best dramatists and poets. . . . [S]he not only acquired more than the ordinary proficiency in some of the branches of an English education but also a correct judgment and taste in literary *merit*. He made it a rule to excite her to throw all her energies into whatever little effort, or essay, she undertook, and thus always to be doing *her best*. (H. R. Schoolcraft, "Notes" 96)

While reading *The Spectator*, Richard Steele and Joseph Addison's news-paper famed for its prose style and cultural criticism, John Johnston and his daughter Jane must have noted Steele's famous story of Inkle and Yarico. Inkle sets out to America, like John Johnston, "to improve his Fortune by Trade and Merchandize" (R. Steele 50). After arriving at the coast, he wan-ders off and finds himself stranded, but is saved by Yarico, a high-born young Indian woman, who cares for him devotedly. Inkle then thanks Yarico, who by then is pregnant with his child, by heartlessly selling her into slavery. Perhaps John and Jane chuckled at, or regretted, the Eurocentric thinness in the story's sense of Native culture. Yarico hides Inkle in a cave. The food she brings him is not prepared food, but merely fruit, and Yarico never appears in the story among her own people, whom she supposes would threaten Inkle. Or perhaps John and Jane, jaded by experience on John's part and reading on Jane's part, took for granted such notions from Europeans who knew nothing of Indian people. Regardless, both John and Jane could hardly read the tale of Inkle and Yarico without recalling Waubojeeg's fear that John would desert Ozhaguscodaywayquay and John's vow to stand by her. They would think of the many fur-trade marriages they had seen, marriages that Jane had seen all her life, and contemplate the difference between those that lasted and the many that broke apart, especially in a world where, as Jane grew up, most marriage partners she might meet would be other fur traders (except during the war). She might well see something of herself in that child of Yarico and the British trader, or think that she could yet find herself to be another Yarico, not exactly sold but still deserted.

For John Johnston as well as for Waubojeeg, this was a fate to fear, and so it is not hard to see why he thought of taking his daughter to his home-land, where he hoped she might meet better chances. In 1809, therefore, John took Jane with him to Ireland and left her in Wexford with his sister Jane Johnston Moore, expecting his sister to provide her with schooling. He con-sidered leaving her in Ireland to stay. But Jane Moore's husband died, leaving her in financial trouble. The sickly young Jane Johnston suffered badly on the voyage and in Ireland (H. R. Schoolcraft, "Biographical" 444), and she missed her home and mother. After three or four months, John returned and brought her to England, where she spent another few miserable months before they took the long voyage back to the Sault in 1810 (H. R. Schoolcraft, "Memoir" 58–59; "Note" 96). Though her stay was brief and trying, contem-porary accounts of Jane Johnston Schoolcraft made much of what they called her Irish education. At a time when few girls attended school, an overseas education was a mark of distinction for any woman on the frontier, still more for an Indian or métis woman. Possibly, like most female poets of her time in Britain and America, she never attended school. Seeming to identify with Portia in Shakespeare's *The Merchant of Venice*, she even copied out a speech where Portia refers to herself as "an unlesson'd Girl, unschool'd, unpractis'd" (LC70). If she did go to school during her short stay in Ireland and under her aunt's straitened circumstances, her schooling was brief. The later trumpeting of her Irish education shows John Johnston's, and then Henry Schoolcraft's, and perhaps Jane Schoolcraft's yearning to exalt their social position.

At the same time, the Ojibwe world of her mother and the multifarious and métis world of the Sault also left their marks on Jane. Her parents' differing worlds offered competing models of femininity, even if Jane would likely have seen Ojibwe and métis models as less prestigious, given the steady encroachment of white authority and the military and political power of upper-class white people like those her father identified with. While we should be wary of romanticizing Ojibwe or métis models of femininity and of supposing that they were more consistent than Euroamerican models, especially given events like Waubojeeg's beating of Ozhaguscodaywayquay to send the unwilling bride back to her arranged marriage, it has to make a difference to our understanding of Schoolcraft's life and writing to keep in mind the range of femininities she lived among. Since we have more record of her mother than of other women around her, and since the sickly Jane (as her letters testify) relied on her mother's attentions even after her marriage, especially during her husband's long absences, it can tell us something to contemplate the model of women's role that Ozhaguscodaywayquay bequeathed her daughter.[14]

Ozhaguscodaywayquay seems to have attracted the respect of everyone who met her.[15] Though her children aspired to a world very different from their mother's, their letters refer to her with relaxed affection and esteem. The fullest account of her, the travel writings of the Victorian art critic and Shakespeare critic Anna Brownell Jameson ("Mrs. Jameson," who would later add to her fame through a close friendship with Elizabeth Barrett Browning and Robert Browning), testifies to Jane's and Henry's devotion to Jane's mother (esp. 3: 70, 184). Ozhaguscodaywayquay carried great influence with Ojibwe leaders, as indicated by the often-told story of how she and George dissuaded them from attacking the treaty delegation led by Michigan Territory Governor Lewis Cass in 1820, convincing them to grant land for an American fort.[16] Jane would have been nearby as Ozhaguscodaywayquay called the leaders to assemble and warned them of the dangers to their people if they attacked the outnumbered American party. She was also renowned for her knowledge of traditional stories and lore. Businesswoman, diplomat, storyteller, and oral historian, she was a physically active woman who caught and preserved the famous local whitefish, regularly paddled her canoe across the broad St. Mary's River, and annually left for the woods to make huge quantities of maple sugar, sometimes returning with as much as two tons.[17] Though Ozhaguscodaywayquay chose not to speak English, when a Presbyterian minister arrived at the Sault, she took an active role in the church (Porter 24 and 31 March 1832; H. R. Schoolcraft, *Personal Memoirs* 400–402, 431). Her assertiveness as a treaty negotiator or a Christian can provoke differing interpretations in contemporary eyes. In one view, she was a traitor to her people. In another, she adapted insightfully to changing times. If she was a traitor, her betrayal at least saved her people from the war that probably would have followed if local leaders had not signed a treaty in 1820.

Ozhaguscodaywayquay/Susan Johnston's nuanced position in the middle ground can help us understand her daughter Jane. While some modern accounts describe Jane as meek, I find another picture in her extensive correspondence, her poetry, and her other writings, a picture that connects more easily to the model of her active mother. Sickly though Jane was, after her marriage she ran the largest household in the area, supervising servants who worked a good deal but also left much work for their mistress, and who required extensive managing. The accounts that describe Jane as meek may underestimate the seriousness of women's work. Much as she may have aspired, as Tammrah Stone-Gordon suggests, to the feminine ideal of "True Womanhood" described in an influential article by the historian Barbara Welter, the prevalence of the cult of true womanhood, with its genteel notions of feminine propriety, has been called into question by scholars who challenge its range outside the privileged classes (which Jane in some ways belonged to), outside white women (a group she belonged to in some ways and in other ways did not), and outside the American northeast. Other traditions of public engagement and self-understanding influenced women's sense of their options both in daily life and in poetry (on poetry, see Bennett), and Schoolcraft took an interest in other models of femininity. Jameson recounts hearing from her "about the female chief" who "fought & headed her people in the last war" (26 Aug. 1837), noting that Schoolcraft "retains a lively recollection of her appearance, and the interest and curiosity she excited" (3: 77). A revealing anecdote also testifies to Schoolcraft's respect for more routine Ojibwe models of femininity. Margaret Fuller, the transcendentalist feminist writer, visited Mackinac in 1843, two years after Jane and Henry left for New York. In her travel account *Summer on the Lakes, in 1843* Fuller recalls observing what she thought was Ojibwe women's "inferior position" and yet also hearing "much contradiction" of her observations. "Mrs. Schoolcraft," Fuller writes, "had maintained to a friend, that they [Ojibwe women] were in fact as nearly on a par with their husbands as the white woman with hers. 'Although,' said she, 'on account of inevitable causes, the Indian woman is subjected to many hardships of a peculiar nature, yet her position, compared with that of the man, is higher and freer than that of the white woman.' "[18] While the term "peculiar" (which may not quote Schoolcraft exactly) takes white models as the norm, the broader claim depends on at least a degree of identification with Ojibwe women.

Indeed, as she grew up, young Jane saw little of white ideals of femininity. Apart from the trip to Ireland and England and her exposure to a modestly wider circle at Mackinac Island during the War of 1812, back home at the Sault, "far from fashion's gaze," as she later put it in one of her poems ("The Contrast," l. 5), Jane, as we have seen, almost never saw a non-métis white woman. Even as an adult, after the Americans visited in 1820 and then took over in 1822 and she lived routinely among English speakers, she was said to speak English with great charm and yet with a curious accent (Jameson 3: 36, Steele 109), which might have had elements of French and of Irish English as well as of Ojibwe.

To get a picture of Jane Johnston's world at the Sault, it can help to consider the local population and culture, largely Ojibwe and French, outside the Ojibwe and British world of her own family. When Jane's parents moved to Sault Ste. Marie in 1793, they found four French families (Anna M. Johnstone, "Recollections") and a seasonally varying number of Ojibwes. For the Ojibwes, the Sault was a summertime hub of people and culture. George Johnston's recollection of the year 1815 describes a typical summer before Henry and the federal garrison arrived. He remembered a

> large and numerous assemblage of Indians at the foot of the falls, and on an eminence was situated the ancient village of the Chippewas, considered as a metropolis during the summer months, and where the Indians living on the southern and northern shore of Lake Superior and its interior portions of the country, congregated to meet on friendly relations, and to spend their time in amusements and in the performance of their grand medicine dance, and to enjoy the abundance of the rapids, yielding such a plentiful supply of whitefish, to warrant sufficient daily food for such assemblages, and at this time the Indians were lords of the soil, free and independent, and fierce as the northern autumnal blast. ("Reminiscences" 606)

In 1814, the Montreal trader Gabriel Franchère described the "inhabitants" of Sault Ste. Marie—meaning the white men—as "principally old Canadian voyageurs married to women of the country. . . . It is to be regretted," he added, "that these people are not more industrious."[19] According to one journal from the 1820 federal expedition, Sault Ste. Marie had fifty Indian families and eighty white men, women, and children (a census that must count racially mixed people as white). According to another, "The inhabitants [that is, the white men] are Frenchmen chiefly, married to *squaws* by whom they have families. There are 8 or 10 houses" (Trowbridge, "With Cass" 144–45; Doty 179). In 1822, John Johnston described the local French and racially mixed population through the lens of his Irish Protestant pride. With what may seem, from the perspective of our own time, like sobering racial prejudice for someone married to and having children with an Ojibwe woman and living in an Ojibwe-speaking home paid for by Ojibwe trade, he wrote: "The Canadians and Halfbloods all over the country are very numerous, and from want of instruction are, if possible, more the slaves of sensuality than the Indians themselves. In fact, they know not what is meant by morality or religion, and from the idea that they are good Catholics would make the task of reforming them arduous indeed" (Letter to David Trimble). As Henry put it, "They work hard as voyageurs, dance away the carnival, and leave all other concerns to the priest" ("Sketches"). By 1826, four years after Henry and the garrison arrived, one hundred and fifty-two civilians (meaning whites and racially mixed people) lived at the Sault, including thirty women, mostly in log cabins weather-boarded with bark (McKenney 158). Even the arrival of troops did not change things enough in Henry's mind. He called Sault Ste. Marie "the Siberia of the American army" ("Sketches"). As late as 1831, a visitor to the Schoolcraft home at Sault Ste. Marie wrote to his brother that "Many & I may say most of the white inhabitants here have Indian wives. There are no young ladies excepting those which are half Chippeway" (Houghton 479). A year later, the new Presbyterian missionary noted in his journal that "There are no unmarried females in the place except two in the mission family who are not of mixed blood" (Porter 15 May 1832). Henry's memoirs describe Mackinac Island, where he and Jane moved in 1833, as the same kind of métis world they had known at the Sault.[20]

Angie Bingham Gilbert, a Baptist missionary's daughter who grew up in the Sault, speaking Ojibwe fluently, late in life wrote a number of talks for women's groups describing her memories of Sault Ste. Marie. A generation younger than Jane, she remembered the years of Jane and Henry's adulthood. For the Indians, Gilbert recalled, Sault Ste. Marie

> was a favorite resort, with its wild romantic beauty of uncut woods, the grandeur of its great Lake, and broad swiftly flowing river with its tossing, clashing, foaming rapids. It was, from the very first, a spot of great romantic interest, both to the Indians themselves, and to their white associates and followers.
>
> At that time, its stationary population of a few hundred, was a curious conglomeration of many nationalities more or less mixed, by intermarriages

with Indians, and represented all classes and conditions of men from almost all parts of the known world: patrician and plebian rich and poor; educated and ignorant; good, bad, and indifferent, *principally*, bad and indifferent. It was the home of a portion of the tribe, and others gathered there in large numbers, at regular seasons of the year. ("Synopsis" 2–3)

Many of the half Indian daughters of the Fur Traders, were beautiful and attractive women; their Indian mothers taking pride in rearing them like white girls, and making their homes, like the homes of white mothers. Some of the women of that region, were famous beauties, their beauty being of a unique type, and their manners quite fascinating. Many married into fine positions at the North, others, going "Below," to compete with their fairer sisters in the fashionable life of large cities. Of course, there were also women of mixed blood, of a plainer sort, and humbler circumstances; but, with the gathering there, of "all sorts and conditions of men" from many parts of the world, some leaving conscience and honors far behind, it can readily be seen, that Romance, might become the Rule, instead of exception; and sad Reality, later, cut with even a keener edge, a trusting heart, than in the greater world outside. ("Basket" 8–9)

Gilbert's exoticizing descriptions suggest the expectations and frames of reference surrounding Jane and her brothers and sisters, especially for women, but they also suggest that what Gilbert paints as exotic must in some ways have seemed routine to those who grew up with it.

The British novelist Captain Frederick Marryat visited Mackinac and Sault Ste. Marie in 1837, scandalizing Henry and many other Americans with his coarse manners (H. R. Schoolcraft, *Personal Memoirs* 562–64; Zanger). Based on the feeble expertise he picked up through gossip from whites and perhaps from métis, he wrote in his diary about the racially mixed social world he found and, without naming names, about Jane and her mother and sisters: "The majority of the inhabitants here are half-breeds. . . . It is remarkable, that although the Americans treat the negro with contumely, they have a respect for the red Indian: a well-educated half-bred Indian is not debarred from entering into society; indeed, they are generally received with great attention. The daughter of a celebrated Indian chief brings heraldry into the family, for the Indians are as proud of their descent (and with good reason) as we, in Europe, are of ours" (Marryat 126). Marryat and Gilbert together offer a picture of the racial and cultural pride, exoticizing romanticization, and defensive sense of backwoods and racial inadequacy that shaped Schoolcraft's daily world and in some ways shaped even her English-identified poetry.

Into this world in 1822 came the ambitious, driven Henry Rowe Schoolcraft as the first federal "Indian agent" for the Michigan Territory, which at that time included present-day Wisconsin and Michigan as well as parts of Ohio and present-day Minnesota, an area far larger than England, Scotland, Wales, and Northern Ireland put together. His charge was to assert American authority against the still powerful British influence, and he came with a garrison of troops to build and occupy a fort. The troops meant more white people in town, including white women, and they brought a garrison library. The Johnstons welcomed Henry into their home until he established his own quarters, and Jane and Henry married in 1823. Some of Henry's and Jane's biographers have speculated that his choice of Jane may have been driven by exoticizing her as romantically Indian or mixed-blood.[21] But that reading unduly lets the general pattern of such stereotypes shape our interpretation in an individual case and in a local world where white men typically married Indian and métis women (Brown, Van Kirk, Sleeper-Smith), and it goes against the extensive record of letters and journals that testify to genuine affection. There was more than mere proximity to draw Jane and Henry together. A stream of visitors from the 1820s and 1830s would testify to her intelligence and charm. He must have had charm, as well, for he made friends easily (though he often had trouble sustaining friendships). Henry's omnivorous intelligence, if not his charm, had made him a budding poly-math, already experienced, at the age of thirty, in manufacturing, the natural sciences, and as an explorer, literary figure, and government official. Jane and Henry both read widely, not a common trait far from cities in an age when books were expensive. They both wrote poetry. (Henry published a good deal of his poetry and wrote much more than he published.)

To be sure, Henry sometimes did exoticize Jane, and, for that matter, most lovers sometimes exoticize their beloveds. Jane could also succumb to the cultural pressure to exoticize herself. Their letters—hers especially—show a playful, mutual exoticizing along with a basking in the literary fun that each must have been excited to find possible with the other. Five months before their marriage, Jane wrote Henry this flirtatious note:

> Miss Johnston presents her Compliments to Mr. Schoolcraft, & desires to tell him that her Mother, begs his acceptance of the accompanying little moc-cucks of maple sugar. Miss Johnston, begs leave to remind Mr. Schoolcraft, of Shakespeare's Merchant of Venice, when Bassanio, comments on the three Cas-kets, one of gold, one of Silver & the last of Lead, in one of which, the picture of Portia, is contained, he repeats—
> "So may the outward shows be least themselves;
> "The world is still deceived by ornament."
> and as he chooses the Leaden one, says—

"Thy plainness moves one more than eloquence."
and is of course fortunate in his choice, Mr. Schoolcraft, may say the same of
the unornamented *moccucks*, they are plain, but the sweet they contain is not
the less fine, & on that account he may be induced to accept them.[22]

In words and objects, this is the métis world: Shakespeare's *Merchant* together with Ozhaguscodaywayquay's moccucks (birchbark containers) of
maple sugar. Modest about her physical charms (her supposed "plainness"),
Jane nevertheless enjoys a pride in herself and her heritage by likening herself
to the wise and beautiful heiress Portia—only then, teasingly, to pretend it is
the moccucks of maple sugar and not her own sweetness that stands in for
Portia. Portia has many suitors from many lands and of several colors, but
she disdains the Prince of Morocco for his "complexion," preferring a white
suitor. To win her hand, a suitor must choose the leaden rather than the gold
or silver casket. Jane's mother, as notes like this one indicate, apparently
approved her daughter's choice, but Jane pretends to run Henry through a
mock test, one she knows he will pass. After all, having won notice for his
writing about lead mining—at that point a labor carried on mainly in the
Midwest and by Indian women (Murphy)—he should know to value the
leaden casket, the plain Jane rather than the golden or silvery white women.[23]

In one of a number of similar notes, apparently penned half a year into
their marriage, Jane moved from *The Merchant of Venice* to *A Midsummer
Night's Dream*: "The Fairy Queen Titania, sendeth greeting to the Powerful
King of Metals," she wrote, "and wishes that his thoughts and diction may
flow as smoothly and as stately as a Swan, on the bosom of an expansive,
beautiful and unruffled Lake, whose plumage he will press whenever he uses
the accompanying Cushion."[24] Here she is exoticized—by herself and perhaps by Henry if her note draws on his conversation—as Shakespeare's fan-
tastic fairy freshly arrived from the "spiced Indian air" (act 2, scene 1)
presumably in India, though the connection to Jane as Indian would not be
lost on either of them. Shakespeare's Titania resists but ultimately must sub-
mit to her king. While the expression "king of metals" usually refers to gold,
Jane as Titania, ready to be mastered by her Oberon Henry, finds her match
in Henry's renown as an explorer for lead and copper.

Six weeks after his arrival at the Sault, Henry recounted a side trip in his
journal. Worth quoting at length, his account gives a feel for the world of
Jane Johnston that was sweeping him away: the Sault among the Johnstons,
the Ojibwe language, the vast northern waterways, the famous Sault rapids,
and the newly emergent American national power that he himself represented. He does not mention the twenty-two-year-old Jane, but her presence

probably contributed to the atmosphere that inspired him to a lyricism outside his usual utilitarian range:

> I went with a pic-nic to Gross Cape, a romantic promontory at the foot of Lake
> Superior. This elevation . . . overlooks a noble expanse of waters and islands,
> constituting one of the most magnificent series of views of American scenery.
> Immediately opposite stands the scarcely less elevated, and not less celebrated
> promontory of Point Iroquois, the Na-do-wa-we-gon-ing, or Place of Iroquois
> Bones, of the Chippewas. These two promontories stand like the pillars of Her-
> cules which guard the entrance into the Mediterranean, and their office is to
> mark the foot of the mighty Superior, a lake which may not, inaptly, be deemed
> another Mediterranean Sea. [T]he Canadians who managed [the canoe], kept
> time in their strokes, and regulated them to the sonorous cadence of some of
> their simple boat songs. Our party consisted of several ladies and gentlemen. . . .
> We moved rapidly. The views on all sides were novel and delightful. The water
> in which the men struck their paddles was pure as crystal. The air was perfectly
> exhilarating from its purity. . . . Directly . . . , the broad view of the entrance
> into the lake burst upon us. It is magnificent. A line of blue water stretched like
> a thread on the horizon, between cape and cape, say five miles. Beyond it is what
> the Chippewas call *Bub-eesh-ko-be*, meaning the far off, indistinct prospect of a
> water scene, till the reality, in the feeble power of human vision, loses itself in
> the clouds and sky. . . . We clambered up and over . . . , till we . . . stood on the
> highest pinnacle, and gazed on the "blue profound" of Superior, the great water
> or Gitchegomee of the Indians. We looked down far below at the clean ridges of
> pebbles, and the transparent water. After gazing, and looking, and reveling in
> the wild magnificence of views, we picked our way, crag by crag, to the shore,
> and sat down on the shining banks . . . , and did ample justice to the contents
> of our baskets of good things. . . . [G]iving our last looks at what has been
> poetically called the Father of Lakes, we put out, with paddles and song, and
> every heart beating in unison with the scene, for our starting-point at Bá-wa-
> teeg . . . , alias Sault Ste. Marie. But the half of my story would not be told, if I
> did not add that, as we gained the brink of the rapids, and began to feel the
> suction of the wide current that leaps, jump after jump, over that foaming bed,
> our inclinations and our courage rose together to go down the formidable pass;
> and . . . down we went, rushing at times like a thunderbolt, then turned by a
> dab of the pole of our guide, on a rock, shooting off in eschelon, and then
> careering down another *schute* or water bolt, till we thus dodged every rock, and
> came out below with a full roaring chorus of our Canadians, who, as they cleared
> the last danger, hoisted our starry flag at the same moment that they struck up
> one of their wild and joyous songs. (*Personal Memoirs* 112–14)

The Canadians—French-Canadian voyageurs and often métis—were now
"ours," beholden to American power, and the vast lakes seemed poised be-

tween inaccessible grandeur and utilitarian reduction to a mere gateway for American destiny.

Henry had come to Sault Ste. Marie looking for a place to settle down, whether in his job at the Sault or in another job that he hoped it might lead to. Born in 1793 into a rising family in central New York state, the precocious young Henry followed his father's work as a supervisor of glassworks, at first successfully, but then he went bankrupt when British imports resumed after the War of 1812. Trading on his scientific talents, he escaped west as an explorer in the Ozarks and then on two trips to what today we call the Midwest, including the 1820 expedition with Governor Cass. Along the way, he gained close connections with Secretary of War John C. Calhoun and with Cass. (Cass, later secretary of war, senator from Michigan, Democratic presidential candidate in 1848, and then secretary of state, remained Henry's major patron.) In 1822 Henry parlayed his connections into the appointment from President Madison to the agency at Sault Ste. Marie. With his new post, for the first time he saw the prospect of financial security and thus felt ready to marry. Of a literary as well as a scientific turn of mind, the energetic, mostly self-educated new agent had canoed up and down rivers and across the Great Lakes, and published two books recounting his travels and the scientific observations that largely motivated them. In his *Narrative Journal of Travels through the Northwestern Regions of the United States* (1821), however, he showed no particular respect for Indian people, and instead saw Indians as interesting savages.[25]

The most authoritative civilian in town and the most eligible bachelor, Henry had the largest income and the best prospects, while Jane was the most eligible woman and the daughter of the previously most authoritative white man. She was raised to marry a white man, and she came with a large dowry. The dowry must have been a strain after the family's financial setback in the War of 1812, but that setback also underlined the advantage of marrying into financial stability. In different ways, both Jane and Henry were social climbers. Henry eagerly sought recognition for his writing and aspired to gentlemanly status. Jane, more delicately, aspired to an upper-class position that her father, proud of his gentlemanly history, tried hard to prepare her for and that, in another sense, growing up on the frontier, away from schools and white women, and with loyalties to her Ojibwe as well as to her European heritage, she could hardly have been prepared for and hardly have had confidence that she could achieve. Each of them must have looked like the other's best chance.

Decades later, rewriting the travel book he published after serving as a member of the Cass expedition that passed through Sault Ste. Marie in 1820, Henry left an impression of the world where Jane Johnston grew up, as well as a sense of his own and Jane's eagerness to testify to their own gentility, on his part crassly and on her part with the charm she was admired for:

> It required but little observation . . . to explore the village of St. Mary's. It consisted of some fifteen or twenty buildings of all sorts, occupied by descendants of the original French settlers, all of whom drew their living from the fur trade. The principal buildings and outhouses were those of Mr. John Johnston and the group formerly occupied by the Northwest Company. . . . There were about forty or fifty lodges, or two hundred Chippewas, fifty or sixty of whom were warriors. . . . Mr. Johnston, the principal inhabitant, is a native of the County of Antrim, Ireland, where his connections are persons of rank. He is a polite, intelligent, and well-bred man, from a manifestly refined circle; who . . . married the daughter of a distinguished Indian chief. . . . [H]is family received us with marked urbanity and hospitality, and invited the gentlemen . . . to take all our meals with them. Everything at this mansion was done with ceremonious attention to the highest rules of English social life; Miss Jane, the eldest daughter, who had received her education in Ireland, presiding. (*Summary Narrative* 76–77)

In the same vein, when Anna Maria Johnston went away to school in Massachusetts, she wrote Jane that she was mortified to find that her hosts "made little difference between Master & Servant" and ate "at the same table" as their servants (16 Oct. 1833), which tells us about the Johnston family's social practices and assumptions. While Jane's letters abound with a solicitude for her servants that seems sincere and unaffected, the Ojibwes and métis could harbor class distinctions and even snobbery like any other people, and the Johnstons' insisted-on gentility must have appealed to the eager-to-prove-himself young Henry.

Henry Schoolcraft would go on to win recognition as one of the first American ethnographers—a pivotal, founding figure in the history of ethnography and folklore.[26] He set about learning the Ojibwe language and writing down traditional Ojibwe stories, and eventually he made the study of Indian people his major life's work. He published a series of books with his versions of Ojibwe stories, uninspiringly titled, in the first version, *Algic Researches* (1839). (Henry liked to make up words. He coined "Algic" by mixing Algonquin and Atlantic.) *Algic Researches*, in turn, was the principal source for Longfellow's *The Song of Hiawatha* (1855), guaranteeing Henry's fame (see Osborn and Osborn). Henry worked hard to study the language and "collect" Ojibwe stories, relying heavily on Ozhaguscodaywayquay, Jane, George, Charlotte, William, Anna Maria, and numerous other Indian people who visited his office over the years and whom he met in his official travels through Indian lands across the Michigan Territory. As Henry wrote in 1822, soon after he arrived in Sault Ste. Marie:

> Fortunately, I have, in my kind and polite friend Mr. Johnston, who has given me temporary quarters at his house, and the several intelligent members of his family, the means of looking deeper into the powers and structure of the language, and am pressing these advantages, amidst the pauses of business, with all my ardor and assiduity. . . . My method is to interrogate all persons visiting the office, white and red, who promise to be useful subjects of information during the day, and to test my inquiries in the evening by reference to the Johnstons, who, being educated, and speaking at once both the English and the Odjibwa correctly, offer a higher and more reliable standard than usual. . . . All [the Johnstons] possess agreeable, easy manners and refinement. Mrs. Johnston is a woman of excellent judgment and good sense; she is referred to on abstruse points of the Indian ceremonies and usages, so that I have in fact stumbled, as it were, on the only family in North West America who could, in Indian lore, have acted as my "guide, philosopher, and friend." (*Personal Memoirs* 107–8)[27]

With his diligence, opportunism, and imagination, Henry was the first person to set out systematically to write down a large body of Native American stories, though in line with the taste of the day, he revised the tales, limiting their value by later standards.[28] As he put it in his memoirs, "I have weeded out many vulgarisms. I have endeavored to restore the simplicity of the original style. In this I have not always fully succeeded, and it has been sometimes found necessary, to avoid incongruity, to break a legend in two, or cut it short off" (*Personal Memoirs* 585; see also 655). Just as Henry's travel writings compromised accuracy, stole from other sources, and snubbed his colleagues to help win him personal fame, so—aided by perspectives easier to reach in our own time, including how such publications can look through the eyes of contemporary Ojibwes and other Native people—we can see Henry Schoolcraft's publication of traditional Ojibwe stories as cultural theft. It seems no coincidence that as he revised the stories for publication, Henry also played a leading role in negotiating a series of treaties to steal Indian lands.[29] Both acts of theft traded on the myth that Indians would disappear, and that if white people did not take over the land and the stories, then both would be wasted. This is not to claim that any publication of stories would be theft; after all, Henry worked with the active collaboration and encouragement of many Ojibwe people. On sending Henry some stories, for example, George Johnston told him that "they can be improved upon at your leisure, & englified. The moral points they contain can be enlarged, as the old man"—Nabunway, the storyteller—"seemed to dwell at lengths upon them" (14 May 1838, LC43). But Henry's extensive rewriting, combined with his minimal crediting of particular Ojibwe people, can lead us to look at his project skeptically. Such skepticism can come also from the last several decades' rethinking of the larger project of cultural anthropology and ethnography and their collusion with international colonialism. With all the eagerness and as little guilt as most white Americans felt in the massive landgrab that led colonialist white America to steal Indian lands and send many thousands of Indian people into forced exile, Henry took cultural and intellectual property to put it on display for the pleasure of white people. He did not prepare the volumes in ways that imagined Indian readers, and his meager acknowledgment of the Johnston family and other Ojibwe collaborators offers only enough credit to particular Ojibwe people as he needed to bolster the supposed authenticity of his own work.

His rationalizing sense that he could achieve a purer Indianness by rewriting what Indian people told him and encasing the tales in genteel sensibilities can also tell our own sensibilities (no less time-bound than his) something about how Henry and perhaps how Jane saw the relation between their social ambitions and Jane's Ojibwe heritage. For although Henry could pressure Jane to adapt to his ways, Jane, like later Native people, could aspire to change and yet also envision change as part of a continuity with the past, both for social ambitions and for literary ambitions.

While some readers will be tempted to read Jane Schoolcraft's poems, with their meter and rhyme, as capitulations to white or canonical ideas of literature, such a response would underestimate and oversimplify her poems, her métis culture, and the history and resources of American Indian literacy and literature. For one thing, many of her poems explicitly participate in Ojibwe language and in Ojibwe cultural self-representation. For another, while the genre of written poetry has non-Indian roots, that does not make it inevitably non-Indian, canonical, or (even when it is European and canonical) bad. Indian writers—like all writers—take what they find and change it, in the same spirit as contemporary Indian writers who rewrite literary history—and who rewrite it with gusto. To tell Indian writers that they cannot use the resources that, like other writers, they inherit from non-Indian traditions would be to lock Indian writers into the worst kinds of small-minded prejudice. English has long since become, among other things, an American Indian language, and its literary traditions are Indian too. We can argue over how Indians rewrite literary traditions, but it only scores cheap and finally harmful points to write Indians out of the chance to produce written literature in the first place, the chance both to remake and even to continue literary traditions as they themselves see fit. Moreover, any claim that Jane Schoolcraft's poetry, not to mention her stories and translations,

Figure 3. The Johnston home, c. 1902. On the right, the wing added
for Jane Johnston Schoolcraft and Henry Rowe Schoolcraft after their marriage
in 1823. Gordon T. Daun Collection, Judge Joseph H. Steere Room, Bayliss
Public Library, Sault Ste. Marie, Michigan.

only reinforced canonical English traditions flies in the face of the massive
effort scholars have undertaken over the last several decades to recover wom-
en's literary traditions, including the heritage of women's romantic poetry.
Schoolcraft wrote poetry in her time and of her time, like any other poet,
and that participation in her own changing and métis world can enhance
rather than diminish the value that her work promises for our recovery of
lost literary, Indian, and American history.

The Personal World

Jane and Henry busily set up a happy marriage. They had a son, William
Henry, eight and a half months after the wedding. Jane's parents built a new
wing onto their house for the couple, an addition that still stands (though
the rest of the house is gone) and is listed on the National Register of Historic
Places (figure 3). Eventually, with federal funding, Jane and Henry built what
for the time and place was an impressive mansion designed to evoke federal
authority in the person of the Indian agent. They named their home Elmwood, and it too still stands and is listed on the National Register of Historic
Places, though remodeled and moved from its original setting to rest next to

Figure 4. Elmwood, built in 1827. Photograph taken before Elmwood was moved to make room for the Michigan Northern Power Canal in 1902. Gordon T. Daun Collection, Judge Joseph H. Steere Room, Bayliss Public Library, Sault Ste. Marie, Michigan.

the Johnston home (figure 4).[30] In the winter of 1824–25, they traveled to New York City. Jane then stayed with friends while Henry went to Washington. Later in 1825, when he traveled back from a treaty council at Prairie du Chien on the Mississippi River, Henry kept a "Private Journal" for Jane. Suffused with affection for her, Henry's private words—which he described as "Thoughts that breathe, & words that burn" (7 Sept.)—sometimes spilled into poetry, silly at times but passionate as well:

> I had been dreaming of home, and stepped in my canoe, with my mind filled with the Subject.
>> Oh Jane, Jane, Jane!
> When Shall I see thee again
>> To smile or to speak, to rejoice or complain
> This may be very bad poetry, but it is good sense. Don't you think so, my guardian Spirit, or rather the guardian spirit of my wife, whom I am sure she has sent to attend *me* on this journey, answer Yes! Then I will go on with my doggerels—

> Thoughts of home will still intrude,
> In the lounsome solitude
> Thoughts of thee, & my return
> In my widow'd bosom burn
> Thoughts of bliss that once was mine,
> Moments passed with thee & thine
> Moments sweet & moments past
> Too sweet to fade, too sweet to last (24 Aug. 1825)

We could see Henry as making light of the Ojibwe notion of a guardian spirit, which figures largely in some of Jane's stories, but his words also seem to appreciate and almost to identify with Ojibwe ideas. And even if we notice that he rhymes "Jane" with "complain," his words, overall, overflow with affectionate enthusiasm. Meanwhile, waiting at home in Sault Ste. Marie and expecting their second child (who would arrive stillborn in November), Jane wrote poems about missing Henry:

> Say dearest friend, when light your bark,
> Glides down the Mississippi dark?
>
> .　.　.　.　.　.　.　.　.　.　.
>
> Say, do thy thoughts e'er turn on home?
> As mine to thee incessant roam. ("Neenawbame," in "Absence")

This was by no means the marriage of convenience that some commentators on Henry have supposed.[31] On the contrary, despite its strains, Jane's and Henry's twenty-year dialogue was in many ways a loving marriage of like minds.

Perhaps it was during their visit to New York earlier that year that someone sketched a portrait of Jane.[32] Henry's memoir records the New York visit in his irrepressibly out-to-prove-himself parvenu's prose, with hints of the trial that the visit wrought on Jane:

> We had held a most gratifying intercourse with a highly moral and refined portion of society. . . . A large part of the interest to others and attention excited arose manifestly from the presence of a person of Indian descent, and of refined manners and education, in the person of Mrs. Schoolcraft, with an infant son of more than ordinary beauty of lineament and mental promise. There was something like a sensation in every circle, and often persons, whose curiosity was superior to their moral capacity of appreciation, looked intensely to see the northern Pocahontas. Her education had been finished abroad. She wrote a most exquisite hand, and composed with ability, and grammatical skill and taste.

Figure 5. Photograph of a portrait of Jane Johnston Schoolcraft. Artist and date unknown, but perhaps from a trip to New York in 1825. The hairstyle matches a date of approximately 1825. Bentley Historical Library, University of Michigan. The original portrait has not been found.

Her voice was soft, and her expression clear and pure, as her father, who was from one of the highest and proudest circles of Irish society, had been particularly attentive to her orthography and pronunciation and selection of words of the best usage abroad. (*Personal Memoirs* 207–8)

We are left to wonder how Jane Schoolcraft would respond to finding her unaccustomed accent and good spelling ("orthography") on display like the teeth of a horse—or a slave—at auction; how that would reinforce her sense of being Indian, being métis, being white; how it might in turn affect her aspirations as a poet who would later write—in Ojibwe—of an isolated spot in Michigan, that

> here, there are no false displays,
> No lures to lead in folly's maze
> Or fashion's rounds to hurt or kill.
> No laws to treat my people ill. ("Lines Written at Castle Island, Lake Superior,"
>   *IL* version)

It is indeed difficult to characterize her aspirations as a poet. She had little chance for "intercourse," to use her husband's word, with literary society. Her best chance for literary conversation would have come on the visit to New York in 1824–25, later visits and several full winters in Detroit, and then a trip to New York and other eastern cities in 1838–39. But there is little sign that she had much to do with literary matters during these modest travels. Mackinac, though much like the Sault, was more bustling and cosmopolitan, with more visitors from afar, but by the time she moved to Mackinac in 1833, Schoolcraft had already completed most of her writings.

Her literary world seems to have consisted mainly of the family library, her father and husband, perhaps her brother George and sister Charlotte, eventually the garrison library (heavy on history, travels, and biography, if Henry's reading notes from his memoirs offer a representative sampling), the occasional officer or officer's wife with literary interests, and now and then a visitor from afar. For a time, the Sault had a Ladies' Reading Club. Schoolcraft's letters show her reading avidly and critically, and taking an interest in style, but—after the early references to *The Merchant of Venice* and *A Midsummer Night's Dream*—not regularly mentioning poetry, drama, or fiction. For literature, she probably relied on her father's books, on newspapers, on the many magazines that her husband subscribed to, and on books that Henry picked up during his travels or that she may have found on their visits to Detroit. Henry's voluminous published and unpublished articles often discuss the full range of writers from the time. His "Private Journal" for Jane in 1825 refers to Alexander Pope and Shakespeare's Falstaff and repeatedly quotes Robert Burns and "our favorite [Oliver] Goldsmith" (25 Aug.), as if he and Jane had a habit of reading those writers together. While Jane Schoolcraft's manuscripts and papers offer no elaborate recognition of other writers, they refer to or quote some of her poetic predecessors: Goldsmith, Thomas Campbell, Hannah More (though More's prose, not her poetry), Hester Chapone, Amelia Alderson Opie, William Robert Spencer, Ann Taylor, and Thomas Green Fessenden. Near the end of Schoolcraft's life, Elizabeth Oakes Smith, at the time a newly popular poet (who would later be forgotten but has started to attract readers again), wrote in response to a letter from Schoolcraft, enclosing a poem to her and calling her "a warm and generous heart self-styled a child of the woods; . . . who has not lost amid the seductions of society, her primitive simplicity and truthfulness of character." As Schoolcraft's reading appears to have ranged across a broad spectrum, so her poetic forms try out a variety of patterns. While her most characteristic lines come in iambic tetrameter and rhymed couplets, her meters and stanzaic forms vary widely. But we have no information outside her poems themselves of anything that Schoolcraft thought about poetry, hers or anyone else's, or how she understood her ambitions or role as a poet. Though she wrote many poems, there is little record of her thinking of herself as a poet by vocation. She was not shy about her poems, however. Contemporary descriptions of her often mention her poetry, so she seems to have been happy to show it to visitors, even if not to editors.

And after a fashion, she did "publish" at least nine poems and five Ojibwe tales in the winter of 1826–27. Winters left Sault Ste. Marie cut off from the rest of the world for five to six months, except for the occasional dogsled or trekker on snow shoes. To help pass the time, Henry put together a magazine, written out by hand. In a letter to C. C. Trowbridge, Henry evoked the long Sault winter and described his new project:

I assure you it is irksome to be shut up for so many dreary months in every year, in this "fag end of creation" . . . secluded from the refinements of civilized society and from all participation in the pleasures of friendly social intercourse. There are times when the mind seeks to unbend itself, recover its elastic[it]y—to live here a person should be a *little over half oyster* that he might *feel* but little,—or *better*, if he were transformed to a swallow, to lie in torpid state till thawed out by the seering [sic] rays of the sun—To get [illegible] this sort of feeling, I have amused myself this winter, or to speak more properly, I have trifled away my time, by writing, once a week, a *jeu d'esprit* paper entitled the "Literary Voyager", which has been brought out on the evenings of the meetings of the Ladies' Reading Club, and afterwards circulated in a select number of families, both *within* & *without* the fort. Believing you will not be displeased to see it, I shall send you the numbers as soon as the navigation opens."[33]

François Audrain, Henry's subagent, wrote George Johnston: "We have had a reading society this winter. Mr. S was the editor of paper [*sic*], (titled Literary Voyager) which was well written and very amusing." Henry filled *The Muz-zeniegun, or Literary Voyager* (as its full name went—"muzzeniegun" is Ojibwe for book, and "voyager" puns on the French-Canadian voyageurs) mostly with his own writing while including pieces from Jane and others in the area. He circulated it beyond the Sault to Mackinac, Detroit, and friends in the East. One copy of most of its pages survives in his papers at the Library of Congress, and Philip P. Mason edited a print edition that appeared in 1962.[34] Nevertheless, Jane Schoolcraft's writing attracted little notice until more recently, and even then the poems and stories in the *Literary Voyager* remained the only writing of hers that scholars took notice of.[35] But much more of Jane Schoolcraft's writing has survived. Much of it is preserved among Henry's papers in the Library of Congress, where a large set of her poetry manuscripts, and additional poems, stories, translations, and other writings appear mixed in with Henry's manuscripts or scattered among their voluminous correspondence. I also found a book of her poetry in Henry's hand in the Illinois State Historical Library, and Henry published an assort-ment of her stories, usually without attributing them to her, in *Algic Re-searches* and various other places. After her death, he published a few of her works in a magazine of his called *Oneota* and two of her poems in his mem-oirs, and there are additional manuscripts and translations from Ojibwe in various other places. (For more information on the surviving copies of her writing, see the annotations to the texts and the appendix on sources and editorial procedures in this volume.)

Despite Henry's carping to Trowbridge, the winter of the *Literary Voy-ager* seems to have been a happy time. Jane and Henry delighted in their son Willy. Jane's exchange with her father, when he wrote a weakly witty poem inviting her to a whist party and she produced a playful, poetic reply, suggests a winning joie de vivre. Jane's poems and prose in the magazine reached out to a wider audience. Then disaster struck. In one day, while Jane was about three months pregnant, Willy caught sick and died, sending Jane and Henry's marriage into a deep sadness, while also launching Jane as poet into that sadly common topic for early nineteenth-century British and American women's poetry, the death of a child. She wrote at least five poems about Willy's death, and for one of those, "To my ever beloved & lamented son William Henry," I have found seven different versions or copies, more than for any of her other poems. Two of the poems about Willy's death appeared in the *Literary Voyager*, along with poems on the same topic by John Johnston, Henry, the presiding doctor (Zina Pitcher, who appears in John Johnston's whist poem and would later be mayor of Detroit), and two others. Though one of Henry's biographers has dismissed Jane's poems about Willy's death, in misogynist terms, as mere "sentimental dirges" wrought from "overstrung nerves" (Bremer 110), in their time and place they attracted interest and admiration. The large number of surviving copies of "To my ever beloved & lamented son William Henry" indicates that Jane and Henry took particular pride in it.

Henry sent Trowbridge a copy, and Trowbridge read it with appreciation and looked forward to seeing the complete set of the *Literary Voyager* on the topic. As he wrote to Henry:

> The lines composed by Mrs. Schoolcraft, which you were so good as to enclose to me, struck me with such peculiar force, as well in regard to the pathos of style as the singular felicity of expression, that I have taken the liberty to submit them for perusal to the Governor [Lewis Cass] and one or two of our other mutual friends. The Governor has advised me to publish them [Trowbridge had connections with the *Detroit Gazette*], and this would accord with my own wish; but a regard to the delicacy of Mrs. Schoolcraft's feelings on this mournful subject, and respect for the continued friendship which you have manifested for me in transmitting this memorial of a mother[']s woe, have induced me to defer their publication until I shall have obtained permission to that effect from Mrs. Schoolcraft and yourself.
>
> Your brother [James] thinks one of the last numbers of the literary voyageur, relating to this occurence, would be very interesting to us, and we indulge the hope that we shall be favored with the perusal of all these fruits of your winter leisure. (11 May 1827)

Henry's response does not survive, but Trowbridge wrote back six months later: "I regret that Mrs. Schoolcraft and yourself decline giving to the world the pleasure of seeing those beautiful lines of Mrs. Schoolcraft's, but I confess that the restriction imposed has rendered them doubly valuable to me," a claim he backed up by saving his copy of the poem.

We probably will never know why Jane Schoolcraft did not publish her writing while Henry published voraciously. There was no market yet for publishing Indian stories, but there was an audience for poetry. While American women poets, led by Lydia Sigourney and numberless anonymous or pseudonymous poets in the newspapers, were thriving in the poetic marketplace (Bennett), still, in many people's minds it was not proper for women to publish poetry (Walker 34–35). In the 1820s, moreover, new poetry was mostly confined to newspapers. Despite Sigourney's growing popularity, the publishing, printing, and transportation industries had not developed enough for a national market in American poetry, which eventually emerged in magazines in the 1830s and then in books beginning about when Schoolcraft died, in the 1840s (Charvat 29–48, 100–105). Poets typically had to fund their own books, and the cost would have made it hard for Jane or Henry even to imagine putting out a book of her poems, though Henry found the money to publish his own work. For all these reasons, though Schoolcraft's choice not to publish remains mysterious, it is not so mysterious as Emily Dickinson's refusal to publish a generation later, because Dickinson had an accessible publishing infrastructure that Schoolcraft never had. Perhaps Henry did not want Jane to publish, but that seems unlikely. He had the usual prejudices of his time and social position, but he took pride in Jane's accomplishments and in their marriage.

While all the many accounts agree on the amiability of the marriage between John Johnston and Ozhaguscodaywayquay/Susan Johnston, the surviving picture of the Schoolcraft marriage is murky. The evidence points in different directions, and the marriage probably vacillated from romance to confusion to stiff, harsh unhappiness and back again repeatedly, perhaps varying, like many marriages, as much from day to day as from any larger patterns of growing tenderness or frosty disengagement. It is often said that the marriage grew cold in reaction to William Henry's death, but the letters argue otherwise, as does Jane's journal from May and June of 1828 (LC60), which overflows with affection for Henry even as she sadly recalls William Henry's death.[36]

It may seem beside the point to speculate about their marriage. After all, they each began to write before they met. But their marriage propelled the writing life that they each grew into, for this was a literary marriage. It gave Henry access to the knowledge about Indian culture and language that he depended on (and exaggerated) for the rest of his career as a public official, writer, scientist, ethnographer, and editor. Henry wrote far more than Jane, and far more publicly, if also, usually, less well. His books about his travels won acclaim in many quarters, though not universally. Despite his modest reputation as a poet, his poetry and especially his articles won enough respect to garner wide publication. Through his omnivorous literary interests as reader and writer, his voluminous correspondence, and even his many subscriptions to periodicals, he offered Jane her main connection to the larger literary world beyond her father's library. Without his encouragement, Jane probably never would have written any stories. He saved her letters and poetry manuscripts, laboriously copied out her poems, even binding them into a handmade volume, and he left two manuscripts of his own writing about her poetry (see the appendices in this volume). There may have been other Indian writers with histories similar to Jane Schoolcraft's, and some of them may have been happier for not marrying someone like Henry Schoolcraft, but with no one to save their manuscripts as Henry saved Jane's, their literary legacy is lost.

Jane's surviving correspondence with Henry shows the vicissitudes of their marriage, and on their own terms the letters, along with Jane's journals, offer a remarkable body of writing; record of a marriage; and record of daily, domestic, intellectual, and spiritual life. While the early letters are touchingly affectionate, as time goes on the letters give way more and more to the practical details of running the household, raising the children, and planning Henry's career. Henry's affection and kindness vary, and across the years, Jane seems more affectionate than Henry. At their most dramatic, Henry's letters sound cold, even cruel. But the harsh moments stand out. More typically, his letters express his love or take care of business. Nevertheless, it may help us understand the misogynist world that Jane Schoolcraft wrote from and wrote about if we look briefly at some of those dramatic moments in their letters. To understand the emotional role of their correspondence, we need to picture a world before telephones, email, faxes, photographs, recorded music, radio, and television: a time when traveling took a long time and often meant going somewhere radically unfamiliar, sometimes with harsh conditions or danger, especially in what was then the West. Jane eagerly, anxiously, sometimes desperately looked forward to Henry's letters, which arrived, if at all, only when a boat happened to reach Sault Ste. Marie or Mackinac Island. Typically, she read them while she was ill, often coughing and bedridden, and overburdened with household responsibilities. She grew to resent being left behind by a husband who traveled for long trips to faraway places for treaty negotiations and legislative sessions that cast the fate of the entire region, and to centers of social, literary, and government life like New York and Washington.

The mixed emotions and hints of their correspondence come across in an exchange from September 1829 as Jane was about to give birth to their son Johnston. In a defensive tone, Henry wrote from Detroit, where he had gone to attend the Territorial Council:

> However long I may be delayed, or wherever it may please providence to carry me, or to put a final stop to my career, doubt not, that you, & you only, are the exclusive object of my undivided love. It is the order of providence that man should be active, & woman quiescent. And it has been our fate to be often separated, and often for considerable lengths of time, since our union. But there

> has ever been but one primary object, in my exertions—to provide a security, *while youth & health remains, for you,* and the *dear little objects* of our love. (12 Sept. 1829, LC36)

While it may be presumptuous to judge Henry's words with confidence, they carry the sound of heavy-handed insincerity. At the least, he is anything but adept in his expression of affection. Jane's response carries more nuance: "I heard of your re-election to the Council, by Mr. Agnew, & have since read it in the Papers, if it is pleasing to you—it is pleasing to me, & I must learn that great virtue of a woman—quiescence" (25 Sept 1829, LC36). Deftly, she submits to his authority, yet at the same time she mocks his misogyny, blames him for taking so long to write when she is supposedly his uppermost concern, and takes pride in an ironic language that he might not recognize (but who can say?)—or else she uses the irony to tease him. This both is and is not the meek woman described by historians and antiquarians of the Johnston family and biographers of Henry. Her words wear the clothing of meekness, but they show a good deal of artful spunk at the same time. In short, in her own way she talked back, and that pattern continued through much of their correspondence.

The harshest moment in Henry's letters to Jane describes the family that she cherished. Writing about "the necessity & importance of a Christian life," he encourages her to join him in his growing faith, and he addresses the obstacles she faced:

> Brought up in a remote place, without any thing which deserves to have the name of a regular education, without the salutary influence of society to form your mind, without a mother, in many things, to direct, & with an over kind father, who saw every thing in the fairest light, & made even your sisters & brothers & all about you to bow to you as their superior in every mental & wor[l]dly thing, you must indeed have possessed a strength of intellect above the common order, not to have taken up some noxious & [*sic*] opinions & feelings, as false & foolish, as flattery & self deceit can be. (24 and 25 November 1830, LC37)

While it seems plausible that John Johnston showed more fondness for Jane than for his other children, it is mean-spirited for Henry to say that to Jane, especially after John had extended preferential treatment to Henry. The phrase "without a mother, in many things" comes across as similarly mean spirited, no less so for its scrupulous qualification, "in many things"; yet it remains true that Jane's beloved mother could not "direct" her in many of the things that Jane aspired to. Regardless, this harsh letter, though revealing, is not typical.[37] Henry continued to show affection for Jane and her mother, and he was devoted to the memory of her father. Her responses to this letter and similar letters of intensifying religiosity joined in Henry's sentiments rather that suggesting a distance between them (7 Mar. 1831, LC37). Revivalism was sweeping the country in those years, a time sometimes called the Second Great Awakening, and Jane often anticipated Henry in his fascination with matters of faith, requesting religious books and writing such pleas as "I anticipate a long, long letter from you—how is your health? how do you spend your leisure hours? but above all, what are your feelings on the great subject of Religion?" (18 May 1828, LC36).

She was interested in other people's views about religion and other topics, but she had her own views as well. One difficult episode in Schoolcraft's family life testifies to her assertiveness and her insistence on women's prerogative in choosing their own course. In 1834, the family went into an uproar about the romance between Jane's younger sister Anna Maria (variably spelled Anna, Ann, and Anné) and Henry's younger brother James, a ne'er-do-well with a history of rakishness, drunkenness, gambling, and violence. According to Henry's biographer Richard G. Bremer, Charlotte (one of the sisters between Jane and Anna Maria) "seized Anne Maria and held her while Mrs. Johnston beat the recalcitrant daughter with the fire tongs. The widow also forbade James the house, an order which he casually disregarded. The frustrated mother then referred the matter to the Agent [Henry] and his wife [Jane], both of whom opposed the match" (157). Bremer's account of the ruckus over what he calls Anna Maria's "infatuation" (in fact it was a long-standing romance that, despite James's faults, led to a happy marriage) does not make visible its dubious reliance on a layered skein of allegations, particularly the report about the violence, which comes from William McMurray's (Charlotte's husband's) denial of Henry's report of James's report of Anna Maria's report of what happened. Though Bremer apparently does not believe William's denial, he relies on William's description of James's conduct, which James's letters deny.[38] We will never know what happened, whether, for example, Ozhaguscodaywayquay/Susan Johnston ("the widow"), herself the recipient of her father's violence to force her into a marriage, resorted to violence to try to keep her daughter from marriage, and did so, ironically, in part because the prospective groom had a history of violence.[39] But we know how Jane responded, for when she read the accusations, and before she saw William's denial, she wrote Charlotte in the firmest terms she could muster[40]:

> But Charlotte there is one thing I cannot palliate ~~much? less~~ approve—& that is your engaging Mamma to ~~such? a? violent course~~ such harsh measures towards Ann, now she is of age no one has a right to lay violent hands on her, ~~don't you~~

~~know that the Law might recover her damages not you~~ she is no longer a minor, neither can she or anyone? be treated as a little child & beside that you cannot find any thing to countenance such ~~harsh~~ treatment in the xxxxxx of our meek & Merciful Redeemer but ~~only~~ all to the contrary & I feel sorry, very sorry that you should have been accessory to such a disgraceful scene for I do not say this to excuse *any* of Ann's conduct for I have condemned it from beginning to end & I have told her so in my last letter but merely express *my* opinion of right & wrong—forgive my frankness & candor you know it is in my nature never to garble the truth xxxxxxx words from an honest & affectionate heart are not quite as bad as *absolute blows* of love— . . . I mourn in dust & ashes—it is indeed bitterness of spirit & sorrow of heart such as I have never known before. ~~Mr. S has lost his favorite sister.~~ (4 Mar. 1834, LC12)

While the families eventually reconciled, in this letter Schoolcraft lays down a rule: no violence in the family, at least not between adults. (The letter was written, in fact, on Anna Maria's twentieth birthday.) She also shows that for basic principles, particularly concerning women's conduct and violence against or by women, she will put aside any supposedly characteristic meekness and speak out frankly. We can see this family squabble as a debate over competing visions of women's propriety. Jane takes a sharp stand on Anna Maria and Charlotte's (and indirectly, their mother's) proper roles. She thinks they should hear each other's views but that in the end Anna Maria is responsible for choosing her own way.

Over the years, she also grew increasingly assertive in questioning or protesting Henry's long absences, both in her poetry and in her letters.

The Boat arrived this afternoon & I was made happy by the reception of your letters, but alas! not as happy as I should have been had you said there was a probability of your returning home.—What necessity is there of your going to Detroit . . . ? A man may be seen too often as well as too seldom for his own good. [B]ut pardon me my dear Husband, I know I have *no right* to speak, but out of the fullness of the heart, the mouth find[s] the utterance—And *if ever* I required support & encouragement since our marriage *it is now.* (22 Nov. 1831, LC37)

I received your letter dated Washington April 10ᵗʰ two or three days ago, & was indeed surprised to find you were still there, & grieved to find you had still to come to New York, & then go back to the Seat of —— (pride & voluptuousness) I was going to say, but I know it is from absolute necessity, & not from the fascinations of such a life that keeps you from your *honorable home*—I believe I never have wished you to act contrary to *duty, public* or *private,* & I would be the last to wish it *now,* though on *many* accounts frequent, *long* absences of the

Head of a *Family* is [sic] injurious, & tho' my own, & the dear Children[']s situation at present, does indeed call for every possible alleviation that common humanity, let alone affectionate care can suggest. . . . I have been just able to get about house, & that is all—& thankful I am to my Manifest God & Father that I am enabled to do that much—but the incessant *trials* I experience daily, to keep up *housekeeping*, with none but the thoughtless, *disobedient* Louisa to assist me, is [sic] wearing out my little remaining strength– If I thought it would possibly meet your sanction, I would this moment break up *housekeeping*—shut up house & go to my dear Mother for awhile, to seek that necessary repose & relief, which, should I not soon get, I should be, "where the wicked cease from troubling & the weary are at rest." (10 May 1836, LC13)

After these words, she then expresses her bitterness that Henry blames her for not writing, when he appears not to have received the letters she has written, and three days later, in another letter, she adds: "I must confess it is worse than Widowhood to be so often, & so long left alone."

As these examples indicate, her protests can take on a sound of petulance or, in more extreme moments, even whining, and often a sound of melancholy, of what today we call depression.

Day after day I drag out a wretched miserable existence toiling against *wind &* *tide*, as it were in the discharge of my domestic duties, which are indeed in their nature (at least some of them) a sore trial to my faith & patience & to mind & body—without the aid & counsel of my natural, *Earthly Protector*,—in a situation & circumstances which would be difficult, or painful to bear even were I blessed with your cheering smile of approbation, encouragement & support——debilitated & worn down as I am—wanting all the little *nameless* kind attentions, so necessary to the comfort of a weak nervous Invalid. Yet in the face of all this—I am obliged to attend *day* & *night, in my own room*, upon Charlotte [a dying Ojibwe third cousin who lived with the family, partly as a servant, not to be confused with Jane's sister Charlotte]. (15 Mar. 1836, LC13)

But the more sympathetically we interpret her loneliness and sickness—along with her work keeping house, running the household, and raising the children—then the more we may see grounds for her complaints. What might look like clinical depression can also look like a sensible concern for genuine difficulties. If "anxious" and "anxiety" sometimes seem like her favorite words, she seems to have good reason for using them. In her story "The Forsaken Brother," Schoolcraft describes the forsaken brother's sister in terms like those she often applied to herself in letters to Henry: "Years, which added to her strength and capability of directing the affairs of the household, also brought with them the desire of society, and made her solitude irksome." Irksome and, we might add, sympathetic.

To help her endure her pains, doctors suggested laudanum, the now-notorious tincture of opium popular at the time but ruinous nevertheless, and devastating for many other nineteenth-century poets from Coleridge to Poe. It appears that some time in the mid-1830s Jane grew addicted, so that the laudanum deepened the pains it was meant to solace. Henry's first biographers, Chase S. Osborn and Stellanova Osborn, draw attention to the remarkable story of *The Black Gauntlet: A Tale of Plantation Life in South Carolina*, an 1860 novel by Henry's second wife, Mary Howard Schoolcraft, which bases part of its plot on a figure like Jane, desperately addicted to opium and abusively sending off her doting children to sneak her surreptitious doses (Osborn and Osborn, esp. 616; Mary Schoolcraft 491–98). But since this episode of *The Black Gauntlet*, like most of the novel, overflows with hatred for black and Indian people, its lurid account of the Jane Schoolcraft character seems anything but trustworthy. It appears that Henry told exaggerated tales of his first wife shaped for the ears of his virulently racist second wife (a white Southerner who fiercely advocated slavery and was horrified, on racial grounds, when her half brother married Jane and Henry's daughter Janee). Nevertheless, though Mary Schoolcraft's story paints an unduly lurid portrait, there are hints in the correspondence that corroborate Jane's addiction. Jane wrote Henry and later her sister Charlotte's husband William asking for laudanum (10 May 1836, LC13; William McMurray); and their friend Dr. Chandler Robbins Gilman, whose 1836 *Life on the Lakes* printed two of Jane's stories from the *Literary Voyager*, wrote Henry about Jane: "I do most earnestly hope that she will persevere in abstaining from the use of all the deleterious matters to which she so unfortunately accustomed herself" (14 April 1839). Perhaps partly because of the laudanum, she wrote far less in her later years.

And perhaps the laudanum contributed to her pattern of avoiding company. Many accounts, including many of her letters, describe Jane as confined from illness. When Jameson recounted her arrival at Mackinac, for example, she wrote that Henry "apologised for whatever might be deficient in my reception, and for the absence of his wife, by informing me that she was ill, and had not left her room for some days" (3: 35). A remark from John Ball, who met Jane and Henry only briefly (indeed this one brief remark is his entire account of them), attributes Jane's seclusion to another cause: "When in Detroit that winter [of 1837] I stopped at the American. . . . Among the boarders were . . . Mr. Schoolcraft, whose wife was a half-breed of the Johnson family. She did not often appear at the table, though well educated in England and a real lady in her manners. When she found herself cut by some of the white ladies when at Washington, she could never get over it, but rather retired from company" (146–47). Ball saw Schoolcraft's isolation as racial. In some ways, he might have been wrong. At the least, he garbled the story. Her family name was Johnston, not Johnson (but that was a common error); she never went to school in England (though she visited England and may have gone to school briefly in Ireland); and she had never been to Washington (but she had been to New York, and she would visit Washington a couple years later). Apart from its errors, however, the gist of the story, that she retired after being cut for her race, has an air of plausibility, suggesting one more reason for her frequent seclusion. We have already seen Henry's story of New Yorkers ogling Jane as the northern Pocahontas. Ball's story carries weight as the kind of story that self-corroborates; that is, if people thought Schoolcraft was ostracized on racial grounds, then that way of thinking in itself helped ostracize her.

While she seems not to have encountered as much racial prejudice as the daughters of Indian women and white fur traders increasingly met across the river in Canada (Van Kirk, esp. 201–30), where her sister Charlotte lived after marrying in 1833, Jane probably heard about the Canadian women's trials, and those stories would have intensified the self-consciousness she felt on her visits east and her stays in Detroit. Early in her lifetime, white traders moved away from their custom of marrying Indians. In 1806, the North West Company forbid its white employees from marrying Indian women, while allowing them to continue marrying métis women. In 1809, two North West agents were fined for allowing a Sault Ste. Marie clerk to marry "a Woman from the Indians" (Brown 97–98). In Jane's adulthood, the expectations continued to shift, with steadily fewer marriages in the northwest fur-trade country between white men and métis women (Brown, Van Kirk). Jane herself transcribed and translated from Ojibwe a song—included in this volume—about an American white man whose love for an Ojibwe "maid" is less than sincere. The middle ground was closing down, and Jane Schoolcraft's once familiar world was disappearing, giving way to a world of Indian removal and racial polarization.

In that painfully shifting climate, Jane's cloistered life of racial, domestic, and sickly isolation and its years-long conversation with Henry's public confidence, fame, and white entitlement had gendered dimensions that went along with her pattern of writing and not publishing and his pattern of writing and ceaselessly publishing. Both of them pondered the relation between gender and their seemingly opposite fates. Jane wrote Henry: "I have often felt the want of your kind support & *authority*[.] . . . *public* duties bring their own fame & reward, when discharged faithfully—but the unobtrusive duties of domestic life are not *even* thought upon with all its cares & troubles & *incessant* appeals to forbearance & patience. Nor is a word spoken, in praise or encouragement to the devoted person who sacrifices health & [illegible] in the fulfillment of those often neglected duties, & yet human nature is the same in *Man* and *Woman*—perhaps the latter requires more in consequence?" (15 Jan. 1838, LC15).

Their self-consciousness about gendered roles drew from and contributed to their thinking about the relation between gender and political life and writing. While I will argue that some of Schoolcraft's poems carry a political dimension, she never wrote about politics in the forthright, more typically masculine style of William Apess. From her depressed and addicted state, and after writing most of her poetry, she even denied the propriety of women's interest in politics: "I cannot enter into the subject of Politicks, I am content to dwell under the dispensations of Providence . . . , & I leave *this* subject to *Men*, altogether, as I think Women have a more appropriate sphere in domestic duties. . . . I care not to be called *unpatriotic*, so long as I obey the laws of the land I live in, without *intermeddling* in the *obvious* duties of the *other sex*—Yet I feel interested in the Canadians. I hope they will succeed in their efforts for freedom, perhaps the U. S. will aid them" (20 Nov. 1837, LC42).[41] She forswears an interest in politics, but cannot resist adding the "Yet." Henry's response, while far from the suffragist or feminist sentiments of a later day, might surprise those who see only his harshness:

> I would have you possess an acquaintance with the general political occurrences of *the age*, and particularly *our own country*. I deprecate the *study* of politics by ladies; but this sentiment is to be received with a proper allowance. There is a great difference between making political events a *study*, and having a general *acquaintance* with them. In Europe there is no discrimination. Neither men nor women are universally intelligent in the subject, but for ladies to pretend to know the difference, between a *monarchy* and a *republic*, a *written constitution*, and a *sovereign will*, is abhorrent! Not so here. Ladies may be intelligent on the subject, without being stigmatized as politicians. Every mother should know her rights, & be able to tell her children theirs. That country where a woman may not allude to state affairs, or entertain an opinion on passing events, is a *despotism*. (22 Jan. 1838, LC43)

For Henry, politics was his daily trade: he was busy administering federal policy for (and against) Indian people, negotiating treaties, writing laws, jockeying for position in federal affairs, and playing the protégé to Governor and Secretary of War Cass. In that context, Jane's relative lack of interest in politics suggests a gendered rejection of—or at least a separation from—Henry's antidomestic busy-ness and careerism.

Still, Henry took it for granted that Jane would share his excited interest in Andrew Jackson, the Democratic president, fabled "Indian fighter," and notorious champion of Indian "removal." When he met Jackson in Washington over the Christmas holiday of 1835, Henry wrote Jane a bubbly, awestruck tale of the meeting. He flattered Jackson and Jackson's secretary's family with gifts from Indian country, including moccasins and "cakes of maple sugar from the north, prepared under the direction of Mrs. Schoolcraft" (25 Dec. 1835 to Mrs. Donelson, 26 Dec. 1835 to J. J. Schoolcraft, LC40). As a Democratic official in federal Indian affairs, Henry actively supported Indian removal. But these many years later, as we recover the legacy of a barely known Indian writer, it gives one pause to think of Jackson and his entourage savoring her gift of maple sugar, and it underlines how Schoolcraft was integrated into the system that exploited her, just as she and her family's cultural and linguistic knowledge were integrated into her Indian-agent husband's efforts to admire, aid, and at the same time conquer, steal from, and diminish her Indian people.

Later Indian readers may recognize the routine complications of mixed allegiances in such a position. Many Indian readers, especially, might also identify with Schoolcraft's sadness in an 1839 poem lamenting Henry's decision to leave their children at eastern boarding schools. Her poem anticipates the widespread practice, especially in later years, of forcibly removing Indian children from their families and sending them off to boarding schools where, in their lonely exile, they often faced beating, cultural and linguistic suppression, and colonialist indoctrination. The practice of sending Indian children to boarding schools had already begun, and Henry opposed it (Bremer 149–50, 183; H. R. Schoolcraft, *Personal Memoirs* 189), though he thought it best for his own children to go to elite boarding schools.

For this poem about her children, Schoolcraft broke her usual pattern and wrote in Ojibwe. She typically spoke to her children in Ojibwe, as her mother had spoken with her, and so the choice of language acts out the poem's lament, and yet we have the poem only because her English-speaking husband, who sent the children to boarding schools, saved it and published it after her death. Henry took pride in his wife's Ojibwe, bragged about her fluency, depended on her and her family for his own frequent writings about the Ojibwe language, and even encouraged her study of Latin and Hebrew.[42] While he sought to cultivate her linguistic skills so that she could help with his research, his linguistic research focused on her Ojibwe language, suggesting a degree of mutuality within his egotistical and opportunistic careerism.

The Literary Writings: Poetry, Stories, Translations

Scholars of American poetry, drawing force from the revolutions of feminist thinking and literary criticism, have extended their studies beyond the charisma of Dickinson and rediscovered the rest of nineteenth-century American women's poetry. A welcome series of insightful studies (Walker, Petrino, Bennett, Gray, Loeffelholz, Richards) has concentrated mostly on women's poetry from the years after Schoolcraft's death, without considering Schoolcraft's work (which was mostly not available). The various and sometimes contesting models that these studies propose may help us understand Schoolcraft, but in the end they do not anticipate her unconventional blend of alternately complementary and competing conventions: "poetess" modesty; Christian piety; eighteenth-century sensibility; Ojibwe and Romantic apprehension of emotion through the natural world; Romantic melancholy; Ojibwe, British, métis, and American family loyalties and rivalries; the patterns and ethos of the English and the Ojibwe languages, both individually and bilingually; and familially based political assertiveness.

For example, she could begin two poems (including one that we looked at briefly above) with the following two sets of extraordinarily different lines.

> Rise bravest chief! of the mark of the noble deer,
>   With eagle glance,
>   Resume thy lance,
> And wield again thy warlike spear! ("Invocation to my Maternal Grand-father")

> The sun had sunk like a glowing ball,
> As lonely I sat in my father's hall;
> I walk'd to the window, and musing awhile,
> The still, pensive moments I sought to beguile:
> Just by me, ran smoothly the dark deep stream,
> And bright silver rays on its breast did beam;—
> And as with mild luster the vestal orb rose,
> All nature betokened a holy repose . . . ("Pensive Hours")

The invocation to her grandfather immediately begins in a Native ethos, defining her grandfather by his totem. It takes pride in his reputation for war and in war's masculine-figured accoutrements, the lance and spear. Along the way, it prolifically mixes meters, boldly shaping a warlike tone by starting with two accented syllables, an imperative verb, and an exclamation mark ("Rise bravest chief!"), then shifting into more melodic anapests capped by an iamb ("of the mark of the noble deer"), followed by two short lines of iambic dimeter before shifting in the fourth line to Schoolcraft's characteristic iambic tetrameter. By contrast, "Pensive Hours" rests more calmly, even musically, in rhymed couplets (roughly following the pattern of an iamb followed by two anapests and then another iamb at the end), as Schoolcraft lingers over emotions recollected in the tranquility of a natural scene like many a Romantic poet of her generation and the generation before her. The Romantic strain continues in "Pensive Hours" as she listens to the river outside her window, but before long it absorbs into its Romantic ethos another sound more like her grandfather's warlike world, for Schoolcraft too had lived through war, and the very home where she reposed had been ransacked and burned by American troops.

> Save the Sound of St. Mary's—that softly and clear
> Still fell in sweet murmurs upon my pleas'd ear
> Like the murmur of voices we know to be kind,
> Or war's silken banners unfurled to the wind,
> Now rising, like shouts of the proud daring foe,
> Now falling, like whispers congenial and low.
>
> .   .   .   .
>
> Such thoughts—the lone moments serenely employed,
> Creating contentment and peace unalloyed—
> Till roused by my harp—which so tremblingly true,
> The soft balmy night breeze enchantingly blew,
> The sounds to my heart as they vibrated clear,
> Thrill'd sweetly and carried the melody tried,
> Softer and sweeter the harmony rings,
> I fanceyed some spirit was touching the strings,
> And answered, or seemed to my hopes, thus to say,
> Let thy Soul live in hope, mortal:—watch still and pray.

Thoughts of war echoing across the murmuring river lead her to that characteristic sound of Romantic poetry, the aeolian harp that catches the wind in the window and transforms it into melody. For her, the harp makes audible an animated universe, a pantheistic apprehension not only Romantic (and a few years later, Emersonian) but also Ojibwe, evoking the Manito- or spirit-populated daily world of the Ojibwe universe. At the last, she holds back the spirit world by a Christian escape clause that tells her that the spirit she fancies only "seemed" to answer her hopes, a turn that Christian readers might take as conclusive and that other readers might take as an unconvincing afterthought. As the next lines reassure her, she rests "At peace with myself, with my God, and mankind," confident that her "prayers were heard and approv'd." Thus Schoolcraft could write in widely varying forms and bring together widely varying ways of thinking, imagining her work through an Ojibwe ethos, a Euroamerican ethos, and a merging of minds that brings Ojibwe and Euroamerican ways of thinking together, making even her most personal, familial, and privately pensive poems reverberate with cultural suggestiveness.

Schoolcraft's datable poems begin in 1815 ("Stanzas Written in 1815") and continue on to the summer of 1840 (several poems included in letters to Henry). Most of them respond to an occasion or place, such as the death of her son or another relative, the waning of a rain shower, a visit to an island or a rock formation, Henry's birthday, his long absences, or in one case, the tragedy of a French family that loses a son to cannibalism. Not planning to publish, she wrote in response to events, rather than following the career plan of a poet before the public. Such a plan would probably have seemed too masculine and egotistical. Schoolcraft could write about private anxieties, including her melancholy sadness and her lonely separation from her husband or children, without fear of censure from the world beyond her marriage or her circle of family and friends. She often wrote, as well, of outdoor pleasures; walking in her beloved garden (described in letters and journals) or escaping to places where she could transform loneliness into pleasure; places such as a "lone glade" ("Nindahwaymau") or a "still retreat" ("Amid the still retreat") where she could find "friendly solitude" ("Relief"), believing that "'Tis the dark shades alone that give pleasure and ease, / 'Tis the union of sombre and bright" ("Lines Written under Affliction"). Often, as well, her poems merge the characteristic pantheism of Romantic poetry, the sense that nature is alive with spirituality, with an Ojibwe sense of a world rife with spirits and animation. Thus she treasures the "Sweet pink of northern wood and glen, / E'er first to greet the eyes of men / In early spring" ("To the Miscodeed"), or she wonders "How wide, how sweet, how fresh and free / How all transporting—is the view / Of rocks and skies and waters blue" ("Lines Written at Castle Island, Lake Superior"). She recalls that she "fanceyed some spirit was touching the strings" of her wind harp ("Pensive Hours"), and she contemplates "watchful spirits in the night," which "guard" or "soothe to rest, where any weeps" ("As watchful spirits in the night").

For her poem in Ojibwe that laments leaving her children at eastern boarding schools, Henry produced what he called a "free translation," expanding her eighteen short lines in Ojibwe to thirty-two long lines in English. Henry's thought-provoking, expanded version probably draws on his interpretation of remarks he heard from Jane. In his version, Jane builds her poem around an opposition between where she and her children come from and where she must leave them, representing where they come from by country, land, her mother, lakes, waters, landscapes of light, winds (suggesting the huge open space of the level Midwestern land and the wind cascading across the wide lakes), song and language ("the lullaby tongue"), her youth, her forefathers with their war lances and plumes, liberty, home, and friends. Henry's version represents the place where she must leave her children by cities, Europe, gloom, learning, and schools, seeing Jane as granting value to schools, but not when they are measured against the pain of separation from her children.

Next to Henry's free translation, a more literal translation (prepared specially for this volume by Dennis Jones, Heidi Stark, and James Vukelich) reads almost like a haiku or an Imagist poem, such as "In a Station of the Metro" (1913), the famous three-line poem that Ezra Pound claims to have pared down from a draft of thirty lines:

Nyau nin de nain dum	As I am thinking
May kow e yaun in	When I find you
Ain dah nuk ki yaun	My land
Waus sa wa kom eg	Far in the west
Ain dah nuk ki yaun	My land
Ne dau nis ainse e	My little daughter
Ne gwis is ainse e	My little son
Ishe nau gun ug wau	I leave them behind
Waus sa wa kom eg	Far away land
She gwau go sha ween	[emphatically] But soon
Ba sho waud e we	It is close however
Nin zhe ka we yea	To my home I shall return
Ishe ez hau jau yaun	That is the way that I am, my being
Ain dah nuk ke yaun	My land
Ain dah nuk ke yaun	My land
Nin zhe ke we yea	To my home I shall return
Ishe ke way aun e	I begin to make my way home
Nyau ne gush kain dum	Ahh but I am sad

The more literal translation can appeal to readers in our own time who might weary of the meter and rhyme that readers of Schoolcraft's day expected, but the difference can also help us appreciate how readers of Schoolcraft's day preferred poems, like her English-language poems, in the style of their time.

In the more literal translation, the lines (apart from the first four lines of stanza 3) are self-contained units of meaning without conceptual or rhythmic continuity between lines, which makes them differ from the usual patterns of European poetry. Without a direct connection between lines, the "you" of line 2 hangs resonatingly open. It can suggest the land as well as the daughter and the son, and perhaps, more openly and mysteriously, it can address whoever might someday read her poem. The separation between lines leaves each line hovering in suspended space, which contributes to the Imagist feeling, yet the lines are empty of images, almost scrupulously spare. Instead of offering images, the poem refers to places, all in the context of the opening line's intransitive act of bare contemplation: "As I am thinking." In that way, the opening line suspends her in thinking without naming or imaging the object that she thinks about, suspends her in the homelessness of a contemplation unmoored from what it contemplates. The opening line's bare, objectless thinking sets off a field of implied object that invites the places referred to later in the poem to reverberate emotionally. Then in the last line, completing the frame that begins with the first line's contemplation, the thinking turns to a direct statement of emotion, instead of the Imagist use of concrete images to represent emotion indirectly.

Within the poem's broader field of intransitive thinking, line 13 stands out for its insistence: "That is the way I am, my being." In that sentence, her being (her ontology) is reflexively its own object. It is not something that she produces transitively (for an object); it is something that is—and not merely is but largely, encompassingly is. It suggests a desire to live in ontological continuity in the midst of what might seem like traumatic cultural change. While that cultural change can seem to render her Ojibwe world as a diminishing past, our readiness to read this poem today, including the readiness of some readers to read it in Ojibwe, gives the lie to any reduction of the Ojibwe and Indian worlds to a state of mere diminishment over the horizon. In that way, this poem registers both Schoolcraft's subjection to cultural self-doubt and an alternative to doubt that she builds by dwelling in the encompassing confidence of being in and of her native land. Indeed, four times she repeats the line "Ain dah nuk ki yaun," translatable as "my land" or (in Henry's translation and in her own translation of the same expression in "To the Pine Tree") as "my native land." It seems no coincidence that two of the three surviving poems that she wrote in Ojibwe, the boarding-school poem and "To the Pine Tree," are about returning to her native land.

While many of Schoolcraft's poems have no forthright political or national dimension, others, such as "To the Pine Tree" and "The Contrast," engage the personal and the familial with what we might call a nationalist commitment to place and people that can resonate powerfully for the later history of Indian literary and political self-consciousness and sovereignty. In notes for a never-written memoir of Jane, Henry recalls Jane describing how relieved and excited she felt to see pine trees again on returning to America from Ireland and England in 1810, and he recalls encouraging her to write a poem about that excitement ("Notes" 96–97; see also "Dawn" in this volume). When Henry put together a manuscript collection of her poems, he began with what must be that poem, "To the Pine Tree," first in Ojibwe and then in her English translation. Recalling her return home after a painful time away, she chose, uncharacteristically, to write in Ojibwe, just as she turned to Ojibwe to write the poem about her children being sent away.

The pine! the pine! I eager cried,
The pine, my father! see it stand,
As first that cherished tree I spied,
Returning to my native land.
The pine! the pine! oh lovely scene!
The pine, that is forever green.

Ah beauteous tree! ah happy sight!
That greets me on my native strand
And hails me, with a friend's delight,
To my own dear bright mother land
Oh 'tis to me a heart-sweet scene,
The pine—the pine! that's ever green.

Not all the trees of England bright,
Not Erin's lawns of green and light
Are half so sweet to memory's eye,
As this dear type of northern sky
Oh 'tis to me a heart-sweet scene,
The pine—the pine! that ever green.

Here in the English version of the poem Schoolcraft recalls her eagerness to verify and legitimate her excitement at the pine trees' confirmation of her return. The poem's repetition seems to search for that same verification and confirmation. Over and over she sings out the pine, the pine! Redundantly, the pine is beauteous and it is happy; it greets and it hails; it is forever green, ever green (twice), and—with the repetition of rhyme—a heart-sweet scene, as if no amount of repetition could be enough to stabilize the child's fearsome discovery that she may be whisked away to another land, far from her mother and her "mother land," perhaps never to return again. While the repetition suggests fear, it also expresses revelry and delight at her return. This is "ain duk nuk i yaun" (line 3), the expression she caresses in the boarding school poem (spelled slightly differently), and which she renders in English here as her "native land" (line 4), the land of her mother. The land seems animated, as well it might to an Ojibwe steeped in Ojibwe patterns of thought and grammar: the trees greet her. Yet more, she feels singled out by their greeting, hailed (line 9) as if the trees spoke not just to anyone passing by but directly to her. In singling out this moment for memory, Schoolcraft also expresses a desire for the trees to speak to her, a sense of her connection to her mother and her mother's land as threatened, and a desire to split that wish off from her needy self and project it onto the pine trees, as if to separate herself from the vulnerability that her own desires might uncover. She wants, as everyone wants, to return to the infant's imaginary world where there is no difference and no absence, to the "forever" (line 6), to the root of generating greenness, the repetition of forever without change. But of course she cannot return to that imaginary world except in the yearning of memory. The world keeps changing regardless of our desires. The personal and familial world changes, and the social world changes, and for Schoolcraft it was easy to identify the two, because her family's union of races and cultures also represented the white world's rapidly growing encroachment on the Ojibwe and Indian world.

That drama of advancing change and difference forms the organizing conflict of "The Contrast." If "To the Pine Tree" yearns to return to a nostalgic sense of a lost Ojibwe childhood and escape from the world of difference and absence, then "The Contrast," right from its title, which contrasts Schoolcraft's anguished present with her happy childhood, admits the impossibility of such return, though it continues to linger in nostalgia for the idealized childhood world that "To the Pine Tree" hopes to recover. Two intriguingly different versions of "The Contrast" have survived. One version—which itself survives in three slightly varying drafts—is self-consciously subtitled "A Splenetic Effusion," with the word "splenetic" implying what we now call depression. Indeed, many of Schoolcraft's poems evoke an air of "pensive" (one of her favorite words) melancholy or loneliness. Schoolcraft's "splenetic effusion" recounts her happy childhood (when "My feelings *ever were* believ'd") and then bemoans how her happiness falls into disarray when she falls in love with Henry, for the drafts of this version are dated March 1823, after Henry's arrival at the Sault in July 1822 and before their marriage in October 1823. The other, apparently later version similarly recounts her happy childhood, but then it decries how her happiness unravels not over her love for Henry but instead over her dismay at the advancing colonial power of the United States.

> But ah! how changed is every scene,
> Our little hamlet, and the green,
> The long rich green, where warriors played,
> And often, breezy elm-wood shade.

How changed, since full of strife and fear,
The world hath sent its votaries here.
The tree cut down—the cot removed,
The cot the simple Indian loved,
The busy strife of young and old
To gain one sordid bit of gold
By trade's o'er done plethoric moil,
And lawsuits, meetings, courts and toil.

Adieu, to days of homebred ease,
When many a rural care could please,
We trim our sail anew, to steer
By shoals we never knew were here,
And with the star flag, raised on high
Discover a new dominion nigh,
And half in joy, half in fear,
Welcome the proud Republic here. ("The Contrast")

As Henry later described the cultural changes that inspired this poem, "The bustle of commerce, and the introduction of courts of law, the establishment of an Indian Agency and of missions for the Indian population, the introduction of schools, churches, elections—these filled the once remote and depopulated village" ("Dawn"). Though the poem never mentions Henry, he was the official and imposing representative of the United States and the new American bustle, so that the second version of the poem implicitly includes and rewrites the first version's personal story in nationalist terms.

If we contrast the two versions of "The Contrast," they suggest that by rewriting her personal, self-consciously splenetic story in nationalist terms, Schoolcraft offers a bracingly colonial reading of her marriage and a personal, conflicted investment in national conflict. On the one hand, she succumbs to identifying with colonialist condescensions in her vision of warriors at "play" and of Indians as "simple." (She also mentions "The simple Indian" in the poem "The Doric Rock.") On the other hand, through more resentful eyes, she sees and fears the coming environmental devastation, the ruthless economic piracy, and the onslaughts of commercialism, legal quagmires, and legalistically rationalized landgrabs. (Her father and her brother George fought seemingly endless legal battles with the federal government, almost along the lines of what Dickens would soon satirize in *Bleak House*.) Schoolcraft's resentment of trade implicates her own family of traders and seems almost to recognize and condemn their role as a leading edge and even a Trojan horse for colonialist conquest. That conquest brought her a marriage that allowed her to enjoy what by local standards amounted to baronial privilege, but at a cost that would lead her to continue second-guessing the trade-offs, the mixture of joy and fear she felt at the "proud Republic" that, with its military garrison right outside her window hoisting "the star flag" every day, loomed suddenly and bewilderingly so very much "here."

Schoolcraft's stories sound sharply different from her poems. She probably approached at least some of her stories more as translations than as her own writing. Either way, they differ from her poems because they come out of a different tradition. Her poems work within Euroamerican models, while sometimes contesting those models. Her stories, by contrast, put the European models of the literary story and the folktale to the service of rendering Ojibwe oral storytelling. While the poems speak in a private voice, the stories speak in a public voice, both as Ojibwe storytelling for Ojibwe listeners and as Ojibwe tales newly written down for an American and even an international, non-Ojibwe public. Through that combination of European and Ojibwe forms, the stories not only tell fascinating tales but also challenge Euroamerican ideas of authorship, so that what it means to say that she wrote her stories, or to call them "hers," or even to call them stories, differs dramatically from what it means to say that she wrote her poems or that, for example, her contemporaries James Fenimore Cooper, Nathaniel Hawthorne, or Catharine Maria Sedgwick wrote their novels. Unlike Cooper, Hawthorne, Sedgwick, or other writers of literary fiction, she wrote versions of traditional oral tales that were first told indefinitely long ago and then passed down through many voices and generations by oral storytellers, who continue to tell them and publish them in other versions.[43] As Henry and Jane started to write down Ojibwe stories, they may have taken indirect inspiration from the growing European rage for folktales. At the least, they responded to the same sense of nostalgic identification with culturally defining stories from the oral past that drove and was driven by tales from such widely varying writers and recorders as Macpherson and the Brothers Grimm. Still, though the first collection from the Grimms appeared in 1812, there is no sign that Jane or Henry knew of the Grimms' stories by the time that Henry published *Algic Researches* in 1839 (though Wilhelm Grimm read Henry's and possibly Jane's work).[44] While in some ways Jane Schoolcraft's stories resemble European folktales more than European literary fiction, nevertheless, traditional American Indian oral stories have their own cultural contexts and patterns.

Schoolcraft grew up hearing Ojibwe stories from her mother, though she probably heard them from others as well, including, for example, her uncle Waishkey. Both Ozhaguscodaywayquay and Waishkey, in turn, would have grown up hearing stories, including from their father Waubojeeg, known for his skill as a storyteller. In this way, Schoolcraft did not make up the stories that she wrote down. According to Henry, "Her mind had in childhood been thoroughly imbued with the lodge-lore and imaginary legends and traditions of . . . the forest . . . , which cover the whole aerial sphere of the heavens, and render the doctrines, the existence of gods and spirits familiar to the youthful ear and eye. They were to her, 'familiar as household work'. She could look, into the heavens, and into the bright tracery of its stars and clouds, and read in them the sublime pictography of the wise men and sages of her forest ancestry" ("Dawn"). On the other hand, when she wrote down stories she did not compose them exactly the same way as earlier storytellers, even apart from writing them in English after hearing them in Ojibwe. In the case of one story, "The Origin of the Robin," one not necessarily reliable source— Gilman—says that "it was taken down by Mrs. S verbatim, from the lips of an old Chippewa woman" (1: 159), but for the most part we do not know if Schoolcraft worked closely from someone else's oral performance as she heard the stories, or soon after hearing them, or if she drew instead on her memory of having heard the stories before. Similarly, we do not know if she tried to reproduce the style and details of particular storytellers or particular instances of storytelling, or if instead she tried to collate or average out the versions she had heard, or certain versions she preferred. Nor do we know whether she sought to translate what she heard or remembered in Ojibwe into a literal English equivalent. Instead, she may have sought a more imaginative rendition with the stamp of her own style. The variety among her stories suggests that she chose different methods for different stories.

Thus if Schoolcraft's authorship draws on the European model, in that she wrote her stories down, it also draws on more communal Native and Ojibwe models passed down orally across the generations. In some ways, Euroamerican writers follow a similarly mixed process, for any given Euroamerican story partakes of various genres that have a long history in many other stories, such as coming-of-age stories, romances, war stories, stories of a bumpkin traveling to the city, and so on. Because most literary readers are so familiar with these models, to the point of taking them so much for granted that they often do not notice them, they notice instead the differences between stories that from a more distant perspective might look more alike. In the same way, in reading Schoolcraft's stories, we might focus on their similarity to other stories of the same kind, stories familiar to many Indian readers, or focus on her own individual role as the author of these particular versions. Here, I seek to introduce "her" stories in a way that can help with both of these approaches, so that we may see their role both as Native, Ojibwe stories and as works from one particular writer's pen.

Like all peoples, American Indians tell stories of everyday life and stories about their history. Indians also have a long, elaborate tradition of telling stories from what is sometimes called "the time before time," or as School-craft puts it in "Mishósha," from "an early age of the world," an age before the world solidified into its present or even its historical patterns. In the time before time, the animal people talked, and people and spirits had powers and vulnerabilities outside the expectations of later times. Such stories include creation stories and other tales about how things changed into their current form. They sometimes evoke comparisons to the biblical story of Genesis or to European folktales and fairy tales, but they are not the same as Bible stories, folktales, or fairy tales. Indeed, Jameson admired Schoolcraft's stories for their difference, for what she called—in condescendingly Eurocentric terms—their "wildness and childishness, and dissimilarity to all other fic-tions" (3: 88). Traditionally, stories of the time before time were oral and could be told only during winter, the longest season in the Lake Superior north country. Beginning roughly with Schoolcraft herself, the stories also come in written form, and they are now often told, written, or read year round. Sometimes they are told with children in mind as listeners, and some-times they play a role in sacred beliefs and rituals. Sometimes that role, or the stories themselves, or particular versions of the stories, are not for public consumption or for the ears or eyes of those who are not designated partici-pants in a particular ritual or who do not belong to a particular people, ritual society, or tradition. Such practices vary across times and places, from one Native nation to another or from one story, set of stories, or version to another, and they vary in the minds of individual Indian listeners, readers, and storytellers.[45]

Schoolcraft's stories weave a range of distinctive patterns within this broader outline of traditional Native and specifically Ojibwe stories. Her sto-ries rarely end in happiness and never end comically; most of them are sad. They usually feature punishment, and their sadness evokes the melancholy that is typical of Schoolcraft's letters and often notable in her poems. Most of the key actors appear at a formative time, more or less at the pivot between childhood and adulthood, an in-between state dramatized with special anx-iousness in the rude and even cruel "boy-man" or "little spirit" in the story of that name. The stories can refer to mundane bodily functions that might not appear in European tales, such as the reference to the young man in "Mishósha" who, we are told, supposedly "stepped out" during the night, or the comic moment when the eagles in "Mishósha" fly over the evil magician and "treated him with great indignity," a "vulgarism" that Henry snipped out from *Algic Researches*. Nor do they shy away from sexuality, but they skip details and minimize the language of sex or bodily functions, and they are never lewd. They often take place on or near a great lake, evoking the visually, ecologically, and culturally central role of water and of Lake Superior in the daily life of Schoolcraft's personal, familial, and Ojibwe world. Indeed, this is the lake world made famous in the lines from Longfellow's *Hiawatha*, "By the shores of Gitche Gumee / By the shining Big-Sea-Water" (157). For readers unfamiliar with the massive presence of Lake Superior and its related waterways in Schoolcraft's part of the world, it may help to note that Lake Superior, the world's broadest freshwater lake, covers an area larger than Scotland, yet it is only one link in the great chain of lakes that surrounds Michigan's upper peninsula.

Like many Indian stories of the time before time, Schoolcraft's stories tell bits and pieces about how the future of the world was made. In the few stories we have from her, however, she does not tell the momentous tale of the world's origin or tell stories of tricksters and culture heroes, which Henry included among the stories that he put together with her help and the help of her family. Instead, Schoolcraft's stories modestly tell what are sometimes called "pourquois tales," like the story of how the camel got its hump or the giraffe its long neck. She tells of the origin of robins or of the spring flower known in Ojibwe as the miscodeed. For the origin of corn, the pourquois tale takes a serious turn, but often the pourquois side of the tales merely winks at an effort to explain the origin of later times, as when they mention casually how sycamores began or how men reached their present size, although even such perfunctory gestures might connect to a larger pattern that takes on more meaning through a ritual or another story. While the stories thus take place before historical time, the "Origin of the Miscodeed, or the Maid of Taquimenon" plays with that pattern by referring to more recent, historical conflicts between Ojibwes and their neighbors the Outagamies (Meskwakis or Foxes) and Dakotas, and by using her great grandfather's name, Mongazida (or Ma Mongazida), for one of the actors, while also setting the scene in the Tahquamenon valley, far from Mongazida's home at Chequamegon but not so far from Schoolcraft's home at Sault Ste. Marie. Such changes in what was most likely an old story may have come across to Ojibwe listeners as playful jabs at the tradition and as traditional ways of remaking and sustaining the story, intensifying its local meaning and infusing the stories and the local ground with a sense of ancient continuity.

The style varies remarkably from story to story. Sometimes, it is burnished into something like a flowing Euroamerican folktale format, as in "The Forsaken Brother," or as in "The Origin of the Miscodeed," with its Christian-sounding reference to a guardian angel (in contrast to the more Indian guardian spirit earlier in the same story and in "The Origin of the Robin"). Other times, the stories follow patterns that would not be recognizable in Euroamerican traditions. Repetitive acts and cadences can retard the narrative flow, as in "Moowis," which may stick more closely than the other

stories to literal translation of an Ojibwe original, or to the repetition produced when someone tries to write down an oral narrative and the storyteller
must pause for the transcriber to catch up, perhaps leading the storyteller to
repeat the previous part before starting again (Tedlock 38). Even if most of
that repetition later gets cut, it can leave a trail in the final text, especially if
the transcriber wants to respect patterns of repetition heard when there is no
transcriber. Like the narrative, time itself in Schoolcraft's stories does not
always flow according to the usual Euroamerican models. Simultaneous actions can progress along different curves in time, as when the young man in
"Mishösha" arrives back at the island before the magician who set out before
him. In "The Little Spirit, or Boy-Man," the little spirit suffers no conse-
quences for his rudeness or cruelty, as readers accustomed to a Euroamerican
model of time, folk narrative, and pedagogical closure might expect. The
story just stops, with the little spirit at the peak of his frightening powers.
Such differences may come from variations in the history behind Schoolcraft's production of the stories, from Henry's editing, or simply from variations in Schoolcraft's taste and her desire to experiment with different
strategies. Perhaps she had more time or desire to Europeanize some stories,
or more desire to retain the Ojibwe feeling of other stories. Or perhaps at
different times she tried more, or tried less, to meet the expectations of white
readers, including her husband, whose expectations themselves cannot easily
be surmised. For just as white readers may have preferred Euroamerican
literary or folktale models, they may also have preferred or even imposed
contrary models that they believed had a more "authentically Indian" sound.

Longfellow responded to the stories in Henry's publications, including
Jane's stories, without knowing that she was the source. In his famous poem
Evangeline (1847), seven years before *The Song of Hiawatha*, a Shawnee
woman warms to Evangeline and tells her a cleaned-up version (with snow
instead of excrement) of Jane Schoolcraft's story "Moowis" (which Henry
published in 1844, after *Algic Researches*), followed by the story of "Leelinau"
from *Algic Researches* (Longfellow, *Evangeline* part 2, section 4). While no
evidence attributes "Leelinau" to Jane Schoolcraft, she may have written or
translated it, or an earlier version of it, and she used the name Leelinau as
one of her pen names in the *Literary Voyager*. Late in life she used the name
to sign letters and notes to Henry. Eventually, the fame of Longfellow's work
took Jane Schoolcraft's writings (however much rewritten by Henry Schoolcraft and Longfellow) around the world, and they came especially to be identified with northern Michigan. Towns, lakes, rivers, counties, schools, and
innumerable businesses across northern Michigan and much of Wisconsin
and Minnesota are named for (or often by) Henry Schoolcraft, or for charac-
ters or places in *The Song of Hiawatha*, but few of the people who live their

daily lives amid those names know of Jane Schoolcraft, and still fewer have the slightest idea how much the writings of Henry Schoolcraft and Henry Wadsworth Longfellow depended on hers.

In the usual European and Euroamerican way that takes credit for "discovering" what millions of Indian people already knew, when Henry first heard the stories told by Ojibwe people at Sault Ste. Marie in 1822, he wrote with astonishment: "The fact, indeed, of such a fund of fictitious legendary matter is quite a discovery, and speaks more for the intellect of the race than any trait I have heard. Who could have imagined that these wandering foresters should have possessed such a resource? What have all the voyagers and remarkers from the days of Cabot and Raleigh been about, not to have discovered this curious trait, which lifts up indeed a curtain, as it were, upon the Indian mind, and exhibits it in an entirely new character?" (*Personal Memoirs* 109). For Henry, such discoveries would turn into a pattern. He made himself famous by asking Ojibwe people to guide him to the source of the Mississippi River and then proclaiming that he discovered it (H. R. Schoolcraft *Narrative of an Expedition*). He made himself famous again by publishing Ojibwe and other Indian stories without attribution. As Cornelius Mathews put it in 1856, introducing a new edition of the stories, "To Mr. Schoolcraft, the large-hearted and able pioneer of the literature of the Indian race, the world is indebted for the discovery of such tales and legends" (iii). The pattern extends across Henry's career. His early travel books routinely included plagiarized material. Breaking an agreement for his second book, Henry cut out his would-be collaborator so that he could take all the credit himself. As federal Indian agent, he negotiated treaties that took land from Indian peoples and funneled money to his own family. In the 1830s he took charge of the Johnston family finances and lost their money in foolish investments (at a time, to be sure, when many people lost money in similar schemes). He followed a corrupt pattern of hiring Johnston and Schoolcraft relatives as federal employees—some qualified, some not—until in 1841 he was dismissed from his post as agent, partly for corruption but probably more because the Democrats lost the presidency to the Whigs.[46] While Henry took too big a share of the credit for his writings as an ethnographer, a student of Ojibwe language, and a presenter of Ojibwe and other Native stories, his work in these areas was nevertheless collaborative compared to the work of other anthropologists in what George W. Stocking, Jr. has dubbed the "Dark Ages" of American anthropology (Bieder xi), and his project of recording and presenting the work was innovative for its time and influential on the later shape of anthropology. In the long run, despite the depredations and misconstruals in his work, in some ways it has also served Indian people who value its contribution to recording their history.

Figure 6. Henry Rowe Schoolcraft, c. 1845–1850. Minnesota Historical Society.

To understand Jane Schoolcraft's role in Henry's work—and his role in hers—it can help to look more closely at how he both presents and masks his dependence on her and her family. Henry's way of presenting the stories that he published in *Algic Researches* and in some of his many other publications tends to make invisible the lives, work, imagination, aesthetic taste, ideas, and interpretations of particular Indian storytellers. Thus when Longfellow begins *The Song of Hiawatha* by asking "whence these stories?" (141), he asks a more searching question than he may have realized. For many of the stories, we will probably never know the degree and form of Henry's dependence on Jane, her mother, the other members of her family, and other Ojibwe people, except to say that he relied on them heavily.[47] Scholars have taken it for granted that we do not have copies of the English translations, produced by Jane and her family, which Henry then revised. Richard Bauman, a leading folklore scholar, at least has the curiosity and frankness to say explicitly what others seem to take for granted. "It is impossible at this late stage," writes Bauman, "to differentiate their editorial work [Jane's and her family's] from his, at least as regards the first published editions of the various narratives" (263). But if we look through the trove of manuscripts that Henry saved, we can find some that he revised for *Algic Researches*, primarily those by Jane, which are included in this volume. There are also several by her brother William, including "Ojeeg Annung; or, The Summer-Maker," the opening story in *Algic Researches*, and "Manabozho," the longest story (LC85).

Just as Henry worked with the Jackson Democrats to support the "removal" of Indian people from their land, so he sometimes seems to try to remove Indian people from their own stories. In a note near the beginning of *Algic Researches*, he says "The materials of these tales and legends have been derived from the aborigines, and interpreted from their languages by various individuals" (56), and then he names twelve people, all of them white men or Indian people with European-derived names. First on the list is "Mrs. Henry R. Schoolcraft," followed by her brother "Mr. William Johnston" and "Mrs. James Lawrence Schoolcraft" (Jane's sister Anna Maria). Eleventh of the twelve is Jane's brother, "Mr. George Johnston." Later, buried within the second volume of *Algic Researches*, he attributes several stories to particular Native storytellers who do not have European names, Chusco and Shagush Koda Waikwa (2: 151, 240).[48] Later, in *Oneota*, Henry shifts procedures, more frequently crediting named Indian people, including Jane and George. Far more typically, though, throughout his work, including *Algic Researches*, he attributes the stories to a generalized Indian nation, usually the "Odjibwa," "Ottowa," or Chippewa. By contrast, in the unpublished *Muzzeniegun, or Literary Voyager*, written out by hand for a circle of friends who would pretty much know or could find out who wrote what, he attributed five stories to Jane Schoolcraft, though he used the pseudonym Leelinau or her Ojibwe name Bame-wa-wa-ge-zhik-aquay. Overall, however, in the published work he tends to offer credit to entire Indian peoples and to himself, not to the storytellers or translators, even though traditional stories of the kind that Henry published vary greatly from one storyteller and translator to another. In some cases, the line between storyteller and translator blurs, because the translator might not rely on a particular performance or transcription of a performance, and instead might retell the story, just as a storyteller retells a story, although the translator would have to adapt it to a different language and a different set of cultural expectations.

In these ways, the stories come to us as if they had little or nothing to do with specific Indian people but instead represented entire "tribes" taken as ahistorical, impersonal lumps and robbed of variation or conflict across people, regions, times, genders, belief systems, and aesthetic temperaments—robbed, that is, of the variations and conflicts that shape the gritty intricacy of any culture. By reading Jane Schoolcraft's versions of these stories as her work, and by reading her other writings, particularly her poetry, we can change our view of the stories that Henry published. Poetry, in particular, offers a kind of writing that we typically read as intensely attuned to the drama of an individual writer's imagination, especially since the era of Romantic poetry that Jane Schoolcraft's writing contributes to. While that way of reading poetry as the direct expression of an individual mind may underestimate poetry's cultural role and heritage, it nevertheless allows us to see poetry as grating against a unitary representation of an entire people, not just now but across their history. In that sense, restoring our sense of Jane Schoolcraft's role in "Schoolcraft's stories" can change our sense of what the wider body of stories published by Henry represents for Indian culture and for the history of anthropology.

In the past, however, Jane's role in the stories has been ignored or seen only minimally and in belittling, derogatory ways. Mentor L. Williams, for example, who edited a modern edition of the stories, defends Henry against the charge that he cut the sexuality out of the stories, pointing out instances where the stories include what a prudish sensibility would have censored. Then, having said that the stories are not prudish, he nevertheless blames Jane Schoolcraft, her sister Charlotte, and other Christian Indians for the stories' prudery: "it must be remembered that part of a complaint such as this must be borne by his [Henry's] informants. The Johnston girls were gentle, secluded, and very Christian; they suffered the same sentimental afflictions to which the females of the time were subject. They were devout and prayerful. . . . It is more than probable that a large number of those stories that were 'marred,' were marred by the teller rather than the recorder" (xx). Williams's misogynist view of the well-read Jane Schoolcraft and Charlotte McMurray as secluded "Johnston girls" devalues Christian Indians, seeing them as inauthentic Indians whose tales of Indian culture are not part of that culture and cannot be trusted. This is a familiar story: whites often see a white who studies Indians as a better, more authentic source of knowledge about Indian culture than a knowledgeable Indian (see Wendy Rose). In much the same way, for many years, later anthropologists have repeated Henry's pattern by cloaking the work of Native colleagues, of "informants" and "assistants," discouraging us from recognizing the learned intellectual work of generations of nonacademic anthropologists of color whose role as anthropologists usually, though gradually less often, remains invisible.[49] The point is not that a given white can never know more than a given Indian, but that many whites overestimate colonialist learning and underestimate, cannot see and respect, Native learning. That underestimation reinforces and is reinforced by the long history of Jane Schoolcraft's invisibility in the production of what has come to be known as (Henry) Schoolcraft's stories.

Again, Henry's contribution to the history of anthropology and cross-cultural understanding was considerable, and I do not want to minimize it so much as to rethink it. He set the pattern for what cultural anthropologists call fieldwork (Bieder), and I would argue that in some ways he also anticipated the later model of participant observation that evolved from fieldwork. In the wake of Henry Schoolcraft's writings, American anthropologists led by John Wesley Powell (Darnell 73) and, more famously, Franz Boas developed fieldwork—going out among the people that a scholar writes about—into an anthropological imperative, whereas later British anthropology, led by Bronislaw Malinowsky, established and also mythologized an imperative and an ethic of participant observation (Stocking), which included not just traveling among the people but actually living with them.

And yet the overestimation of Henry's contribution to the history of anthropology, which masks Jane Schoolcraft's contribution to his work, also masks a deeper incapacity to see Indian culture. While the recovery of Jane Schoolcraft's individual contribution dramatically changes the picture of the dawn of American anthropology, the new picture has to do with much more than her individual role, because it also offers, more broadly, a cultural picture. That is to say, when Williams, whose view of Jane Schoolcraft's role I take as typical, disparages the way that she supposedly let her Christianity and sentiment contaminate the pure Indian stories and culture that Henry recorded for posterity, Williams's reliance on a romantically idealized notion of Indian culture as pure and stable, pagan and unfeeling (unsentimentally "masculine"), misses the fact that Jane Schoolcraft's supposedly impure position is itself a stance within Indian culture. For Indian cultures, like any cultures, have always been changing, and while her sentimentality—if that is what it is—hardly derived from Indian sources alone, Indian cultures' adaptation to the white invasion does not necessarily make their new forms any less Indian, even though they are differently Indian. Native cultures were not changing for the first time, right then at the Schoolcraft moment, solely because of what white people did to them, though that is what many white people fantasize, exaggerating their own agency out of their inability to see Native agency. The stories that Jane and Henry recorded are stories of change going back to the beginnings of human culture, and the stories themselves change, and have changed for millennia, every time a storyteller tells them or an audience hears and interprets them. Jane Schoolcraft's middle-ground Indianness was as Indian as her maternal ancestors' Indianness, but it was differently Indian, just as the Ojibwe-speaking Henry was still white, though his whiteness found itself reshaped by his and his American ancestors' contact with Native peoples.

Moreover, just as Henry was a participant observer in the changing Ojibwe culture, in many ways hostile to that culture yet still anticipating the gradually emerging model of participant observation that came to define modern cultural anthropology, so too, we can now see, was Jane Schoolcraft an ethnographic participant observer in the changing colonialist culture. In her day-to-day life she helped make new models—and in her writing she scripted new models—for Native people and, more generally, for people of the middle ground to interpret the conquering culture. And at the same time, she made available to the conquering culture new models of ancient American history that it would draw on as it struggled for ways to imagine its colonialist self-image—nationalist, guilt-obsessed, and often, as in Longfellow's *Hiawatha* and so much of popular colonialist culture, appropriating, lyrical, and narrative.

Though Schoolcraft's stories vary a good deal, it may help to look at one in particular for an example of questions to ask as we read her stories. "The Forsaken Brother" takes shape through a series of paired oppositions. The first paragraph ends in movingly paired repetitions of rhetoric and character. While the sinking sun echoes the dying man's passing, he speaks in parallel phrases, first to his son and then to his daughter. They respond in a paired phrase, "Never, never!" and he responds in turn by pairing his words to theirs, repeating the pair of words they have spoken, "Never—never!" The father and husband's death then finds its echo in the death of the mother and wife, which itself is then echoed in the brother's departure and then in the sister's departure. Soon, they each marry, sustaining the pattern of pairs. The forsaken brother's song, as well, builds itself out of paired repetitions.

Schoolcraft's little brother William, age fifteen when the story appeared in the *Literary Voyager*, was also named Miengun or Wolf, which would have made the story of a little brother changing into a wolf more memorable to Jane. (The connection to Miengun takes on added poignance given that he and his brother-in-law Henry later forsook each other, becoming bitter enemies.) Ozhaguscodaywayquay and perhaps other family members, including Jane, had probably told him this story, perhaps even teased him with it. He would surely have read it in the *Literary Voyager*, and a copy of the story survives in Miengun's hand. The older brother's astonishment at his brother's turning into a wolf complicates the familiar idea that Indian people take for granted the fluidity of the boundary between people and animals, for both brothers see the transformation as a shock and a crisis. In yet another paired repetition of repetitions, when the older brother calls back to his younger brother's song with the very words from the song, "My brother, my brother," the symmetrical response changes the meaning of the words, substituting resignation for the younger brother's desperate plea for help. At last, after so many pairings and repetitions, the younger brother, the third sibling of three and the odd one out, is the only one who cannot fit into any pairing. He is indeed the forsaken brother.

With her knowledge of the Ojibwe and English languages and traditions, and her experience and skill as a writer of prose and poetry, Schoolcraft was well positioned to translate oral Ojibwe texts into written English texts. Her translations, usually of Ojibwe songs, sound dramatically different from her poems or stories, accenting the distinctiveness of her work as well as her readiness, as a translator, to put her own aesthetic in the background. Yet a good deal of that difference also comes from the contrasting aesthetic traditions of Ojibwe song and English poetry, including contrasts in language, culture, and genre.[50] About two-thirds of her translations are love songs of various sorts. Many of them come in multiple versions, with an Ojibwe text followed by a literal translation and sometimes by a poetic translation. Across the distance of years, with the intervening revolutions of poetic language and form, the literal translations—in a way that no one could have anticipated when they were written—strike a chord more in tune with modern poetry, like the new translation of the boarding-school poem. In that way, the literal translations might appeal to the taste of modern readers more than the metrical poetic translations.

The literal translation of the "Song of Okogis" offers a striking instance:

See how the white spirit presses us,—
Presses us,—presses us, heavy and long;
Presses us down to the frost-bitten earth.

Alas! you are heavy, ye spirits so white,
Alas! you are cold—you are cold—you are cold.
Ah! cease, shining spirits that fell from the skies,
Ah! cease so to crush us, and keep us in dread;
Ah! when will ye vanish, and Seegwun return?

These many years later, readers can probably not resist wondering whether to read this song as an anticolonial protest against white, Euroamerican imperialism. To tell ourselves that this is the song of a frog lamenting how the long northern winter overstays its welcome seems impossibly anticlimactic. Nevertheless, it is indeed the song of a frog complaining about the oppressively cold, lingering winter snow. The repetition suggests the drone of frogs, and the intensity of emotion might evoke what readers of modern poetry, of Robert Frost, for example, have learned to critique as the ceaseless human desire to project our human emotion onto the natural world. And yet we might ask, what is a frog, in a world where a forsaken boy transforms into a howling wolf, and we might wonder whether we can expect the Ojibwe nature of Schoolcraft's world to match the nature of Frost's wintry landscapes or Wallace Stevens's snow man,

For the listener, who listens in the snow,
And, nothing himself, beholds
Nothing that is not there and the nothing that is. (Stevens 10)

It seems unlikely that Henry Schoolcraft ever read a racial reference into the "Song of the Okogis, or Frog in Spring," and not necessarily likely that Jane Schoolcraft did. Probably later readers should not either, but that cannot stop us from wondering whether we might. We read in a world very different from Schoolcraft's world, as evidenced merely by the desire to publish her writings that she never chose to publish, let alone by the desire to read her work in such contexts as early American women's writing, American Indian literature, mixed-race culture, modern literary criticism, Irish-American literature, and college English classes. The song's commanding act—beginning with the opening imperative, "See"—of identifying with a melancholy frog who feels the white spirit pressing, pressing, pressing heavy and long, who feels that white spirit as heavy and cold, cold, repetitively cold, who wants that crushing spirit to go away yet knows that, even after it goes, the spirit will nevertheless continue the ominous repetition and return again—that commanding act calls on us to see what we otherwise might not believe that we could see.

The Final Years

In her last years, Schoolcraft's life changed in many ways. In 1839, her children left for their boarding schools, and *Algic Researches* appeared, the book that was supposed to—and in many ways did—make Henry's fame. Henry got embroiled in the fierce dispute with William and the federal government (1840–41, Bremer 196–206) and was dismissed from office. Jane and Henry left her homeland and family for New York City, where they had to start their lives over, and where Henry had no job. Over these years, the letters between Jane and Henry vary a good deal. Often, their affection comes across, as in a letter addressed to *"My dearest Husband"*: "I hope you will come home soon. I feel lost in this big house without you, & feel very lonesome at times, especially in the evenings. Try & get some new *publications* to read. Ever most truly your affectionate Jane J. Schoolcraft" (11 July 1839, LC44). Some of Jane's letters from 1840 sound cheery and charming. Perhaps they indicate an extra effort to support her husband during the federal investigation. In a letter of 8 June 1840, for example, signed in three places with her old pen name, Leelinau, she twice breaks into flirtatious verse, as in this couplet that she squeezes into a margin: "My ear-rings are gone, in the Wars of Fate—/ And a pair of red-drops I would not hate. Leelinau." When Henry next travels, however, almost a year later, she resumes their correspondence with trepidation, as if something had happened to strain their relations: "In accordance with the practice of days of 'Auld lang syne', when I used to count the months, days & hours, during the many long absences you have made from me & my little ones, I again have recourse to pen, ink & paper, prompted by love as well as duty, to use them as the medium of reiterating the long established feelings of days of *yore*—& to tell you, how we are . . . —trusting that, reciprocal feelings of interest still exist to justify the demand on your time, patience & indulgence & of my expression of them" (24 Apr. 1841, LC46). But again, such letters stand out. They are not typical. Indeed, in her next letter (10 July 1841, LC46, almost three months later), she writes to him with eagerness.

The investigation into Henry's corruption and the loss of his job as agent hit hard at Jane Schoolcraft's pride. Even the servants treated her differently, as she wrote Henry:

I feel very anxious indeed to have you & the dear children around me once more, after experiencing the disagreeable effects of being left alone with those who make me constantly feel, that I am not at liberty to ask for *that aid*, a household incessantly requires from persons who feel & express that it is out of their line of duty, as servants of Government to do any thing, *in* or *out* of the to preach there — I am sorry I could not go to hear him yesterday, tho' he preached twice in church, he told me just now, that he had a full meeting - that some Officers & Soldiers attended — My Brother John arrived last friday & speaks with delight of the Traverse, The Indians there, are anxious to have him remain with them & say they would be glad to have Ma & Waishky go & live among them The chiefs were not satisfied till John left a trunk & his Rifle as a token for his return — — — John has commenced hoeing, & weeding the Garden & is to pole the Peas & Beans tomorrow — I can hardly tell, what will thrive, & what not, from the rankness of the Weeds, but the poor Straw berry beds are a complete failure this year — I have got through cleaning, with the exception of this room I am still in, & upstairs, but that can be done any time after the more important work in the Garden is done

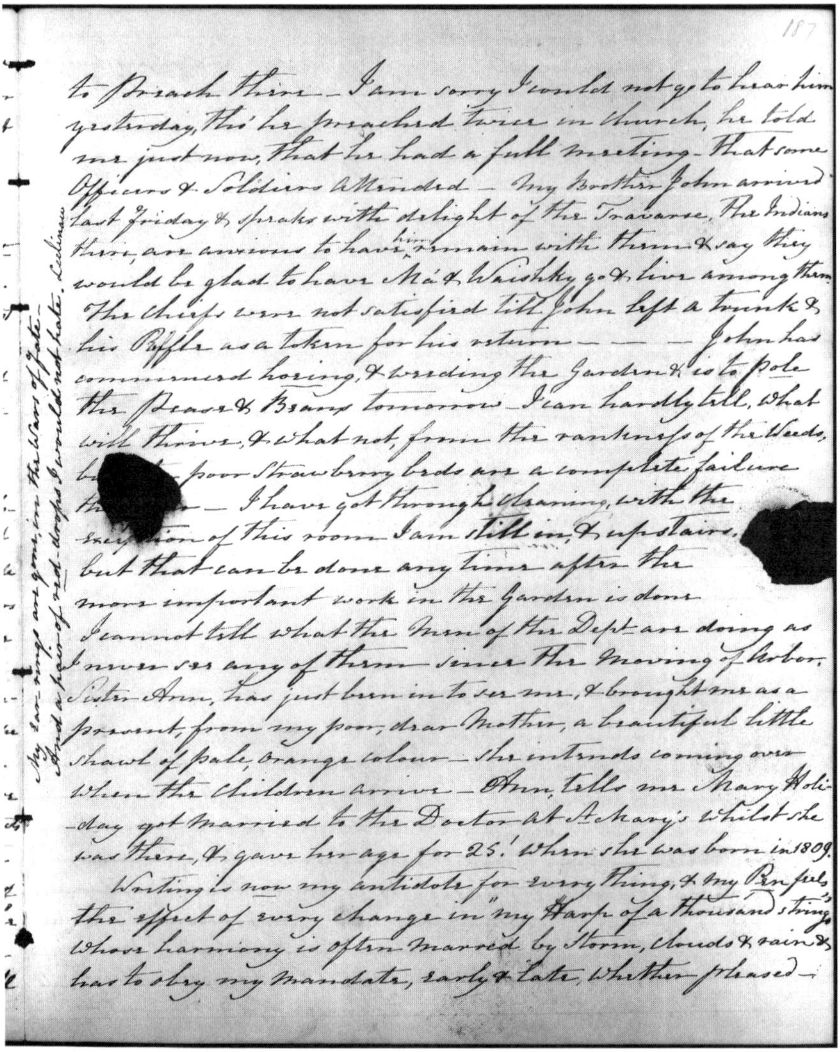

I cannot tell what the Men of the Dept are doing as I never see any of them — since the moving of Harbor, Sister Ann, has just been in to see me, & brought me as a present, from my poor, dear Mother, a beautiful little shawl of pale orange colour — she intends coming over when the children arrive — Ann, tells me Mary Holiday got married to the Doctor at Achary's whilst she was there, & gave her age for 25. When she was born in 1809.

Writing is now my antidote for every thing, & my Rienfels the effect of every change in my Harp of a thousand strings whose harmony is often marred by Storm, clouds & rain & has to obey my mandate, early & late, whether pleased —

Figure 7. Manuscript page of a letter from Jane Schoolcraft in Mackinac to Henry Schoolcraft in Detroit, 8 June 1840. See the short poem in the margin, in this volume titled "My Ear-rings." Henry Rowe Schoolcraft Papers, Manuscript Division, Library of Congress, Washington, D.C.

house which is not strictly within the prescribed limits of their obligations. . . . [N]othing now can be done without first ascertaining whether it is *Public* or *Private* service that is demanded, & *not a little* pride, is manifested when any thing is to be done for the house—it is hard to bear refusal, with the addition of *jaw* & impudence from that cause. I would rather do all, & every thing myself, if I could, than have to put up with such *nice* distinctions—(2 July 1840, LC45)

Her anger exposes a sense of entitlement and class privilege. A year later, forced to move, she would suffer the prying eyes of people coming into their home to buy the furniture, or just using the excuse of the sale to poke into the house and invade her privacy (10 July 1841, LC46). Her sense of superiority could even take on racial connotations that evoke—for her time, place, and history—an understandably conflicted sense of her own Indianness. In one of these same anxious letters, as her familiar world unravels, she paints a revealing picture of herself and the world she lived in:

There is a great *deal of talk*, I am told, going on in the place, about the Indians attempting *hostilities* this summer after the payments are over, it is said, some have been imprudent enough to say that they will set fire to the Agency &c. &c.—

It would be well however to be on guard against the treachery & fool-hardiness of drunken Indians, set on by the exasperated feelings of some of the Traders, & where so many are congregated together under their present excited state of mind, they dare & encourage one another to desperate deeds—

. . . I, have to be *spry*, & *some times* we have turns of *fear* at night, sur-rounded by the yells of inebriated french & Indians, & often by the riots of *Sailors* on shore, I have often wished for a good *Brace of Pistils* beside my little bed, & by the way, it would not be amiss to add a pair to your list of purchases for private use, set jesting aside—for I am afraid that the *threats* made & making will end in, *no joke*. (2 July 1840, LC45)

We might react against this way of thinking about "the Indians." Yet she also addresses "Indians" without the generalizing "the," and she chastises others as well: the French, sailors, and traders who have egged Indians on. Instead of seeing a weakness for alcohol as definitionally Indian, she implicates the traders, implicitly condemning the role their alcohol plays in the onset of colonialism.[51]

Jameson gets at Jane Schoolcraft's blend of racial pride with internalized anti-Indian dismay (to call it internalized racism might, at least in this case, smack too much of seeing through the eyes of a later time): "She is proud of her Indian origin; she takes an enthusiastic and enlightened interest in the welfare of her people, and in their conversion to Christianity. . . . But there is a melancholy and pity in her voice, when speaking of them, as if she did indeed consider them a doomed race" (3: 69–70). Years later, in his self-righteous version of Christianity, Henry remembered Jane in similar terms: "Her heart," he wrote, "sympathized deeply with her woodland people whom she viewed as pursuing false objects, through false hopes. The fires of truth that flashed upon her own mind had, as it were, burned out the pictur-esque tapestry that adorned the temple of her native mythology, and left its frame standing as a collapsed wreck at which she gazed, often with pensive and often with melancholy thoughts. She perceived and regretted their fate, and often became pensive in and sad in view of the many unsuccessful efforts to win them over to civilization and christianity" ("Dawn"). Perhaps some-thing of Jane's sense of her Indianness, and its dependence on immediate contexts, comes out in the words of her sister Charlotte after a session of hymn singing, as recorded in Jeremiah Porter's journal: "'Why is it' said Charlotte, 'that singing is so much better in Indian than in English?' This she uttered with her usual enthusiasm, & added, 'there is no doubt but I am an Indian'" (7 June 1832). While there was no doubt, there was still enough pressure on the Johnston siblings for Charlotte to want to say that there was no doubt. Even in Jane Schoolcraft's poems, such as the "Invocation To my Maternal Grand-father on hearing his descent from Chippewa ancestors misrepresented," she is prouder of the Indian past than of the Indian present (not an unusual form of nationalist or racial pride), but in her writing and daily life she remained engaged in the Indian present. Calvin Colton's eyewit-ness, if romanticized, account of Schoolcraft's reunion with a group of In-dian people, perhaps including relatives, on her return to Sault Ste. Marie in 1830, recalls them as "delighted, and overjoyed" to see her, and recalls her "delight" at returning to "a people, whom she was not ashamed to call her own" (82, 87).

Indeed, the separation from her home and people made the move to New York trying. When Henry, needing income and eager to promote *Algic Researches* and related projects, decided that it was time to fulfill his dream of voyaging to Europe, Jane, remembering her miserable childhood trip to Ireland and England, decided to spend Henry's absence with Charlotte in Dundas, Upper Canada (now Ontario). On 22 May 1842, Charlotte unex-pectedly found Jane sitting dead in a chair. From London, after hearing the news, Henry wrote their daughter Janee:

> Reflect, that your mother herself, had not the advantages of a mother (in the refined sense of the term) to bring her up, that her education & manners were, in a great measure, formed by *her father*, and that she had many & peculiar trials to encounter on coming into the broad & mixed circle of society. When I first

saw her in 1820, her refinement, taste, propriety of manners, purity & delicacy of language, & correctness of sentiment, were such as few females, in any rank or station possess. . . . As a mother, she was, so long as her health permitted, a most devoted mother to you & your brother; and her attention & care, in the superintendence & management of the house &c, during my frequent & long absences as a public agent, while we lived at St Mary's & Mackinac, were such as few, are able successfully to *encounter*. Her taste in literature, was chaste. She wrote many pretty pieces, which I have carefully treasured. Let us cherish her memory. (16 June 1842, LC46)

He tries to soften the jarring comment about Ozhaguscodaywayquay by par-enthetically explaining away the harshness in some ways, yet he digs the hole deeper in others, echoing his earlier letter about the "importance of a Chris-tian life." Even so, if his affection for Jane seems tempered by condescension and social arrogance, designed to encourage his daughter's assimilation into white privilege, it still seems like genuine affection, and he touchingly, if euphemistically, recounts Jane's forbearance through racial self-consciousness and harassment. Here, Henry's praise for Jane's writing as "pretty pieces" seems only modestly appreciative of her work and its historical resonance. Later, introducing a book manuscript of her poems (included in this vol-ume), he describes her poetry's "claims, as emanations of aboriginal mind, under the influence of education." In the one case he sees her writings as pretty, yet perhaps only as pretty; in the other, he sees them evoking a cul-tural point, but only as specimens, as instruments for a racial argument. Nearly two centuries later, we are past ready to cast aside such oversimplifi-cations and read Jane Schoolcraft's writing with a mutually reinforcing ap-preciation of its cultural and its aesthetic suggestiveness, not separating those interests but merging them.

The Literary Legacy

Today, we are likely to approach the literary legacy of Jane Schoolcraft in different terms from those that Henry brought to it. With her writing mostly unpublished and unread, she has so far had hardly any literary legacy. This book promises to change that. What possibilities, then, does School-craft's work offer for reinterpreting literary history? I would like to suggest that it speaks to urgent contemporary interests about American Indian liter-ary and aesthetic representation, languages, and literacies.

Schoolcraft was an Indian writer, a female writer, an Irish-American writer, a white writer, a métis writer, but she did not set out to be those things programmatically. She did not set out to be a writer at all. She simply wrote, and except for her stories—which were published, eventually, without her name attached to them, and after Henry's editing and rewriting—she wrote without envisioning a public audience. Readers from our own time are bound to ask her to represent American Indian people and American Indian writing, regardless of how far such thoughts were from her own thinking, with no model before her of previous Indian writers. Yet as we consider that process of representation, it can make a difference to keep in mind that such thoughts were far from how she seems to have imagined her writing, and perhaps far from how she could have imagined it. While it is a commonplace in African American literary studies to note how early African American writing was expected to testify to the intellectual abilities of African peoples, there is no evidence that Jane Schoolcraft (as opposed to Henry Schoolcraft) saw her writing as testifying to the intellectual abilities of Indian peoples. In "To my maternal grand-father on hearing his descent from Chippewa ancestors misrepresented," she worries about the representation of herself and her relatives as Ojibwe (Chippewa) people, not as "Indian" or "Native" people, for she insists on her family's heritage as purely Ojibwe against what she sees as the malicious rumor that her grandfather—and thus she herself—were part Sioux. While at times, especially when she found herself away from home and among white people, she must have felt their eyes on her as an Indian, at home in Sault Ste. Marie she seems to have thought of herself far more as Ojibwe than as Indian.

Indeed, in her poems, as we have seen, she was capable of referring to Indian people from a superior distance, as "the simple Indian," while also capable of referring to Indians as "my people." Apparently she saw herself as Indian, but not as one of the simple Indians. She was, after all, and as the poem about her grandfather can remind us, from the elite on both sides of her family, and proud of it. She was also Christian, and while she was far from alone in that respect among Indians and métis, she was also far from typical. And yet, for Schoolcraft not to imagine herself as a typical or representative Indian is itself in some ways a typical and representative Indian act. For Indian people, probably even more so in her time, often take note of their differences from other Indian people and often rest a good deal of their cultural identity in band, clan, tribal, regional, or linguistic affiliations and not only in the broad category of Indian. The category of Indian derives not from "Indian" thought by itself but instead from contact with non-Indians, for without a concept of non-Indians there could be—and indeed there was—no concept of Indians.

In a variety of ways, Schoolcraft's writing makes concrete this paradox of at once representing and not representing Indian people, or even representing Indians by not representing them. Writers who focus most on representing Indians to a wider reading audience, such as Henry Schoolcraft and the anthropologists who followed him, take an ethnographic approach. That is, they focus on explaining Indians to non-Indian audiences. But Jane Schoolcraft's writing does no such thing. Ethnographic writing, moreover, including Henry Schoolcraft's, often describes Indian ceremonies or religious and sacred ritual and belief, descriptions that many Indian people view with alarm. Again, Jane Schoolcraft's writing steers clear of such topics. She does not present herself as explaining Ojibwe or Indian life to non-Ojibwe or non-Indian readers any more than, say, Nathaniel Hawthorne or Edgar Allan Poe presents himself as explaining American life to Ojibwe or Indian readers. She shows no lugubrious self-consciousness about her Indianness, and no compensatory urge to "celebrate" it. That may not be what readers will imagine when they hear about the first known American Indian literary writer, but perhaps it reverberates more meaningfully than we might stereotypically have expected. Schoolcraft lived her imaginative life as an Indian (and as many other things) without reducing herself to her Indianness. Paradoxically, that probably goes a lot farther to represent the ordinariness of daily American Indian life than the typically obsessive representations that crowd literary history. In that way, Schoolcraft's writing lays out a model of aesthetic and cultural rather than identitarian representation for Indian writing, while nevertheless carrying forth identitarian representation in its engagement with Indian language and literacy.

Unlike Phillis Wheatley (after her early childhood in west Africa), and unlike Anne Bradstreet, Schoolcraft lived much of her daily adult life in an indigenous language. Though she usually wrote in English and focused on personal topics, she also wrote in her indigenous language and wrote about her indigenous culture. At a time when most indigenous writers in the United States cannot speak, let alone write in, an indigenous language, a time when many languages are disappearing, and also a time of great activity furthering the continuity and revival of indigenous languages, Schoolcraft offers a history and a specially valuable model of bilingual and multilingual life and writing for American Indians and for American culture and literature at large.

The textbook market in literature anthologies testifies to American readers' (including teachers and scholars') desire for a longer history to American Indian literary writing. To fill out that history, American literature anthologies have begun to include a good many Indian texts. Nevertheless, in the process, editors often present transcribed and translated oral texts as the earliest American Indian literature, and often as the earliest American literature. While those transcribed, translated texts often carry great literary value, the disproportionate focus on them in many anthologies and in representations of early American literary history can seem to single out Indian people, or sometimes Indians and African Americans, as oral as opposed to literate. Such representations also neglect to recognize that the transcribed and translated oral texts called on to represent pre-Columbian traditions also represent a variety of more recent traditions, for they follow the dominant literary styles of the times when they were told, transcribed, or translated rather than the indigenous and not necessarily literary traditions that produced them. For all these reasons, if we are to represent American Indian literary history, there is much to gain from concentrating more on the long history of Indian literacy and on actual writing by particular Indian writers.

It only awaits for us to make that writing available. Increasingly, we are doing just that, and that's where Schoolcraft and this book of her writings come in. I hope that readers will take this volume as an invitation to continue interpreting the writings that it presents, to uncover more writing by Jane Schoolcraft, and also to reconsider our ideas of early American and American Indian literacy and art, and thus to recover additional writers whose work still awaits our looking for them.

Notes

[1] These characterizations require a measure of caution. The term "literary" is of course subjective; I use it here in the traditional, narrow sense for poetry, drama, and fiction, but it can bear other usages, not least for autobiography. For a welcome reading of Native American nonfiction prose as literature, see Robert Warrior. When I characterize Schoolcraft as among the first Indian writers, I cast a wide net to include such figures (all men) as Samson Occom (Mohegan, 1723–92), the famous minister; Hendrick Aupaumut (Mohican, 1757–1830), who wrote accounts of his extensive diplomatic work and a history of his people; and Schoolcraft's near contemporaries David Cusick (Tuscarora, d. c. 1840), whose *Sketches of the Ancient History of the Six Nations* appeared around 1825–28; Elias Boudinot (Cherokee, 1802–39), who founded the bilingual *Cherokee Phoenix* in 1828 and twice that year reprinted references to Jane Schoolcraft from other newspapers ("Indian Ladies"—printed in many newspapers—and "Religion Tames the Savage"); and William Apess (or Apes, Pequot, 1798–1839), whose first publication, *A Son of the Forest*, appeared in 1829. We might also mention Occom's colleague Joseph Johnson (Mohegan, 1751–76), whose large body of letters have recently been published.

John Rollin Ridge (Cherokee, 1827–67, known as Chees-quat-a-law-ny in Cherokee, which he translated as Yellow Bird, a name he sometimes used to sign his writings) is often cited as the first Native American poet. He published in periodicals beginning in the late 1840s, and after his death his wife published a book of his poems in 1868. While Schoolcraft was writing poetry well before Ridge was born, there were other Indian poets before Ridge and by some measures before Schoolcraft. I use the term "first known" Indian poet rather than "first" to suggest skepticism regarding the notion of firstness and to evoke confidence that our notion of what is first will change. Indeed, while I have been working on this volume, Joanna Brooks has offered excellent readings of six hymns that she notes have been attributed to Occom (Shaw; Brooks, *American Lazarus* 51–86, 189–94; "Six Hymns"). Since hymns are sometimes considered poems, we could say that Occom wrote poetry before Schoolcraft. Brooks, who reviews the attribution of these hymns to Occom and notes other surviving hymns that Occom might have written, is less cautious, calling Occom "the first Native American to write and publish poetry in English" (*American Lazarus* 74), though she notes as well that he published other hymns that might have been written by Joseph Johnson (*American Lazarus* 75) or by their colleagues David and Jacob Fowler (Montauk) ("Six Hymns" 71). (While Occom's authorship of these hymns and others is plausible, I do not find Brooks's argument that he definitely wrote them convincing.) Wolfgang Hochbruck and Beatrix Dudensing-Reichel have also called attention to a poem from 1679 in Latin and Greek published by Cotton Mather in his *Magnalia Christi Americana* (1702), which Mather attributes to Eleazar, an Indian student at Harvard whom we know almost nothing about.

Of additional note among early Native writers is the recently recovered Betsy Chamberlain (1797–1886), a mill worker in Lowell, Massachusetts, who might have been Native (perhaps Narragansett and/or Abenaki). Two years younger than Schoolcraft, Chamberlain published fictional and autobiographical sketches in women's journals for mill workers beginning in 1840 and as late as 1850. On Chamberlain, see Judith A. Ranta. (It is tempting to make analogies between Schoolcraft and Chamberlain or between the recoveries of their works; still, because Schoolcraft's life is so much more documented, and because, like all the other writers named here, Schoolcraft seems to have identified so much more actively with Native people than any record shows for Chamberlain, the similarities seem minimal.) Rufus Anderson's *Memoir of Catharine Brown, a Christian Indian of the Cherokee Nation* (1825) has sometimes been characterized as a book by Brown (Cherokee, c. 1800–1823), which is a stretch, as it is a memoir about, not by, Brown though Anderson includes letters by Brown. While I offer the comparisons to Bradstreet and Wheatley with caution, such comparisons can help bring out the magnitude of Schoolcraft's work and the challenge of interpreting its earliness. Still, I recognize that there are considerable differences between Schoolcraft and these writers.

[2] For examples of this historical work, see Richard White and Lucy Eldersveld Murphy. White's wide-ranging book suffers from underusing and undervaluing Native sources while overvaluing white sources, but his concept of a "middle ground" between traditional Native and Euroamerican cultures remains crucial for understanding the region's history. Murphy's approach is more balanced. While "métis" is the usual term today, it has varied in pronunciation and spelling over different times and regions. In Sault Ste. Marie during Jane Johnston Schoolcraft's lifetime, the more familiar variant may have been *métif*.

[3] On Chequamegon, La Pointe, and Waubojeeg, see Henry Schoolcraft, "Waub Ojeeg," based on information from Ozhaguscodaywayquay. For a valuable source not mediated through Ozhaguscodaywayquay, see the mid-nineteenth-century Ojibwe historian William W. Warren. See also (Mrs.) Anna Brownell Jameson; most accounts of Waubojeeg and Ozhaguscodaywayquay rely on Jameson, whose source was Ozhaguscodaywayquay herself, translated and perhaps supplemented by Jane Johnston Schoolcraft, Henry Schoolcraft, and Charlotte Johnston McMurray. The only extended source on Oz-

haguscodaywayquay's early life and marriage besides Jameson is Thomas L. McKenney, who like Jameson relies on Ozhaguscodaywayquay's family as source. C. H. Chapman's lengthy account claims to depend partly on oral sources but mostly repeats printed sources word-for-word.

[4] I draw here on Janet Lewis's (147) and Bruce M. White's observation that the Mrs. "Jayer" in the published transcriptions of Johnston's letter (341) should be transcribed as Mrs. "Sayer," for, as White notes, Obemaunoquay married John Sayer (White, "Trade Patterns and Gender Roles" 134, 146–47). Following that lead took me to additional information in Thwaites (173–74) and on genealogical web sites that do not cite sources but that corroborate the connection. Obemaunoquay's marriage to Sayer ended some time in the 1790s and thus could have influenced Waubojeeg's skepticism about Johnston's wish to marry Waubojeeg's daughter. In 1849, a son of Obemaunoquay and John Sayer, Jane Schoolcraft's second cousin Pierre-Guillaume Sayer, also a fur trader, found fame when he was accused of illegal trading at Red River, Assiniboia (now Manitoba). His trial, "a landmark in the history of the Canadian west" (Morton 777), served as something like the first act of the famous métis rebellions later led by Louis Riel. On Guillaume Sayer, see W. L. Morton. On John Sayer, see Douglas A. Birk.

[5] McKenney 157, Jameson 3: 210–11. Both McKenney and Jameson offer supposedly direct quotations of Waubojeeg's actual words, presumably drawn from family stories, but the supposed quotations sound so stereotypically like white clichés of Indian English that they probably depend on McKenney's and Jameson's paraphrases. According to the protofeminist Jameson, Waubojeeg said that if Johnston returned, "we will talk farther" (3: 211), whereas according to McKenney, who had a reputation for what we now call sexual harassment (Brazer 191–92), Waubojeeg said that if Johnston returned, then he "will give you my daughter." In interpreting the arrangement between Waubogeeg and Johnston, I am drawing on the landmark scholarship about men's exchange of women by Gayle Rubin, Eve Kosofsky Sedgwick, and Luce Irigaray. Some thirty-five years after her marriage, Ozhaguscodaywayquay (presumably through Jane Schoolcraft) told Jameson the story of Ozhaguscodaywayquay's youthful vision quest, saying that she dreamed of a white man as her guardian spirit (Jameson 3: 211–13). I read that story as a suspect reconstruction that fits the way events turned out; all the more suspect because she would have been violating custom by revealing the dream from her vision quest (Landes 9). For another reading of that story, taking Jameson's account at face value and supposing that it explains Ozhaguscodaywayquay's political influence by granting her a special spiritual power, see Cleland, "Cass."

[6] On Ojibwe marriages and Ojibwe fur-trade marriages, for example, see Ruth Landes, Jennifer S. H. Brown, and Sylvia Van Kirk. (Brown and Van Kirk also describe non-Ojibwe fur-trade marriages, not to be confused with Ojibwe marriages.)

[7] Jeremiah Porter, a Presbyterian missionary in Sault Ste. Marie in 1831–32, recounts in his journal "a most delightful instance of conjugal affection" when, almost four years after John Johnston's death, Porter was stunned and impressed to stumble upon Mrs. Johnston sitting on her husband's grave and weeping with grief. Then, he adds, "I met the daughter, Mrs S on her husband[']s arm retiring to the same sacred spot to weep" (10 May 1832).

[8] The premier fur trade companies, varying over the years and depending on which side of the border they worked, were the Hudson's Bay Company, the North West Company, the XY Company, and the American Fur Trade Company. See Brown and Van Kirk. For John Johnston's career as a fur trader, see the assorted references in David Lavender (who does not always cite his sources), the summary account in Hambleton 12–14, and Bernard C. Peters's criticism of Johnston's complicity in trading liquor for furs.

[9] Brown; Van Kirk; Sleeper-Smith; White, "Trade Patterns and Gender Roles." See also Buffalohead, who does not focus on fur-trade marriages but offers a helpful historical perspective on Ojibwe women's cultural, technological, and political roles.

[10] H. R. Schoolcraft, "Memoir" 68–71, "Notes for Memoir" 98–99. Lavender offers the fullest published account of John Johnston's role in the War of 1812. In a letter of 16 July 1844, George Johnston details his father's role in the British attack on Mackinac in 1812. John Johnston's own accounts appear in a letter of 8 Aug. 1814 to George, in his claims letter to Sir Gordon Drummond, and in his memorial to the British government seeking compensation for his losses. The account of his commanding officer, Lt. Col. Robert McDouall (often misspelled in various ways, including McDonall) comes in accompanying letters. For Susan Johnston/Ozhaguscodaywayquay's much fuller account of the American troops' ransacking of the home and business, see her petition to the U.S. House of Representatives for reparations (S. Johnston). See also Brazer 109–17, 126–36. Some accounts mention the burning of the house, but some do not.

When Jane sewed linen shirts during the American siege of Fort Mackinac, she shared the task with Josette LaFramboise, whose story deserves mention for the way that it illustrates how Jane's can represent a larger métis elite, as well as a local elite that would soon shift its allegiance from the British to the Americans. Josette LaFramboise (1795–1820) was the daughter of Joseph LaFramboise, a French trader, and the famous Magdelaine Marcot LaFromboise, an Ottawa better known as Madame LaFramboise. (The Ottawas, or Odawas, are an Indian people closely related to the Ojibwes.) When her husband was murdered, Madame LaFramboise took over his business and ran it with unusual success, building a sizable fortune. Her spacious home still stands on Mackinac, serving as a popular hotel. Josette was well educated at Montreal schools. Two years after the siege, she married the American commander at Mackinac, Captain Benjamin K. Pierce, son of a New Hampshire governor. In 1818, John Johnston wrote George Johnston that he, Jane, and Jane's sister Charlotte "have been on a visit to Capt and Mrs Pierce. The kind friendly and hospitable reception we had from them . . . could not be surpassed anywhere." Captain Pierce was also the brother of Franklin Pierce, future senator and president of the United States and classmate and close friend of Nathaniel Hawthorne, who wrote his campaign biography, and—to complete the circle—the close friend of Longfellow, who would later base much of his most famous poetry on the writing of none other than that same young Jane Johnston who sewed shirts with his friend's sister-in-law.

[11] Indeed, his son George took great pride in John's continuing loyalty to Britain. In 1844, outraged at the old accusation that because John had served the British cause in the War of 1812 he had betrayed the United States, George wrote a letter "To the public of the state of Michigan" defending his father's loyalty to Britain. "In the year 1807 or 8,"

George wrote, "The American commander, Capt. Dunham at the post of Michilimackinac" invited John "to dine with him, and his officers, at the fort, together with a large
party of . . . six and thirty gentlemen, in the course of the conversation, Capt. Dunham
proposed to obtain a commission of Justice of the peace for my father, to act at Saut Ste.
Marie; My Father rose up from his seat, thanking Capt. Dunham for the honor he intended conferring upon him, . . . and he had wished, to be distinctly understood that
he was born a british subject & would die one, and that if he were made president of the
United States, he would not accept the office, much less would he that of Justice of the
peace; but said he: Gentlemen so long as I remain within the limits of your territory, I
will be amenable to your laws, but so soon as a sword is drawn between the two countries;
you see that I am lame; and if I should not be able to walk, I will creep on all fours to
have a shot at you: Upon this flow of feeling Capt. Dunham, his officers and the American
gentlemen present, rose from their seats, and gave my Father a hearty shake of their
hands, expressing their esteem for his loyalty and praised him for his noble feelings"
(G. Johnston, "To the public"). Susan Johnston/Ozhaguscodaywayquay's petition seeking
compensation for the properties seized and destroyed by American troops also denies the
allegation by business rivals that John betrayed the United States by trading in ways that
unfairly helped the Indians who fought against the Americans (2, 9–10).

[12] The guide to the Papers of Henry Rowe Schoolcraft in the Library of Congress says
that the volume of John Johnston's poems is transcribed by Jane Johnston, but that is not
correct (*Henry Rowe Schoolcraft: A Register*).

[13] George left a variety of notebooks. Those I refer to here are in the Bayliss Public
Library in Sault Ste. Marie. Charlotte's notebooks, owned by the Chippewa County Historical Society, are housed in the River of History Museum, both in Sault Ste. Marie. The
unattributed, not-yet-traced poems in Charlotte's notebooks do not sound to me like her
own writing, but perhaps she wrote some of them.

[14] The best account of Jane Johnston Schoolcraft is a master's thesis by Tammrah
Stone-Gordon, which calls itself a literary biography but takes a more historical than
literary approach. Stone-Gordon's work is valuable for its overdue politicized and feminist
perspective, as compared to the unwittingly colonialist assumptions of other historians. But
she tends to idealize Ojibwe notions of women, as in her account of Ozhaguscodaywayquay. Still, she provides the best account of Ozhaguscodaywayquay that I have seen. While
Stone-Gordon and I take broadly similar approaches to interpreting Schoolcraft's life, we
see many details differently, and my account has been able to draw from more extended
research and a wider theoretical platform than could have been possible even for this
excellent master's thesis. The best published account of Jane Johnston Schoolcraft is the
brief discussion by A. LaVonne Brown Ruoff.

[15] Both the Johnston and the Schoolcraft families hosted innumerable travelers, and
most visitors who wrote about Sault Ste. Marie or Mackinac Island when the Johnstons
and Schoolcrafts were there left an appreciative record of them. Especially notable descriptions appear in John Ball, John J. Bigsby, Abel Bingham (Jan.–Feb. 1829), Calvin
Colton, Ross Cox, Joseph Delafield, Peter Dougherty, Anna Jameson, Thomas L. McKenney, Jeremiah Porter, and Eliza R. Steele.

[16] The best accounts are George Johnston, "Reminiscences" 609–11; and H. R.

Schoolcraft, *Narrative Journal* 135–40 and *Summary Narrative* 78–81. See also Cass; Trowbridge, "With Cass" 145–47 (which, like Cass's letter, credits George but not Ozhaguscodaywayquay); Trowbridge and anonymous; McKenny 150–51; Gilbert, "Tale"; and Gilbert, "Memories." This story has been told many times. The first five accounts I cite are by participants or witnesses, while McKenney's is based on talking with participants. Gilbert grew up in the Sault a decade later and heard the stories orally. Schoolcraft's, McKenney's, and perhaps Trowbridge's accounts appear to be the sources of the many other published versions. Except for a speculative account by Charles Cleland ("Cass"), most versions by white observers or dependent on them ignore or underestimate Ozhaguscodaywayquay's role and take white, masculine, and United States authority and conquest as self-evidently superior, inevitable, and just, as if reluctance to sign away Indian lands could come only from savage foolishness. For an excellent recent account that draws on Canadian Ojibwe perspectives, see Chute, *Legacy* 31–36.

[17] Jameson, esp. 3: 217; Chapman 313. Jeremiah Porter left a notable account in his journal of Ozhaguscodaywayquay's sugar making: "The Miss Johnstons made out a party this morning to visit their mother whose sugar camp is on an island in the River about six miles below. They felt that I must go with them & therefore called for me. I feared to go; but on the whole thought it best. Our party consisted of sixteen, disposed in four sleighs. . . . It was delightful sleighing on the ice. Such a collection of sleighs, with every thing around appearing like Febru', appeared strange for the fifth of April. We walked from the River to Mrs J. lodge, about half a mile thro' a beautiful maple orchard, the trees of a noble growth. Mrs J has been on that island to make sugar every year for the last 28. She makes usually more than three thousand pounds. Her lodge made of bark & mats spread on poles, is larger than many a house. Probably it is 35 feet long & 25 broad & high. On each side are beds raised from the ground. A fire in the middle extends from end to end of the lodge & when there is sufficient sap, kettles are hanging over the whole, the sugar is thus all boiled within the house (for so it may be called) it seems a scene of industry indeed. The Indian women are all around sewing Mococks, made from birch bark, to contain the sugar. We dined in the lodge, on a fine dinner prepared by Charlotte, sung several of our favorite 'village Hymns,' talked rationally for two or more hours, & then leaving Mrs J. to pass another month at her camp, returned to our houses, pleased with our excursion" (5 Apr. 1832). While Jane Schoolcraft, unmentioned here, may not have joined this particular excursion, Porter's tale describes part of the world where she grew up and spent much of her adult life. For Henry Schoolcraft's account of a similar expedition in 1823, which probably included Jane Johnston, see his *Personal Memoirs* 162–63.

[18] Fuller 108–9. On the common misperception by whites in the early republic that Indian women were degraded drudges, and the role that misperception played in rationalizing colonialist dispossession of Indian lands, see Theda Perdue 105–22.

[19] Franchère 279, my translation. Franchère's expression "femmes du pays" (women of the country) has no exact English equivalent. The 1854 English translation renders it "half-breed or Indian women" (276), adding a sometimes derogatory connotation (via "half-breed") and a differentiation ("or Indian women") not in the original and perhaps more representative of the United States in 1854 than of Schoolcraft's métis world and upbringing.

[20] *Personal Memoirs* 458. There are many corroborating accounts of Mackinac (also called Michilimackinac). For especially readable descriptions of the métis world in and around Mackinac, see Juliette M. Kinzie, who passed through a few years before 1833, and Frederick Marryat, who passed through a few years after 1833.

[21] Bremer 97, Stone-Gordon 34. Bremer is unusually hostile toward Henry School-craft for someone who has put so much research into writing a biography, and it is often hard to tell how justifiable his hostility is. His assessment of Jane Schoolcraft's attractions is patronizingly grudging: "If not beautiful, she did combine tolerable looks with a certain element of grace" (96). Osborn and Osborn see the marriage as loving, though if anything they err on the opposite side from Bremer, seeing Henry as one of the most admirable figures in American history. Brazer's account is more balanced.

[22] 19 May 1823. Beginning with Lewis Theobald's emendation in his 1733 edition of Shakespeare, many editions render the word "paleness" in this passage from act 3, scene 2 of *The Merchant of Venice* as "plainness," so no special meaning accrues to what might otherwise seem like a racially suggestive revision on Jane Johnston's part.

[23] Perhaps it was at more or less the same time that Jane copied out Portia's words to her soon-to-be husband Bassanio a moment later in the same scene:

> the full sum of me
> Is sum of something; which to term in gross,
> Is an unlesson'd Girl, unschool'd, unpractis'd:
> Happy in this, she is not yet so old
> But she may learn; and happier than this,
> She is not bred so dull but she can learn;
> Happiest of all, is that her gentle spirit
> Commits itself to yours to be directed
> As from her lord, her governour, her king.
>   (text from LC70, dated "1823?" in Henry's hand)

These words can suggest submission to Henry. On the other hand, if we consider Portia's flirtatiously loving defiance of Bassanio in the remainder of the play, then Portia's—and Jane's—sense of submission can cut both ways.

[24] Signed "Fairy Cabinet 6th May," with the year 1824 added in brackets, apparently by Henry, though other, similar notes date from 1823 (LC35). For a less literary treatment of Jane's notes, crediting her with far less wit, see Brazer 157–59.

[25] Here and throughout, my account of Henry is my own interpretation, relying heavily on Bremer but also on my reading in Henry's voluminous papers in the Library of Congress and elsewhere, and on his voluminous published writings, as well as on Osborn and Osborn and the many other sources cited throughout.

[26] The most comprehensive accounts of Henry Schoolcraft's role as a founder of American anthropology are Hallowell, "Beginnings," esp. 42–48, and Zumwalt. See also Bieder. Some accounts, whether more or less skeptically, refer to Henry Schoolcraft patri-archally as the father of American anthropology. See Freeman 302.

[27] In calling the Johnstons his "guide, philosopher, and friend," Henry quotes Alex-

ander Pope's "An Essay on Man" IV, line 390, from 1733–34, and "Imitations of Horace," Epistle I, Book I, line 177, from 1738.

[28] For a helpful and partially sympathetic reading of Henry as trying to bring out the literariness he saw in the stories by presenting them in what he was accustomed to understand as literary language, see Clements 120–28.

[29] As Jeremy Mumford has noted (13–15), Henry also took a leading role in efforts to make one treaty award 640 acres apiece to the Ojibwe wives of white men, even naming Ozhaguscodaywayquay as first on the list. Officials in Washington, Mumford supposes, would not have recognized the name Ozhaguscodaywayquay and so did not realize that Henry's wife, in-laws, and son would have reaped enormous benefits from that provision, but the Senate, presumably smelling a rat, rejected the provision anyway. This was not a particularly surreptitious act, however, and Henry himself would have seen such a provision as deserved, rather than corrupt. Besides singling out Ozhaguscodaywayquay as first on the list, the treaty also singled her out as the only woman whose grandchildren were equally provided for, and as the only person specifically named in the article granting the lands, which also granted her and her descendants different (and presumably better) lands than it granted the others ("Treaty").

[30] When I began this project, both houses were closed, awaiting funds for restoration. In the summer of 2004, the remaining piece of the Johnston house, the original home of Jane and Henry's marriage, opened for visitors, staffed by knowledgeable impersonators of John and Susan Johnston/Ozhaguscodaywayquay.

[31] In a typical example, Michael T. Marsden supposes that "the marriage was one of convenience" (157). Osborn and Osborn argue convincingly that it was a loving marriage (528ff.), but perhaps their worshipful approach to Henry kept them from convincing later commentators, who rely on Henry's published, public writing, and perhaps on assumptions about cross-racial marriages, without considering the private, primary documents.

[32] Consultation with experts in the clothing and hair styles of the time corroborates the impression that the date of the portrait is approximately 1825.

[33] Letter to C. C. Trowbridge. See also *Personal Memoirs* 240. We could say that Schoolcraft genuinely published her work if showing her friends the *Literary Voyager* manuscripts, and perhaps a few other manuscripts, counts as publication. Harold Love makes such an argument for what he calls "scribal publication" in seventeenth-century Britain, but Love describes an institutionalized process that its participants recognized as publication, whereas Schoolcraft's small showing of manuscripts seems self-consciously opposed to publication, which was identified with printing.

[34] No evidence indicates how many copies there were. Over two years after the last known issue, a friend wrote Henry from Detroit: "Your Literary voyage has been travelling around among your friends here, and having lately been returned to me, I shall ask your brother to take it home with him" (Whiting). Probably, additional material by Jane Schoolcraft appeared in the issues or pages that have not survived. I have searched widely across many libraries for additional copies of the *Literary Voyager*, without success. Henry produced a number of manuscript magazines at various times before and after his marriage, but no others on the scale of the *Literary Voyager*; see Kinietz. The brief existing discussions of Jane Schoolcraft—perhaps repeating each other—sometimes credit her

with coediting the *Literary Voyager* with Henry. Perhaps she did, but so far as I can tell that is wishful thinking on the part of later scholars. They offer no evidence, and all the evidence that I have seen credits only Henry as editor. With none of the puffery that often betrays Henry's moments of self-inflation, his memoirs casually refer to the magazine as his own production (*Personal Memoirs* 240, 257).

[35] The one exception that I know of is the unpublished masters thesis by Stone-Gordon, which transcribes several additional poems from Henry's papers in the Library of Congress and one from Henry's memoirs.

[36] Stone-Gordon sees the marriage as painfully unhappy after its initial years, but she relies on the assumption that "Lament," a poem in Jane's hand (LC19), is by Jane and about her marriage, when in fact it is by Amelia Opie (*Lamp* 40–41). Opie's "A Lament" is a eulogy for a dead loved one and not, as Stone-Gordon supposes, Schoolcraft's lament for a figurative death in her marriage. Schoolcraft's children also thought that she had written the poem, though I have found no evidence that they thought it was about their parents' marriage. After her death, Schoolcraft's children produced a hand-written, manuscript magazine called *The Garland*, recalling the *Literary Voyager*. In the 14 Dec. 1844 issue they included "Lament" and—probably drawing on the manuscript in Jane's hand—misattributed it to Jane Leelinau, combining Schoolcraft's first name with her Ojibwe pen name (LC66). There are minor differences between the versions in Opie's books and the version in Schoolcraft's hand. Perhaps Schoolcraft copied it from a version she found in a newspaper or journal. It is easier to track whether materials in Schoolcraft's hand were written by her or merely copied by her, now that we have the internet and literary databases, which were not available to Stone-Gordon.

[37] Henry's biographer Bremer, who despises Henry with cause but perhaps too relentlessly, makes much of this letter. He sees the marriage as without intimacy after William Henry's death, believing that this particular letter, unmitigatedly cold and compassionless, describes a turning point in Henry's religious faith, even a moment of conversion. But that seems to ignore the evidence of continuing affection in later letters; Jameson's testimony to Henry's affection for Jane's mother; Henry's frequent religiosity in earlier years; his remark in his *Personal Memoirs* that 7 Feb. 1831 marked his public acknowledgment of "the divine atonement for human sin" that he had first recognized in 1824 (343); and his remark in a letter of 7 Feb. 1838 that "it is *seven years* this day, since I took the important step of coming out on the Lord's side." The widely accepted argument that Henry underwent a religious conversion at this time seems to oversimplify the story. In short, Henry's life—and with it Jane's—was more intricate and nuanced than can be suggested by our desire for readily comprehensible narratives shaped by convenient turning points.

[38] For the relevant letters, all from 1834, see James Schoolcraft to Henry Schoolcraft, 9 Feb. (twice), 27 Feb., and 1 Mar.; John Hulbert to Henry Schoolcraft, 9 Feb.; William McMurray to Henry Schoolcraft 11 Feb., 4 Mar.; and Jane Schoolcraft to Charlotte Johnston McMurray, 4 Mar. (LC12).

[39] James had been jailed for killing a man in a fight over a woman. He slipped out of jail and footed it from Mackinac to Sault Ste. Marie through the snow, nearly dying from the journey. He was hidden by the family in Canada, and then, to his surprise, had the

charges dropped when his victim recovered from the brink of death. In 1846, in a yet more famous episode, he would himself be murdered, probably again from jealousy over a woman, though competing stories circulate around his mysteriously unsolved murder.

[40] Jane's letter seems to have survived in Henry's papers only because he kept her rough draft, and that she wrote and kept a draft shows that she gave the letter special concern. As a draft, it is hard to transcribe; in the quotation that follows, x-marks indicate illegible words, and question marks indicate uncertain transcriptions.

[41] Schoolcraft refers to the beginnings of the Patriotes Rebellion, a revolt of French Canadians against the British authorities. Having grown up with French Canadians, and now identifying with Henry and the United States that he worked for and that had already fought against the British twice, she seems to have switched from her British family's loyalty in the War of 1812, now identifying instead with those who resisted British colonialism.

[42] H. R. Schoolcraft, *Personal Memoirs* 646. His interest in establishing a link between American Indian languages and Hebrew came partly from his stance in the ethnological debate between "polygenists," who saw different peoples as having different origins, and "monogenists," including Henry, who saw different peoples as deriving from the same origin, ultimately the origin described in Genesis. See Bieder.

[43] While I have not tried to track every published instance of other storytellers' versions of the stories that Schoolcraft tells, "The Origin of the Robin" may be the story she tells that is told most frequently. There are other versions, for example, by Jacques Le-Pique (Kawbawgam, Kawbawgam, and LePique 89), Basil Johnston (128–31), and Charley Batiste (Barnouw 159), and a similar story by John Barnes (Helbig 210). At least for this reader, comparison with these other versions speaks well for Schoolcraft's sense of narrative and dramatic craft. Basil Johnston also tells a version of the "Corn story" (34–38). For other versions of "Moowis," see John Peastitute and Wasagunackank. While later storytellers have sometimes read Jane Schoolcraft's work in Henry Schoolcraft's *Algic Researches*, they typically draw on oral sources, as Jane Schoolcraft did.

[44] Hallowell, "Beginnings" 43. Wilhelm Grimm notes that he read translations from *Algic Researches* in 1844: *Grimm's Household Tales* 2, 531. He does not name the stories, but he refers to several issues of what he calls *Lehmann's Magazin*. The *Magazin für die Literatur des Auslandes*, edited by J. Lehmann, published German translations of "Peboan and Seegwun" (possibly by Jane Schoolcraft, and included in this volume), "Puk Wudj Ininee," and "The Red Swan," all stories from *Algic Researches* that Henry Schoolcraft leaves unattributed.

[45] The literature and scholarship on Native American oral storytelling is enormous and varies greatly in kind and quality, requiring a skeptical eye. The most influential more or less modern accounts include Paul Radin, Dennis Tedlock, Dell Hymes, Jarold Ramsey, and many of the contributions in the collections edited by Karl Kroeber, by Brian Swann, and by Arnold Krupat and Swann, which offer a wide-ranging sample of approaches. For these accounts and for crucial, more recent accounts by Native writers, see especially Barre Toelken, Toelken and Tacheeni Scott, Greg Sarris, and Leslie Marmon Silko. For a contrast between traditional Native American oral stories and Euroamerican literary stories, from an anthropologist who has studied the stories that Henry published, see Hallo-

well, "Myth" 547–48. On the Ojibwe logic for telling traditional stories only in the winter, see H. R. Schoolcraft, *Personal Memoirs* 678–79.

[46] On these details, see esp. Bremer. After Henry hired and then fired William Johnston, William went on a vendetta against Henry, accusing him of corruption and helping to set off a federal inquiry into the charges. The inquiry cleared Henry of the more serious accusations but also noted his hiring of relatives and the blurry line he sometimes drew between federal expenses or employees and family funds or servants, a practice he began earlier in his career when a blurry line was probably expected. Though Henry claimed that the inquiry fully exonerated him (*Personal Memoirs* 685–86), it proved humiliating for both Henry and Jane (Bremer 196–206; J. Schoolcraft to H. R. Schoolcraft, 2 July 1840, 10 July 1841).

[47] See George L. Cornell. Bremer says that Jane Schoolcraft translated most of the tales in *Algic Researches* (249), but he does not indicate how he knows that. Whether or not his estimate is high, she may have consulted on the translations of many stories even when she was not the primary translator. For the full listing and text of Native stories that Henry published, see Mentor L. Williams.

[48] Henry tells more about Chusco in other writings, including "Mythology" (97–102) and *Personal Memoirs* (449–50, 510); see also Jameson 3: 61–64.

[49] For famous examples of "informants" and "assistants," see Roger Sanjek. For the legacy that such a history leaves Native anthropologists, see Beatrice Medicine, "Learning to Be an Anthropologist and Remaining 'Native'" (3–15) and "American Indians and Anthropologists: Issues of History, Empowerment, and Application" (323–32).

[50] Given the continuing popularity of song and music among Ojibwe peoples, it seems curious how little extended scholarship there is about Ojibwe songs, a gap that will no doubt be remedied as more Ojibwe scholars write about their traditions. The landmark work of Frances Densmore is still of great interest. And despite his use of words like "primitive," there remains value in the work of Frederick R. Burton, especially—as we think about Schoolcraft's translations—in his discussion of Ojibwe lyrics (145–76).

[51] For a view different from my own, see Brazer: "Jane, for her part, did not consider herself an Indian. Dear Mama was not to be classed with 'the poor, benighted children of the forest,' who, having lost the self-reliance and dignity of their forebears, had become dependent upon the trader's alcohol and the Agent's handouts, too frequently shed one another's blood, and were becoming the most conspicuous members of the race. She shared the enlightened white man's patronizing pity for these demoralized people, but her own pride in her heritage reached back from the contemporary scene to her illustrious ancestors, of whom her mother and a handful of dignified older chieftains remained the few living examples" (179). Brazer lets certain habits of thought—habits that are indeed bracing for modern readers and worth keeping in mind—represent all of Schoolcraft's thinking, against the larger story told by her writings and translations. Brazer cannot fathom that Indian people, like other people, see hierarchies (if not classes) among themselves. Her reading seems self-contradictory, supposing that because Schoolcraft did not see herself as an ordinary Indian, therefore she did not see herself as Indian, and yet continuing to refer to her as "of the race," proud of her heritage, and identifying with her mother and other Indian leaders. In general, Brazer's ways of addressing Indian people differ considerably from my own.

ABBREVIATIONS

AR: Henry Rowe Schoolcraft, *Algic Researches, Comprising Inquiries Respecting the Mental Characteristics of the North American Indians. First Series. Indian Tales and Legends*, 1839. References to *AR* include these volumes and also the set of manuscripts for these volumes in *LC57–59*. The manuscripts come mostly in HRS's hand but in many other hands as well, possibly including paid copyists. Most of the stories in *AR*, along with additional stories, were reprinted in later editions under varying titles: *The Myth of Hiawatha* in 1856 and *The Indian Fairy Book*, edited by Cornelius Mathews, in 1856, 1857, and 1869, and then again under the title *The Enchanted Moccasins and Other Legends of the Americans* [*sic*] *Indians* in 1877.

Baraga: Frederic Baraga, *A Dictionary of the Ojibway Language*, 1878–1880. Rpt., with foreword by John D. Nichols, 1992. The classic, nineteenth-century dictionary by a Catholic bishop who was Schoolcraft's close contemporary and studied the language in regions close to the linguistic roots of Schoolcraft's own Ojibwe, particularly in La Pointe, where Schoolcraft's mother grew up, and in Northern Michigan, including Sault Ste. Marie. His last house now stands next to the Schoolcraft and Johnston houses in Sault Ste. Marie.

"Dawn":   Henry Rowe Schoolcraft, "Dawn of Literary Composition by Educated Natives of the aboriginal tribes," included in this volume.

HRS: Henry Rowe Schoolcraft.

Jameson: Mrs. [Anna Brownell] Jameson, *Winter Studies and Summer Rambles in Canada*, 1838.

JJS: Jane Johnston Schoolcraft.

IL: Jane Johnston Schoolcraft, *Poetry, 1815–1836* (the Jane Johnston Schoolcraft Papers). This bound manuscript in the Abraham Lincoln Presidential Library (where it moved in 2004 from the Illinois State Historical Library), Springfield, Illinois, consists of carefully transcribed poems by JJS, along with two poems by HRS from his book of poems *Indian Melodies* (1830). The manuscript is in HRS's hand and has an introduction by HRS, included in this volume. It dates one poem, "Lines written at Castle Island, Lake Superior," 1838, suggesting that the book was prepared after that date. Probably it was prepared after JJS's death in 1842. (The dates in the title were supplied by librarians.)

LC or LC: Henry Rowe Schoolcraft Papers, Manuscript Division, Library of Congress, Washington, D.C., which I have accessed on microfilm. Italicized in the annotations (*LC*); otherwise in roman type (LC). Numbers identify the container that holds the materials. For example, *LC70* refers to a manuscript in container number 70.

McKenney: Thomas L. McKenney, *Sketches of a Tour to the Lakes, of the Character and Customs of the Chippewa Indians, and of Incidents Connected with the Treaty of Fond du Lac.* 1827. Rpt., 1972.

Oneota: Oneota, or The Red Race of America. Ed. Henry R. Schoolcraft, 1844–45. An anthology of American Indian-related materials later reprinted under various titles.

Writings

To the Pine Tree

on first seeing it
on returning from Europe

Shing wauk! Shing wauk! nin ge ik id,
Waish kee wau bum ug, shing wauk
Tuh quish in aun nau aub, ain dak nuk i yaun.
Shing wauk, shing wauk No sa
Shi e gwuh ke do dis au naun
Kau gega way zhau wus co zid.

Mes ah nah, shi egwuh tah gwish en aung
Sin da mik ke aum baun
Kag ait suh, ne meen wain dum
Me nah wau, wau bun dah maun   10
Gi yut wi au, wau bun dah maun een
Shing wauk, shing wauk nosa
Shi e gwuh ke do dis au naun.

Ka ween ga go, kau wau bun duh e yun
Tib isht co, izz henau gooz ze no an
Shing wauk wah zhau wush co zid
Ween Ait ah kwanaudj e we we
Kau ge gay wa zhau soush ko zid

Translation

The pine! the pine! I eager cried,
The pine, my father! see it stand,
As first that cherished tree I spied,
Returning to my native land.
The pine! the pine! oh lovely scene!
The pine, that is forever green.

Ah beauteous tree! ah happy sight!
That greets me on my native strand
And hails me, with a friend's delight,
To my own dear bright mother land
Oh 'tis to me a heart-sweet scene,
The pine—the pine! that's ever green.

[Handwritten annotations:]

Use of diction that is parental father = pine, mother = land

uniformed stanza(s) LP ALL in the same set up.

Pine = is special bc it reminds her of her home, brings back loving memories - must be in an unfamiliar place

Variation kind of like a refrain

Why the repetition to returning home - cherishes her love for her native land

A B A B C C (margin letters)

Not all the trees of England bright,
Not Erin's lawns of green and light
Are half so sweet to memory's eye,
As this dear type of northern sky
Oh 'tis to me a heart-sweet scene,
The pine—the pine! that ever green.

To the Pine Tree. Text from *IL.* In his "Notes for a Memoir of Mrs. Henry Rowe Schoolcraft," addressed to Anna Jameson, HRS tells the story behind this poem. When JJS returned from Europe as a child in 1810, "On the home route from Quebec to St. Mary's, her father was impressed with the pleasure she appeared to derive from the scenery of her native country (always a strong point of admiration with her) but when, in crossing the Niagara ridge, in the route from Queenston to Fort Erie, she saw the pine, she could not resist the expression of impassioned admiration. 'There pa! see those pines!' she exclaimed, 'after all I have seen abroad, you have nothing equal to the dear pine.' At a later period, I asked her if she could not recal[l] her feelings at the moment, on which [s]he gave me some lines in the Indian language, of which, you [Jameson] will find a translation appended" (96–97). For another version of the same story, written about a decade later, see "Dawn" in this volume. The later version makes it sound as if JJS wrote the poem at a time closer to the event that provoked it, which seems unlikely, given that the event came when she was only ten years old.

The title was at first written as "To the Pine Tree. / seen at Queenston Heights, U. Canada / on returning from Europe." (U. Canada is an abbreviation for Upper Canada, which is now southern Ontario.) The second line of the title is crossed out and replaced with "on first seeing it". Between "returning" and "from" is added "with my father", which is then crossed out (leaving illegible the word that I am supposing is "my").

The English text, with its meter and its different pattern of rhyme, is not a literal translation of the Ojibwe text.

Ojibwe text. **1** Though it might not matter for this poem, Shingwauk, The Pine (also called Shingwaukonse, Little Pine), was the name of a prominent and eventually revered Ojibwe chief on the Canadian side of Sault Ste. Marie, well known to the Johnstons and Schoolcrafts. On Shingwauk, see especially Janet E. Chute, *Legacy*, and Chute, "Shingwaukonse," including p. 93 for his connection to the Johnston family. **5** *lovely*: loveliest with "est" crossed out and "i" changed to "y". **17** *Ween*: added in the left margin.

English text. **3** *cherished*: written above "darling", which is crossed out. **9** *a friend's*: written above "unmixed", which is crossed out.

To the Miscodeed*

Sweet pink of northern wood and glen,
E'er first to greet the eyes of men
In early spring,—a tender flower
Whilst still the wintry wind hath power.
How welcome, in the sunny glade,
Or hazel copse, thy pretty head
Oft peeping out, whilst still the snow,
Doth here and there, its presence show
Soon leaf and bud quick opening spread
Thy modest petals—white with red   10
Like some sweet cherub—love's kind link,
With dress of white, adorned with pink.

*The C. Virginica.

To the Miscodeed. Text from *IL*. The asterisk and note are in the manuscript. One of the first spring wildflowers, the miscoded (in Ojibwe), Claytonia Virginica (in Latin), or spring beauty is typically white with pink veins, though sometimes it is all pink. See also JJS's "Origin of the Miscodeed or the Maid of Taquimenon." HRS's poem "To Mrs. Schoolcraft. On the Anniversary of Her Birth-Day" includes the lines: "Search the Shadow-border'd mead, / For the blush-lit, *miscodeed*, / Native flower, of odor sweet, / Lover of the calm retreat" (*LC65*). Readers might like to compare "To the Miscodeed" with such once widely read early American poems about wild-flowers or blossoms as Philip Freneau's "The Wild Honey Suckle" (1786), William Cullen Bryant's "The Yellow Violet" (1821) and "To the Fringed Gentian" (1832), and Ralph Waldo Emerson's "The Rhodora" (1847).

 11 *love's*: the cherubic Cupid, the god of love, often referred to simply as "love." **12** *dress*: written above "frock", which is crossed out. **12** *white*: another word, now hard to read but perhaps "pure", is crossed out before "white". **12** *adorned*: another word, now illegible, is crossed out before "adorned".

Lines written at Castle Island, Lake Superior

Here in my native inland sea
From pain and sickness would I flee
And from its shores and island bright
Gather a store of sweet delight.
Lone island of the saltless sea!
How wide, how sweet, how fresh and free
How all transporting—is the view
Of rocks and skies and waters blue
Uniting, as a song's sweet strains
To tell, here nature only reigns.   10
Ah, nature! here forever sway
Far from the haunts of men away
For here, there are no sordid fears,
No crimes, no misery, no tears
No pride of wealth; the heart to fill,
No laws to treat my people ill.

Lines written at Castle Island, Lake Superior. A translation, by HRS or JJS, of
a poem in Ojibwe by JJS. The Ojibwe version has not survived. There are
three versions, all in HRS's hand. One version appears, untitled, in "Castle
Island," a prose manuscript by HRS in *LC62*, recounting a visit to the island
on 14 Aug., without naming the year. Another appears in *IL*, and a third
and considerably different version appears in "Dawn." Because the prose
manuscript's detail gives it the air of having been written soon after the event
and during JJS's lifetime, I have chosen its version for the text. Since "Dawn"
was written later and includes revisions on the manuscript, HRS probably
revised the poem for "Dawn." I take the title from *IL*. The revisions in *IL*
might come from JJS, HRS, or both of them. In the prose manuscript, HRS
describes a voyage with JJS and their children west across Lake Superior off
the coast of Michigan's Upper Peninsula, focusing on their day trip to an
isolated island "due north" of Granite Point. He describes the poem as "a
free translation of some lines in the Odjibwa language, handed me by Mrs.
S. the original of which is cherished as a morceau of Indian literature."
"Finding the island without a distinctive name, among the Odjibwas," he
adds, "Mrs. S. proposed the appropriate one of Castle Island, in allusion to
its castellated appearance at a distance." "Dawn" refers to it as "a volcanic
little island called Nebiquon in the entrance of lake Superior" and describes
the voyage as an "inspiring" and "invigorating" effort to restore JJS's health.

Identifying the exact island has taken some sleuthing. Castle Island lies to the northwest off the coast of Isle Royale, much too far to be the island in question, and there is no island due north of Granite Point. But it turns out that the place names have changed over the years. In 1820, HRS himself provided the name Granite Point for what is now called Little Presque Isle; his 1821 *Narrative Journal* of the Cass expedition even includes a hand-colored geological cross-section of Granite Point (158–60), and Thomas L. McKenney describes exploring Granite Point with HRS in 1826 (McKenney 193–95). Seven miles northwest of the present Marquette, Michigan, Little Presque Isle was connected to the mainland as late as the early twentieth century, and until then it was called Granite Point, not to be confused with the current Granite Point, farther northwest. Due north of Little Presque Isle lies Granite Island, which fits the description in HRS's account, and which in Ojibwe is called Na-Be-Quon, which translates into English as ship or vessel (Baraga 2: 262; H. R. Schoolcraft et al., *Vocabulary*, LC61; AR 2: 46). HRS's *Personal Memoirs* clinch the identification and the year, recalling a visit on 6 Aug. 1838 to "the dimly seen island in the lake, off Presque Isle and Granite Point, called *Nabikwon* by the Indians, from the effects of mirage. Its deep volcanic chasms, and upheaved rocks, tell a story of mighty elemental conflicts in the season of storms" (603). On the history of the name for Little Presque Isle, see Bernard C. Peters 56, 61, 63–64. (For another reference to Granite Point, see the note to next poem, "On the Doric Rock, Lake Superior.")

Schoolcraft begins this poem with a revealing identification with her region, as in "The Miscodeed" and "To the Pine Tree," and with a sense of her own "pain and sickness" that many of her letters and other poems reveal as characteristic. The resentment of cosmopolitan artificiality fits what we might expect from someone who preferred life away from the cities and resented the exoticizing gaze she met in New York. Even so, the resentment of laws that mistreat her people stands out with its uncharacteristically direct political statement. HRS may have written it; if so, he presumably sought to express something that he sensed or wanted to sense in JJS's poem. But in the absence of any evidence that HRS wrote those words (as opposed to translating them), it seems telling that poetry in general and poetry about her devotion to the region in particular would bring out from JJS this passionate anticolonialist lament.

5 *island*: islet *IL*. **6–9** How vast is all around—how free! / The waves come dashing clear and bright / The heavens are blue—the sky is bright / And all unites in sweetest strains *IL*. **13** *sordid fears*: false displays *IL*. **14–15** No lures to lead in folly's maze / Or fashion's rounds to hurt or kill. *IL*. **16** *treat*: the word "treat" can evoke the sorry history of treaties between the U.S. government and Indian nations. **16** Two more lines follow line 16 in *IL*: But all is glorious, free, and grand, / Fresh from the great Creator's hand.

On the Doric Rock, Lake Superior

To a Friend

Dwellers at home, in indolence and ease,
How deep their debt, to those that roam the seas,
Or cross the lands, in quest of every art
That science, knowledge, pity can impart
To help mankind, or guild the lettered page
The bold discoverers of every age.

This spirit—in thy breast the ardent guide
To seek new lands, and wastes as yet untried
Where none but hunters trod the field before
Unveiled the grandeur of Superior's show   10
Where nature's forms in varied shape and guise
Break on the view, with wonder and surprize.
Not least, among those forms, the traveller's tale,
These pillared rocks and castle pomps prevail
Standing, like some vast ruin of the plain,
Where ancient victims by their priests were slain
But far more wondrous,—for the fair design
No architect drew out, with measured line
'Twas nature's wildest flower, that graved the Rock,
The waves' loud fury, and the tempest's shock   20
Yet all that arts can do, here frowning shine,
In mimic pride, and grandeur of design.

The simple Indian, as the work he spies,
Looks up to nature's God above the skies
And though, his lot be rugged wild and dear,
Yet owns the ruling power with soul sincere,
Not as where, Asia's piles of marble high,
For idol gods the beast was doomed to die,
But, guided by a purer-led surprise,
Points to the great good sovreign of the skies   30
And thinks the power that built the upper sphere,
Hath left but traces of his fingers here.

Figure 8. Front view of the Doric Rock, Lake Superior. 1826 water color copy by Fielding Lucas of an 1826 sketch by James Otto Lewis. American Philosophical Society, Philadelphia, Pennsylvania.

On the Doric Rock, Lake Superior. Text from *IL*. As early as the first European record of the region, by the French adventurer and trader Pierre Esprit Radisson in 1661, the Doric Rock was noted as a place of veneration and sacrifice (Radisson 190–91). The voyageurs called it La Chapelle, a name still in use in English as the Chapel. The Chapel still stands, despite some accounts to the contrary (Peters 49–50). HRS opened his 1821 *Narrative Journal*, which would have been familiar to JJS, with an illustration of the Doric Rock on the frontispiece, followed by a detailed description later in the book (152–53). In the summer of 1831, he led a large federal expedition west from Sault Ste. Marie to the Mississippi River; Galena, Illinois; and Prairie du Chien in present-day Wisconsin to negotiate a treaty, vaccinate Indians against small-pox, and conduct scientific exploration. JJS and the children accompanied the expedition on the beginning of the voyage as far as Lake Superior (H. Schoolcraft, *Personal Memoirs* 350). Among the party were JJS's brother George Johnston, Douglass Houghton, Melancthon L. Woolsey (a young printer from Detroit, according to HRS's *Personal Memoirs* 350), and Lieu-tenant Robert Clary. For an account of the expedition, see Bremer 123–26.

Both HRS and Woolsey wrote JJS letters that described the Doric Rock, part of the Pictured Rocks region on the Michigan coast. On 3 July, HRS wrote from Granite Point: "We passed the Pictured Rocks that morning, and I have only to name them to remind you that granduer [*sic*] here puts on such varied forms, as to keep the eye constantly on the stretch. We took our dinner in the little cove near the Doric Rock, partaking of one of your pies, for a desert. And I took a new view of the interesting object, showing it in quite another point of view. Mr. Clary was perfectly delighted with it . . . and said he was repaid for the voyage, if he saw nothing else. But the boldest scenes were beyond. The outer arch of the main point, which we saw in 1820, has fallen down, but I passed with my canoe, [illegible word] standing, beneath the inner arch, turned about in it, & came out out [*sic*], as the fallen rocks on the other side prevented our going out" (*LC37*).

Woolsey's effusive letters to JJS suggest that he had something of a crush on her. His description in a letter of 5 July, while lengthy (though only part of a much longer letter), together with HRS's letter suggests a source or at the least a closely contemporary analog for the description in JJS's poem: "we commenced a minute examination of the celebrated Doric Rock. The principal arch, under which we were, is about twenty feet in height; and while standing under its crumbling walls, our sensations were not lessened by the idea that in an instant it might be said of us, *we had been*. At our left, and in the centre of one of the large pillars another arch is formed,—upon entering this we still find one more at our right, and which commands a view of the lake. Between the two stands a pillar of stone, near four feet in height, entirely detached at the sides, and composed of thin plates of sand-rock. As we go out from these, for the purpose of ascending the roof, a large urn of nature's own design and workmanship, appears before us. It might be a fit depository for the ashes of some of those mighty men, who before the children 'with a white, white face,' overran their country, strode through these forests, or, in their light canoes bounded over these vast waters—but alas, their graves and those of their fathers are mingling with the common dust! Near this urn are the remains of an Indian's fire, which he had lighted at the close of his fast, when propitiating his Manito—a place well calculated to foster the wildness of superstition, and which to a mind more enlightened than that of the poor wanderer of the wilderness, would not be deficient in suggestions of mystery. Who can wonder that the untaught natives of a region like this, should make to themselves a Deity in the rushing stream or the beetling cliff? They act from the impulse of nature, and well will it be for those who enjoy every advantage that civilization and Christianity can bestow, if when weighed in the balance, even with the pagan Indian, they are not found wanting. We were soon at the top of the Doric Rock, and from its dizzy height the prospect was such as to preclude all attempt at delineation, at least by language. Your brother expressed his emotion as well as it was in the power of any mortal to do. Clapping his hands together, and putting a peculiar emphasis upon the last syllable, he exclaimed "Oh! *Oh!*" Nothing more could be said. But while enjoying the grandeur of the scene, I wished that M. was at my side, for my pleasure would have been increased ten-fold by sharing it with her. The summit of the arch is itself a curiosity. It does not appear to be more than three feet in thickness, and yet it supports and nourishes several lofty pine trees, whose weight alone I should think would crush it to atoms. The root of one of them winds around the outer edge of the rock, as if to support the source of its existence. But we had not long to indulge our admiration, for our table was spread under the shade of one of these immense rocks, and all the sublimity around us could not satisfy the imperious demands of appetite; so after regaling ourselves on some of the dainties furnished by our excellent friends at the Sault, we departed to behold new wonders, and utter repeated exclamations of, *Oh! Oh!*" Perhaps these letters provoked JJS to write this poem. (Woolsey's letter of 5 July does not survive in manuscript, but in 1836 it appeared, with his other letters to JJS—and with an introduction by HRS, next to a poem by HRS—in the *Southern Literary Messenger*, a leading journal edited by none other than Edgar Allan Poe. HRS later reprinted Woolsey's letters in *Oneota*.)

HRS passed by the Doric Rock again the following year with another expedition, and James Allen's journal from that expedition, which was soon published and reprinted, includes yet another detailed description of the Doric Rock (169). JJS would also have seen the description in Thomas L. McKenney's *Sketches* (185–86).

8 *wastes as yet*: written above "seas before", which is crossed out. **15–16** Ancient ruins were a preoccupation of eighteenth- and early nineteenth-century British and American poetry; see Goldstein, *Ruins and Empire*. **20** *waves'*: editor's emendation of "waves". **32** *but*: written above "the", which is crossed out. "But" would seem to diminish the value of the "traces" compared to the vast force of even so modest a figure of the "power" as its "fingers".

"My humble present is a purse"

My humble present is a purse,
  Of little worth 'tis true;
Without, 'tis plain, and what is worse
  Within, 'tis empty too.

But not to cost, in Friendship's eye,
  The gift its value owes;
And oft we prize a trifle high,
  When 'tis the heart bestows.

This claim at least, I do aver,
  And promise by this billet,   10
Take you the purse tho' empty now,
  And when I can I'll fill it.

"My humble present is a purse." Text from *LC70*. Untitled. This humble but delightfully witty and metrically skilled poem follows a style that is not characteristic of JJS's poetry. While I have found no corroboration of her authorship beyond the manuscript in her hand, I have also found no sign that anyone else wrote it.

10 *billet*: ticket or note.

Invocation

To my Maternal Grand-father on hearing his descent from Chippewa ancestors misrepresented

Rise bravest chief! of the mark of the noble deer,
      With eagle glance,
      Resume thy lance,
And wield again thy warlike spear!
      The foes of thy line,
      With coward design,
Have dared with black envy to garble the truth,
And stain with a falsehood thy valorous youth.

They say when a child, thou wert ta'en from the Sioux,
      And with impotent aim,   10
      To lessen thy fame
Thy warlike lineage basely abuse;
      For they know that our band,
      Tread a far distant land,
And thou noble chieftain art nerveless and dead,
Thy bow all unstrung, and thy proud spirit fled.

Can the sports of thy youth, or thy deeds ever fade?
      Or those e'er forget,
      Who are mortal men yet,
The scenes where so bravely thou'st lifted the blade,   20
      Who have fought by thy side,
      And remember thy pride,
When rushing to battle, with valour and ire,
Thou saw'st the fell foes of thy nation expire?

Can the warrior forget how sublimely you rose?
      Like a star in the west,
      When the sun's sunk to rest,
That shines in bright splendour to dazzle our foes?
      Thy arm and thy yell,
      Once the tale could repel   30
Which slander invented, and minions detail,
And still shall thy actions refute the false tale.

Rest thou, <u>noblest chief!</u> in thy dark house of clay,
    Thy deeds and thy name,
    Thy child's child shall proclaim,
And make the dark forests resound with the lay;
    Though thy spirit has fled,
    To the hills of the dead,
Yet thy name shall be held in my heart's warmest core,
And cherish'd till valour and love be no more.   40

Invocation To my Maternal Grand-father on hearing his descent from Chippewa ancestors misrepresented. Text from the *Southern Literary Messenger*, 1860. There is also a text in *LC66* with the same words and minor differences of punctuation and spelling; I have chosen the *Southern Literary Messenger* version rather than *LC66*, because *LC66* is not in JJS's hand, and because the *Southern Literary Messenger* version was prepared for publication but did not undergo meddling revision. Another version survives in two drafts that follow next in this edition. At the bottom of *LC66*, on the left, is written "[1823.]", and on the right, "Rosa," one of JJS's pen names. JJS's maternal grandfather, Waubojeeg, had two Sioux half-brothers. Between the title and the text, the 1860 printing says "BY THE LATE MRS. HENRY R. SCHOOLCRAFT, / An educated descendant of WABJEEG, through Irish parentage, who died in 1842." Metrically, this is probably JJS's most intricate poem.

    1 *mark of the noble deer*: Waubojeeg's totem, or clan, was the reindeer.

Invocation to My Maternal Grandfather, Wabojeeg, on hearing his descent misrepresented
[shorter draft]

Rise bravest chief! of the mark of the noble deer,
Resume thy lance, and again wield thy warlike spear!
The foes of thy line, have dar'd to speak an untruth
Their tongues with black envy, throw a stain on thy youth,
They say, when a child, thou wert stol'n from the Sioux,
And thy lineage they cowardly, basely abuse.
For they know that our kinsmen, a distant land tread,
And thy spirit has fled—to the hills of the dead!
Can the sports of thy youth, and thy deeds ever fade,
From the minds of those men, who had oft with thee stray'd,   10
Who have fought by thy side, and remember thy pride

When to battle you led, and the ground you have dy'd
With the blood of thy foes, and ensured the repose
Of thy country long trembling with dread. Till you rose,
Like a star in the west, when the sun's sunk to rest,
You shone in bright splendor, to thy kindred oppress'd.
The mem'ry of thy deeds can refute the false tale
Which slander invented and base-born souls detail
But, noblest chief!—thy child's, child thy praises shall sing
The dark forests and plains with loud echo shall ring   20
Tho' thy spirit has fled to the hills of the dead,
Yet thy worth?, in remembrance long, long shall be led?.

[longer draft]

Rise bravest chief! of the mark* of the noble deer,
Resume thy lance, and wield again thy warlike spear
The foes of thy line, throw a stain on thy youth,
And their tongues with black envy, they garble the truth
They say, thou wert ta'en, when a child from the Sioux*
And thy blood they most cowardly, basely abuse.
For they know that our kinsmen, a distant land tread,
And thou, noble chieftain! art nerveless and dead

   Can the sports of thy youth, or thy deeds ever fade?
From men's xxxxxx, who with thee, have oft lifted the blade   10
Who have fought in thy band, and have bled at thy side
When to battle you led them, and triumphed with pride
When the war cloud hung black, o'er the plains of the west,
And tribe after tribe, on your hunting grounds prest,
When the false Outagami, leagued fast with our foes,
And panic and dread spread around, til you rose
Like a Star in the West, and with weapons in hand,
Drove dauntless and reckless the foe from the land.

   The renown of thy deeds, can refute the false tale,
That cowards invented, and minions detail   20
Thy child's child, thy praise shall triumphantly sing.
And make thine own Lake,* with the loud echo ring.
Then rest, noble chief! on thy scaffold of state,

With war bonnet crowned, and with war trophies great,
Whilst thy daring, thy prowess, thy battles, thy songs,
A tribe's recollections repeats and prolongs
Thy kindred, thy country, one impulse en-league,
And vie in the praise of the brave Odjeeg.

*Totem
*Pronounced *Sooz.*
*Superior.

*cousin)
a form of
his name*

Invocation To my Maternal Grandfather, Wabojeeg, *on hearing his descent mis-represented.* Text of the shorter draft from a manuscript among HRS's poems in *LC70,* where it has no title. Text of the longer draft, which provides the title, from *IL.* There, "from Odjibwa ancestors" is crossed out between "descent" and "misrepresented," and after the title, "1827" is crossed out. The asterisks and notes in the longer draft are in the manuscript. See the other version of this poem immediately just above in this edition.

We have no way to tell which came first, the version in *LC66* (from 1827, and repeated in 1860), or the version in *LC70* in JJS's hand, but we can surmise that both came before *IL,* because HRS probably wrote out *IL* after JJS's death in 1842. Perhaps the version in *IL* is HRS's enlargement and revision of JJS's poem; the last lines of *IL* evince a heroics that seems closer to HRS's more stereotypically masculine style than to JJS's more stereotypically feminine style. But such characterizations of gendered and individual style risk distorting JJS and HRS to make them fit culturally habitual preconceptions. Moreover, the shorter and longer drafts have other differences besides the possible difference in gendered style. The shorter version, for example, favors internal rhyme (lines 8, 11, 13, 15, and 21), which the longer version abandons. For some reason, HRS chose one version as the basis for *IL* and another version for publication in 1860.

By proclaiming JJS's role as a memorialist of her grandfather, these poems suggest a commitment to family history and pride, including pride in her grandfather's "warlike lineage." Matching the pride with worry about betrayal, enemies among her own people, "envy," resentment, rumor, and "slander," these poems also suggest a vulnerability over family reputation in JJS's and her mother's Ojibwe world.

Longer draft. **10** *men's*————: not legible and could be mistranscribed in the manuscript, or might read "memory," which, however, strains the anapestic rhythm, though it offers a nice internal rhyme for "who with thee." **15** *Outagami:* an Ojibwe name for the people who in English were called the Fox. They call themselves the Meskwaki, a term now gaining wider use. The

Meskwaki are closely related to the Ojibwe culturally and linguistically, de-spite their history of conflict. **23** *scaffold of state*: written above "dark house of clay", which is crossed out. **24** written above "The sting that assails, its own bosom shall slay", which is crossed out. **28** "warlike" is crossed out between "brave" and "Odjeeg."

To a Bird, Seen Under My Window in the Garden

Sweet little bird, thy notes prolong,
    And ease my lonely pensive hours;
I love to list thy cheerful song,
    And hear thee chirp beneath the flowers.

The time allowed for pleasures sweet,
    To thee is short as it is bright,
Then sing! rejoice! before it fleet,
    And cheer me ere you take your flight.

To a Bird, Seen Under My Window in the Garden. Text from *Oneota* (345). There is also a version in *IL* called "To a Bird in the Garden" and otherwise differing only in minor variations of punctuation. I use the text from *Oneota* because HRS followed it through to publication. Between the title and the first line of the *Oneota* version appears the explanation "By the late Mrs. H. R. SCHOOLCRAFT, who was a grand daughter of the war chief WABOJEEG."

    The sense of pensive, lonely sadness in this poem, with its plea to "cheer me," recurs frequently through JJS's poetry. The garden is also a characteristic setting for her poems, matching what her letters and HRS's letters and memoirs indicate about their interests and activities. Given JJS's role as a poet, figuratively a singer, and her frequent sense that she will lead a short life, this poem suggests a touching identification with the bird. While animals frequently populate her poems, it seems curious that this bird remains vaguely just a "bird" rather than a particular kind of bird. Many other nineteenth-century American poets wrote poems that in various ways identified themselves with birds (Walker 46–49).

Lines to a Friend Asleep

Awake my friend! the morning's fine,
Waste not in sleep the day divine;
Nature is clad in best array,
The woods, the fields, the flowers are gay;—
The sun is up, and speeds his march,
O'er heaven's high aërial arch,
His golden beams with lustre fall,
On lake and river, cot and hall;—
The dews are sparkling on each spray,
The birds are chirping sweet and gay,   10
The violet shows its beauteous head,
Within its narrow, figured bed;—
The air is pure, the earth bedight,
With trees and flowers, life and light,
All—all inspires a joyful gleam,
More pleasing than a fairy dream.
Awake! the sweet refreshing scene,
Invites us forth to tread the green,
With joyful hearts, and pious lays,
To join the glorious Maker's praise,   20
The wond'rous works—the paschal lamb,
The holy, high, and just I Am.

Lines to a Friend Asleep. There are four manuscripts, one in *LC65*, two in *LC70*, here labeled *LC70-1* and *LC70-2*, and another in *IL*. *LC70-1*, just nine lines long, appears to be the earliest surviving draft, followed by *LC70-2*. *LC65* and *IL* are closer to each other than to *LC70-2*, and both incorporate most of the revisions in process in *LC70-2*. Because *LC65* was probably prepared for readers with JJS's approval, even though it may include changes suggested or imposed by HRS or introduced by the *Literary Voyager* copyist, I have chosen it for the text. At the end of the poem, *LC65* is attributed to "Rosa," one of JJS's pen names. It is not clear whether *IL* was transcribed from *LC65*, *LC70-2*, or another version. HRS gives his view of the poem in "Dawn": "Her sense of the beautiful in nature, and her warm, yet simple appreciation of those beauties, as unfolded by the landscape, is expressed in some lines, addressed to a female friend, who yet coveted the downy pillow of repose, on a summer's morning." On the same small sheet of paper as the early draft in *LC70-1*, and slightly overlapping the last line of the poem,

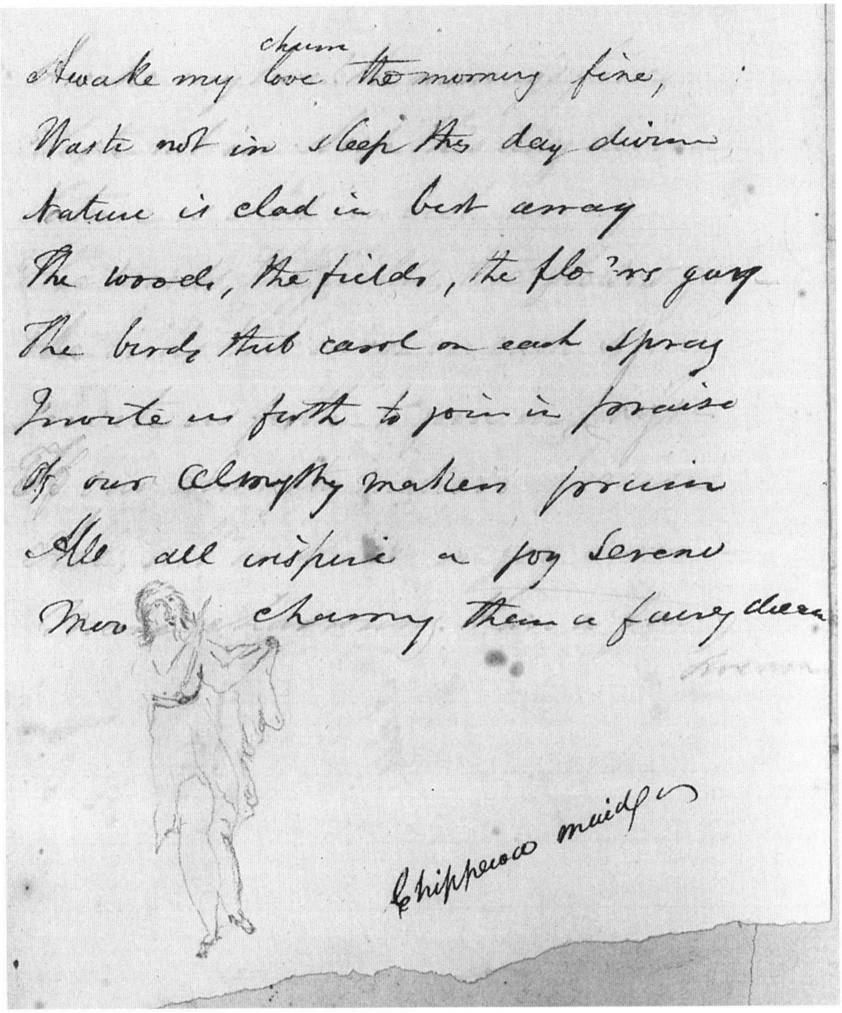

Figure 9. Manuscript of "Lines to a Friend Asleep" with sketch of a "Chippewa maiden" who appears to be dancing. Henry Rowe Schoolcraft Papers, Manuscript Division, Library of Congress, Washington, D.C.

appears a rough sketch of a dancing woman wearing an animal pelt, with the words "Chippewa maiden," probably in HRS's hand, next to the drawing. See figure 9.

title To a female friend—*LC70-2*. **7** *LC70-2* has "piercing" crossed out and "golden" written above it. **8** *lake*: copse *IL*. **11** Before this line, *LC70-2* has crossed out "The air is balmy pure, and violets sweet / Show these gay heads", with the last four words very uncertainly transcribed. Compare the note to line 13. **12** *narrow, figured*: figured flowery *LC70-2* and *IL*. **13** *pure, the earth bedight*: ~~balmy~~ pure ~~and pure~~ the skies serene *LC70-2*. **14** And light and life completes the scene *LC70-2*. **16** *More pleasing than a*: Bland as a lightsome *IL*; "Bland" is an approximate transcription for an illegible word. **21–22** not in *IL*. **21** "Paschal" means passover, and the paschal lamb, sacrificed in the Jewish Passover, is often a figure for the sacrificed Jesus, the "Lamb of God" (John 1:29). **22** *LC70-2* has "The high, almighty, great *I AM*." "*I AM*" is written on top of something else, now illegible. Above "almighty, great" is written "the inscrutable"; below it is written "the holy—, just", and below "just" is written "dreading" ("dreading" is an uncertain transcription), all without crossouts.

By an *Ojibwa Female* Pen

Invitation to sisters to a walk in the Garden, after a shower

Come, sisters come! the shower's past,
The garden walks are drying fast,
The Sun's bright beams are seen again,
And nought within, can now detain.
The rain drops tremble on the leaves,
Or drip expiring, from the eaves;
But soon the cool and balmy air,
Shall dry the gems that sparkle there,
With whisp'ring breath shake ev'ry spray,
And scatter every cloud away.   10

Thus sisters! shall the breeze of hope,
Through sorrow's clouds a vista ope;
Thus, shall affliction's surly blast,
By faith's bright calm be still'd at last;
Thus, pain and care,—the tear and sigh,
Be chased from every dewy eye;
And life's mix'd scene itself, but cease,
To show us realms of light and peace.

By an Ojibwa Female *Pen, Invitation to sisters to a walk in the Garden, after a shower.* Text from *LC64*. There is another version in *LC70*, less legible and mistake-free than JJS's usual drafts, suggesting that it is an earlier version, though readers might prefer some of its variants. *LC64* was probably prepared for readers with JJS's approval, even though it may include changes suggested or imposed by HRS or introduced by the *Literary Voyager* copyist. At the end of the poem, *LC64* is attributed to "Rosa," one of JJS's pen names.

title "By an *Ojibwa Female* Pen," seems to have been added later, perhaps more as explanation than as part of the title, as was "sisters to". "after a shower of rain" is crossed out, and "after a shower" is written above it. *LC70* has the title as "Invitation to a walk in the Garden after a light Shower of rain." 4 *nought*: naught. 4 *within*: in *LC70* "at home" is crossed out, and "within" is written above it. 4 *now*: us *LC70*. 10 *scatter every cloud*: wipe and scatter them *LC70*. 14 *calm*: lamp *LC70*. 15–16: Thus tears, and cares, and envys cry / Be denied and chased from every eye *LC70*. In this sometimes difficult-to-read manuscript, "envys" and "denied" are uncertain transcriptions, and "chased" is apparently written as "chasped". 17 *mix'd*: dull *LC70*.

Pensive Hours

The sun had sunk like a glowing ball,
As lonely I sat in my father's hall;
I walk'd to the window, and musing awhile,
The still, pensive moments I sought to beguile:
Just by me, ran smoothly the dark deep stream,
And bright silver rays on its breast did beam;—
And as with mild luster the vestal orb rose,
All nature betokened a holy repose,
Save the Sound of St. Mary's—that softly and clear
Still fell in sweet murmurs upon my pleas'd ear   10
Like the murmur of voices we know to be kind,
Or war's silken banners unfurled to the wind,
Now rising, like shouts of the proud daring foe,
Now falling, like whispers congenial and low.
Amidst such a scene, thoughts arose in my mind;
Of my father, far distant—of life, and mankind;
But slowing, receding—with awe most profound
They rested on God, and his works spread around,
Divine meditation!—and tear drops like dew—
Now moisten'd my hand,—for His mercy I knew: 20
Since even a leaf cannot wither and die,
Unknown to his care, or unseen by his eye;
Oh how much more then, will he hear when we mourn,
And heal the pierced heart that by anguish is torn,
When he sees that the soul to His will loves to bend,
And patiently suffers and waits to the end.
Such thoughts—the lone moments serenely employed,
Creating contentment and peace unalloyed—
Till roused by my harp—which so tremblingly true,
The soft balmy night breeze enchantingly blew,   30
The sounds to my heart as they vibrated clear,
Thrill'd sweetly and carried the melody tried,
Softer and sweeter the harmony rings,
I fanceyed some spirit was touching the strings,
And answered, or seemed to my hopes, thus to say,
Let thy Soul live in hope, mortal:—watch still and pray.
A holy tranquility spread o'er my mind.

3- *Religious*
Like father,
son + Holy Ghost

At peace with myself, with my God, and mankind.
I felt that my prayers were heard and approv'd,
For the speedy return of my father beloved;   40
For the health I so priz'd, but so seldom enjoyed.
That the time yet in store—should be wisely employed.
And my mind ever feel, as I felt at that time,
So pensively joyful, so humbly sublime.—

If only my mind could feel like she does today

Interesting way to end

Pensive Hours. There are two manuscripts in *LC70*, here labeled *LC70-1* and *LC70-2*, and another in *IL*. In issues number 1 (*LC64*) and number 16 (*LC66*) of *The Literary Voyager*, the title "Pensive Lines" appears above a space for the poem, but the space is blank; it might have been filled out in other copies of those magazine numbers that have not survived or been found. The pattern of revisions suggests a sequence from *LC70-1* to *LC70-2* to HRS's transcription in *IL*. The *IL* version may include revisions from HRS, from JJS, or from HRS and JJS jointly. *LC70-1* and *LC70-2* differ far more from each other than *LC70-2* and *IL*. The text could come from *IL*, because it is more finished than *LC70-2*, without the revisions of a draft in process, but I have followed the text from *LC70-2*, the last version in JJS's hand, because it seems more likely to match JJS's writing and preferences. Still, potentially substantive variants from *IL* are noted below, followed by a full transcription of *LC70-1*. Most readers will probably be struck by an improvement between *LC70-1* and *LC70-2*, and the difference between them offers a window onto JJS's process of composition and revision.

title Beneath the title, *IL* has "Written during my Father's last visit to Ireland, in 1820." The word "last" is added above the line. **6** *And*: The *IL*. **6** *beam*: "b" and "g" are written in the same space, as if JJS hesitated between "beam" and "gleam"; *IL* has "gleam". **7** "All nature" is crossed out, and then the line begins again beneath the cross-out. **7** *vestal orb*: "vestal" is written above "silver", which is crossed out. Alluding to the vestal virgins of ancient Rome, "vestal" was a typical poetic term for a chaste woman. *IL* has "night orb*" and a note at the bottom of the page that reads: "**Pibik Geezis*—night-Sun. Odjibwa." Baraga has the following entry: "*Tibikgisiss, or tibikigisiss.* Night-sun, that is, the moon; which is also called *gisiss*; only for a distinction from the sun, they will call the moon *tibikgisiss*, when a distinction becomes necessary" (Part II, 386). **9** *St. Mary's*: the St. Mary's River at Sault Ste. Marie. **9** An illegible word, perhaps "honey", is crossed out, and "softly" is written above it. **10** *sweet*: written in above "soft". "Soft" is not crossed out, but before it appears a deliberately drawn mark resembling a "Z", except that the line in the center is disproportionally long and runs straight up and down. Since the rhythm does not allow for both "sweet" and "soft," the neat mark may indicate that JJS had not decided between them. In that context, I have emended in accord with *IL*, which has "sweet" but not "soft." **12** *war's*: written above "the sound", which is crossed out. **12** "Or the broad leafy forest disturbed by a wind" *IL*. **12–14** This description and the parallel passage in *LC70-1* probably draw on JJS's memory of the War of 1812 at Fort Mackinac, though it could also draw on a fabled moment of crisis at Sault Ste. Marie in 1820, when war almost broke out after Sassaba, a pro-British, anti-American chief, raised a British flag in defiance of Lewis Cass's expedition, which had come to assert federal authority and demand a treaty. The outnumbered Cass marched unarmed into the Ojibwe village and trampled on the British flag. As recounted in the introduction to this volume, JJS's mother, Ozhaguscodaywayquay, and her brother George then averted war by convincing the local Ojibwe leaders to agree to Cass's treaty. In *IL*, transcribed and possibly revised by HRS, the official representative of national and federal power, the allusion to war and national conflict disappears. **15** "pensive" is crossed out between "thoughts" and "arose"; "fill'd" is crossed out between "thoughts" and "my", and "arose in" is written above it. **17** "passing, they fi-" [with the hyphen representing an illegible letter] is crossed out, and "slowing, receding—" is written above, with the rest of the line following at the same height above the earlier start of the line. **17** *awe*: "thought" is crossed out before "awe" in *IL*, which thus considers a revision and then returns to the earlier version. **19** "Sweet solace—" is crossed out, and the line begun again below it. **20** *Now*: Be *IL*. **21** *wither*: fall *IL*. **22** *care*: power *IL*. **25** "is resign'd" is crossed out, and "strives to bend", is written above it; "strives" is then crossed out, and "loves" is written above it. **27** An illegible word, perhaps "well", is crossed out, and "serenely" is written above it. **28** This line appears below another version that is crossed out and partly illegible: "And I felt it imported? a pleasure xxxxxxed, unalloyed." **29** At around this point the revisions proliferate, and the writing starts to look rushed, as if ideas were coming too quickly for JJS to continue with her usual neatness. **29** three or four illegible words (the first beginning with "wh") are crossed out, and "which so tremblingly true," is written above them, except that "so" is an emendation from *IL* for an illegible word. **29** harp: *IL* has an asterisk at "harp" and a note at the bottom of the page that reads, "*The Eolian Harp." An aeolian harp, named for Aeolus, the Greek god of the winds, is a box with gut strings placed in a window and tuned to produce harmony when the wind blows, like a wind chime. It was a popular metaphor of poetic inspiration for Romantic poets and—as in this poem—a nature-inspired way to defeat dejection, as in "The Eolian Harp" (1796 and later) and "Dejection: An Ode" (1802) by Samuel Taylor Coleridge (1772–1834), or in "Stanzas Written under Aeolus' Harp" (1795 and later) by Amelia Alderson Opie (1769–1853). This is not to suggest that JJS necessarily drew on Opie (though she copied out a poem of Opie's, without noting Opie as its author *LC19*) or on Coleridge (whom her allusion seems closer to and whom she would probably have read), for the aeolian harp was a routine object and metaphor in Romantic poetry. See M. H. Abrams's essay "The Correspondent Breeze." In about 1910, Anna M. Johnstone [*sic*], daughter of JJS's youngest sibling, John, wrote a recollection of the Johnston house that JJS grew up in, that HRS lived in on first moving to Sault Ste. Marie, and that JJS and HRS lived in at the beginning of their marriage. As a child, Johnstone—who was born in 1844 (Weaver 32)—would visit her Aunt Eliza, JJS's sister, who stayed in the family home. Describing what is probably the same harp that JJS writes about in "Pensive Hours," Johnstone's unpublished typescript recalls "the old Eolian harp which Aunt would place in the open windows," remembering that "the wind in blowing over the strings made such strange, indescribable music." **32** *sweetly*: written above "deep on my breast", which is crossed out. **32** "tried" is an uncertain transcription. **32** *carried the melody tried*: blest the wild melody dear. *IL.* **33** "thy, melted away" ("thy," is an uncertain transcription) is crossed out; "in air," is crossed out above "away"; and "the harmony rings" is written above the entire crossout. **34** *touching the strings*: written above "whispering there", which is crossed out. **36** "still" is written before "watch" and is crossed out, with "mortal:—" written above it. The words after "watch" include some writing on top of other writing, so that the "and" (an ampersand) is uncertainly transcribed. In *IL* the line is in quotation marks, and reads: "Live mortal in hope—let thy soul watch and pray." **37–38** A mark resembling an "X" two lines high appears near the left margin, apparently to cross out the last two lines of this draft, which read "At this instant, I felt my prayers heard, and approved, / For the speedy return of my father beloved—". Beneath those lines is "1820." And beneath that, with a different pen and in smaller, calmer writing, appear eight lines (here rendered as lines 37–44) apparently written in place of the cancelled two lines. **39** *heard and*: divinely *IL.* **40** *speedy return of my*: boon I implored, and a *IL.* **42** *the time*: my days *IL.* **44** *joyful*: trustful *IL.* **44** *humbly*: written above "sweetly", which is crossed out.

Following is the text of *LC70-1* (see figure 10):

(Pensive Lines.)
The sun had sunk like a glowing ball,
As lonely I sat in my Father's hall;

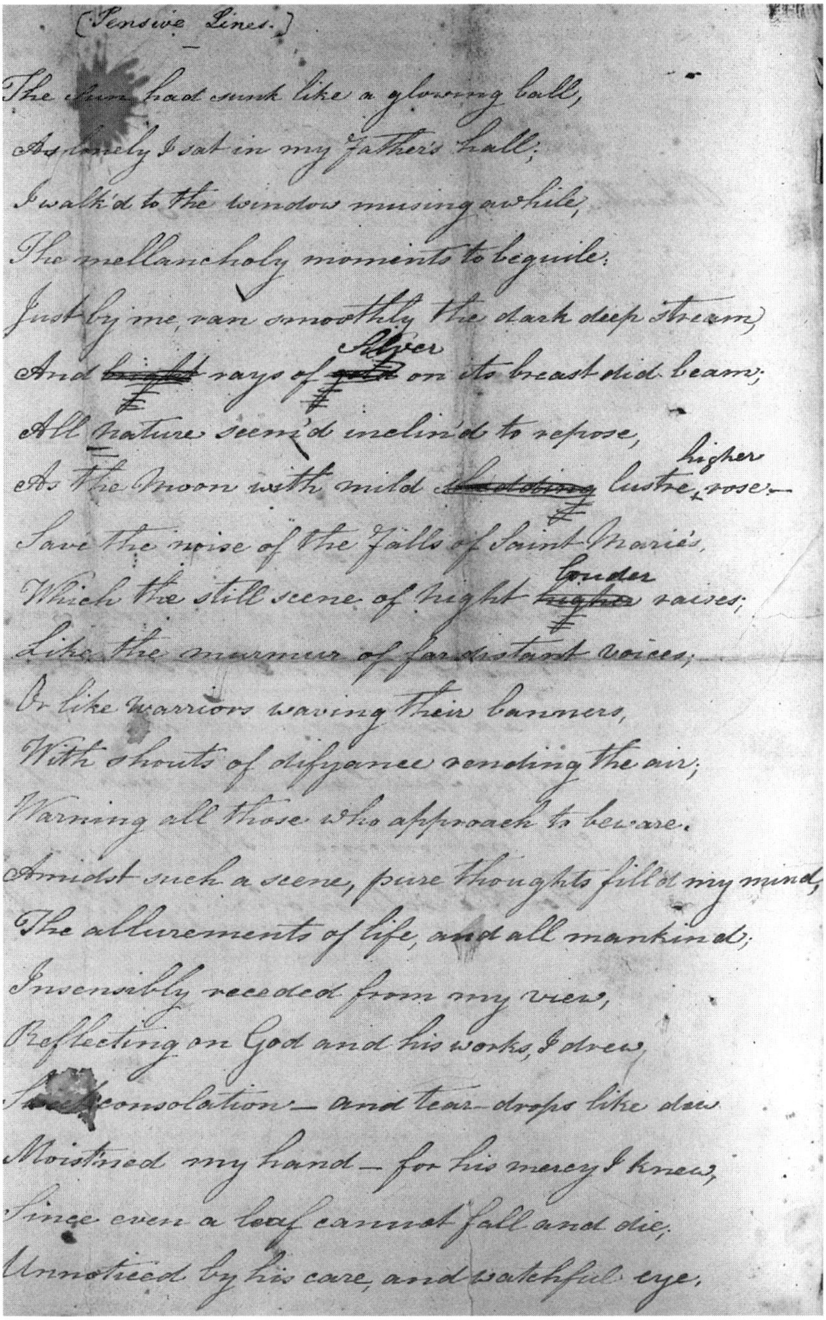

[Pensive Lines.]

The sun had sunk like a glowing ball,
As lonely I sat in my father's hall;
I walk'd to the window musing awhile,
The mellancholy moments to beguile:
Just by me, ran smoothly the dark deep stream,
And bright rays of silver on its breast did beam;
All nature seem'd inclin'd to repose,
As the Moon with mild lustre higher rose,—
Save the noise of the Falls of Saint Marie's,
Which the still scene of night louder raises;
Like the murmur of far distant voices;
Or like warriors waving their banners,
With shouts of defyance rending the air;
Warning all those who approach to beware.
Amidst such a scene, pure thoughts fill'd my mind,
The allurements of life, and all mankind;
Insensibly receded from my view,
Reflecting on God and his works, I drew
Sweet consolation— and tear-drops like dew
Moistned my hand— for his mercy I knew;
Since even a leaf cannot fall and die,
Unnoticed by his care, and watchful eye;

Figure 10. Manuscript page of "Pensive Lines." Henry Rowe Schoolcraft Papers, Manuscript Division, Library of Congress, Washington, D.C.

I walk'd to the window musing awhile,
The melancholy moments to beguile:
Just by me, ran smoothly the dark deep stream,
And ~~bright~~ rays of ~~gold~~ Silver on its breast did beam;
All nature seem'd inclin'd to repose,
As the moon with mild ~~xxxxxing~~ lustre higher rose—
Save the noise of the Falls of Saint Marie's,
Which the still scene of night ~~higher~~ louder raises;   10
Like the murmur of far distant voices;
Or like warriors waving their banners,
With shouts of defyance rending the air;
Warning all those who approach to beware.
Amidst such a scene, pure thoughts fill'd my mind,
The allurements of life, and all mankind;
Insensibly receded from my view,
Reflecting on God and his works, I drew
Sweet consolation—and tear drops like dew
Moist'ned my hand—for his mercy I knew,   20
Since even a leaf cannot fall and die,
Unnoticed by his care, and watchful eye.
Oh! how much more will He hear when we mourn,
And heal the heart that by anguish is torn;
When he sees the Soul to his will resign'd
Patiently Waiting his love ~~which~~ to the end ~~will shine~~.
Such thoughts as these, the lone moments beguil'd,
I felt peace in having them thus employ'd;
Till aroused by my harp which lay exposed,
To the soft breath of the night breeze that blows: 30
The mingl'd melody vibrating sweet,
Thrill'd round my heart a holy joy and heat;
Softer, and sweeter it melted away,
I fancy'd its whisperings seem'd to say
Like a passing spirit that could not stay,
Let thy soul live in hope, watch still and pray.
At that moment I felt my prayrs were heard
For the return of my Father beloved.
1820.   Rosa.

6 *Silver*: written above "gold", which is crossed out. 8 *xxxxxing*: this crossed
out word is not fully legible. 8 "higher" is added above the line, and a comma

is crossed out after "lustre", suggesting that before the crossing out, "lustre" was the end of the line. **10** *louder*: written above "higher", which is crossed out. **10** "raises" is an uncertain transcription. **26** "Patiently" is written in the left margin; "will shine" is an uncertain but plausible transcription. **closing Rosa**: one of JJS's pen names.

The Contrast, a Splenetic Effusion. March, 1823—

With pen in hand I shall contrast,
What I have felt—what now has past!
Slights from my friends I never knew,
Serenely sweet my hours then flew—
Or if by chance one gave me pain,
The wish to grieve me not again;
Express'd in terms endearing, kind,
Infused a joy throughout my mind—
That to have been one moment pain'd,
Seem'd more like bliss but just attain'd.   10
With gratitude my heart has mov'd,
In fault—by them to be reprov'd:
So mild and gentle were their words,
To me more sweet, than songs of birds:
For well I knew that each behest,
Was warm'd by love—convincing test!
    Thus pass'd the morning of my days;
My only wish to gain the praise,
Of friends, deserving of my love—
By actions kind, I strove to prove,   20
That all I did, was them to please,
The sweetest source of all my ease!
My efforts kindly were receiv'd—
My feelings ever were believ'd.
    But ah! how soon the scene has chang'd,
Since I have in love's mazes rang'd.
Oft in tears I sigh and languish,
Forc'd to bear in silent anguish—
Looks strange—expressions oft unkind—
Without an intercourse of mind.   30
Constrain'd to bear both heat and cold—
Now shun'd—now priz'd above all gold.
In converse now, we take delight,
Oft joining in fair fancy's flight.
Now elate—with pleasure smiling,
Kindness mutual—time beguiling.
    But how transient! oh how soon,
Every bliss is turn'd to gloom!

The Contrast, a Splenetic Effusion, March 1823——. There are four manuscripts, one in *LC35* among HRS's and JJS's letters, two in *LC70*—here labeled *LC70-1* and *LC70-2*—and one in *IL*. Text from *LC70-2*, but the three manuscripts in *LC35* and *LC70* are all similar. Each is dated March 1823 and written in similar handwriting, corroborating the impression that they were produced at about the same time. The version in *IL* seems later and is sufficiently different to print as a separate text; it follows next in this edition. HRS wrote yet another version: his poem "Love," in his collection of poems called *Indian Melodies* (1830), seems loosely based on JJS's "The Contrast," and he concludes "Love" with a note saying that "These lines were sketched by a Lady, and retouched, with additional lines, by the author of this little collection" ([H. R. Schoolcraft], *Indian Melodies* 29–30 [the pages are incorrectly numbered as 24–25]). Under the title "Sagiahwin. / From 'Indian "Melodies'","," he included a shorter version of "Love" in *IL* immediately after "The Contrast," and he also marked a version for inclusion in "Dawn" under the title "Sageawin. (Love)."

The Contrast

With pen in hand, I shall contrast,
The present moments with the past
And mark difference, not by grains,
But weighed by feelings, joys and pains.
Calm, tranquil—far from fashion's gaze,
Passed all my earliest, happy days
Sweetly flew the golden hours,
In St. Mary's woodland bowers
Or my father's simple hall,
Oped to whomsoe'er might call   10
Pains or cares we seldom knew
All the hours so peaceful flew
Concerts sweet we oft enjoyed,
Books our leisure time employed
Friends on every side appeared
From whose minds no ill I feared
If by chance, one gave me pain
The wish to wound me not again
Quick expressed in accents kind
Cast a joy throughout my mind   20
That, to have been a moment pained,
Seemed like bliss but just attained.

Whene'er in fault, to be reproved,
With gratitude my heart was moved,
So mild and gentle were their words
It seemed as soft as song of birds
For well I knew, that each behest,
Was warmed by love—convincing test.

  Thus passed the morning of my days,
My only wish, to gain the praise   30
Of friends I loved, and neighbours kind,
And keep a calm and heavenly mind.
My efforts, kindly were received,
Nor grieved, nor was myself aggrieved.
But ah! how changed is every scene,
Our little hamlet, and the green,
The long rich green, where warriors played,
And often, breezy elm-wood shade.
How changed, since full of strife and fear,
The world hath sent its votaries here.   40
The tree cut down—the cot removed,
The cot the simple Indian loved,
The busy strife of young and old
To gain one sordid bit of gold
By trade's o'er done plethoric moil,
And lawsuits, meetings, courts and toil.

Adieu, to days of homebred ease,
When many a rural care could please,
We trim our sail anew, to steer
By shoals we never knew were here,   50
And with the star flag, raised on high
Discover a new dominion nigh,
And half in joy, half in fear,
Welcome the proud Republic here.

The Contrast. Text from *IL*. Compare the other and seemingly earlier version of this poem immediately above. In "Dawn," HRS describes the newfound American bustle of commerce and conquest that inspired the revision.

On Henry's Birthday

Greek mythology

Unaided by the Muses heavenly fires—how vain,
Tho' strong the wish, to write in a sweet poetic strain.
Artless and unadorn'd, my numbers, you must flow,
Inspired alone by ardent Love's extatic glow—
To hail, and bless the day which gave my Henry birth
And wish success and joy might ever crown his worth— ⎤
Oh may the dew of Heaven descend and softly shed ⎬ *Slant Rhyme*
Its own mild influence—with blessings on his head. ⎦
Hallow'd by love an Amaranth wreath I would entwine

mixing diff divinities?

                        offering at affection's shrine   10

On Henry's Birthday. Text from *LC70.* Untitled fragment; title provided by the editor. The manuscript is torn at the bottom of the page, removing the beginning of line 10 and any lines after line 10. Above the poem, in smaller, less formal writing, possibly HRS's, is written "Where hopes fears" and then several faint, illegible words. This poem's use of hexameter lines is unusual for JJS.

3 *numbers*: metered poetry—a poetic term for poetry. **9** *Amaranth*: a poetic metaphor for a flower that supposedly never fades and thus represents immortality.

Absence

No. 1
NINDAHWAYMAU

Pensive and sad I glide along
    St. Mary's woodland shades,
While fancy pictures clear and strong
    A form that never fades.

From eyes, that long have viewed that form,
    And known the mind within,
Whose feelings noble, generous, warm,
    A heart more cold might win.

Gladly I seek the woody shade,
    To steal away from care   10
And seat me down in some lone glade
    While memory follows there.

It speaks of him whose worth so rare
    Deserves my every thought
His image follows me with care
    With equal pleasure sought

Waft him, ye winds, in safety back,
    Dispel my anxious tears,
Then doubt no more, my mind shall rack,
    I'll smile at all my fears.   20

No. 2
NEEZHICKA

Anxious I count each coming day,
As time glides on *too* slow away;
Tardy I feel the hours to move,
Those hours to me, so lonely prove:
Whilst fears possess my troubl'd soul,
Without the power to control:
While Henry strays far from my sight,
Stranger I am to all delight,—

Save when I gaze upon my child,
Cheerful, sportive, gentle, mild; 10
Then lost to every other care,
To heav'n I breathe a fervent pray'r:
That He the God of love and pow'r,
May bless and guard him through each hour,
Make him in health and strength to grow—
Teach him from whence his blessings flow—
Teach him the heav'nly will to trace,
Early to seek his Saviour's face:
And on his mind this truth to write,
Knowledge of God is Wisdom's height. 20

No. 3
NEENAWBAME

Say dearest friend, when light your bark,
Glides down the Mississippi dark?
Where nature's charms in rich display,
In varied hue appear so gay
To wrap your mind and gain your eye,
As light and quick you pass them by,—
Say, do thy thoughts e'er turn on home?
As mine to thee incessant roam.
And when at eve, in deserts wild,
Dost thou think on our lovely child? 10
Dost thou in stillness of the night,
By the planet's silvery light
Breathe a pray'r—to the Spirit above,
For thy wife, and thy child, my love.

No. 4
NINGWISIS

When a boat my dear Willy spies,
Eagerly to the shore he hies;
    With thrilling voice crys "my Papa!"
Joy sparkling in his speaking eye,
But sad he turns, "Pa' gone—bye, bye,"
    And closer clings to his Mamma.

Then haste thee home my Henry dear,
My weary, pensive moments cheer—
    And share the bliss a mother feels,
At the dawn of intelligence,   10
That lights the brow of innocence
    As he, to each parent appeals.

maternal again [handwritten marginal note]

Absence. Together and separately, these poems express JJS's longing for HRS's return to her and their son, one-year-old William Henry Schoolcraft, from a treaty council at Prairie du Chien by the Mississippi River in present-day Wisconsin during the summer of 1825. See the introduction for a sample of HRS's poetry about longing to return home during the same trip. The only manuscript version of "Absence" is in *IL*, but sections 2, 3, and 4 appear as separate poems, with their own titles or with no titles, in other manuscripts. That raises the question of whether to present the four sections as one poem or as separate poems, but we do not need to resolve this question entirely. An edition could print the multiple drafts, as I have done for some other poems, but the differences between drafts, while sometimes of considerable interest, do not seem great enough to call for printing separate versions. Therefore, I have included the poems together under the general title "Absence" and with their individual titles, as in *IL*, because that more easily allows readers to envision them both together and separately. There is also the question of whether to use the text from *IL* for the three sections that are also separate poems outside *IL*, thus using the same manuscript for all of "Absence," or to follow my usual practice of privileging manuscripts in JJS's own hand or produced during her lifetime and with her likely approval. In the abstract, either way seems appropriate, but the particular array of differences between manuscripts leads me to believe that readers would prefer the versions transcribed during JJS's lifetime, with a record of substantial variants listed below the poems. The drawback to this choice is that "Absence" appears here in a form that it never follows in any manuscript, a common editorial practice but one that an increasing number of editorial theorists have begun to reject, and a practice that I have avoided for other poems. The advantage is that each section or poem in "Absence" (though not "Absence" as a whole) still appears in a form that exists in manuscript and that, I believe, will prove the most interesting to the most readers, while still allowing readers ready access to the other forms from other manuscripts.

    Nindahwaymau. Text from *IL*.

    title *nindahwaymau* means "my sibling of the opposite sex." Since the reference is to JJS's husband, the usage is not exactly the same as in the

English translation. Presumably, this is the same poem that HRS calls "Nindawamin" in "Dawn." There, in the place of a translation he offers an English title that is not a translation: "(Knowledge)." **15** *His*: editor's emendation of "With", which seems like an accidental carryover from the next line.

Neezhicka. There are two manuscripts, one each in *LC70* and *IL.* Text from *LC70*, which has no title and is signed "Jane *Schoolcraft.*"

Title *neezhicka* means "alone." **2** *on* too *slow*: heavily *IL.* **4** *to me*: that all *IL.* **5–7** Whi[l]st fears, without my power's controul / Possess in full, my troubled soul / Long as thou tarried from my sight, *IL.* **10** Sportive, cheerful, happy, mild *IL.*

Neenawbame. There are three manuscripts, one each in *LC70*, *LC66*, and *IL.* Because *LC66* was probably prepared for readers with JJS's approval, even though it may include changes suggested or imposed by HRS or introduced by the *Literary Voyager* copyist, I have chosen it for the text. At the bottom of *LC66*, on the left, is written "[1825.]", and on the right, "Rosa", one of JJS's pen names. *LC70* is signed "J. S. July 4ᵗʰ 1825—". *LC70* is slightly more personal than *LC66* or *IL*; *LC66* may have been made less personal because it was distributed to friends, and *IL* sustained the less personal approach perhaps because it followed from *LC66* and was prepared for wider distribution.

Title In "Dawn," HRS spells the title differently and provides a translation: "Neenábame, (a husband's absence)." *LC70* is titled "To Henry—"; *LC66* is untitled. **5** *gain*: please *IL.* **6** *light and quick you*: quick you sail and *LC70.* **7** *home*: me *LC70.* **7** *turn on*: wander *IL.* **8** As mine do constantly to thee! *LC70.* **12** By the Planets' bright twinkling light *LC70.* **11–12** Dost thou, by the planets' light / In the still and solemn night *IL.* **14** *my love.*: *my love!* *LC70.* **14** *and thy child*: and child and home *IL.*

Ningwisis. There are two manuscripts, one each in *LC70* and *IL.* Text from *LC70*, which is untitled and is signed "Sunday Evening 14ᵗʰ of Augt— 1825—". *LC70* is more personal; *IL* may be less personal because it was prepared for wider distribution.

title *Ningwisis* means "my son." In "Dawn," HRS spells the title differently and offers a loose translation: "Ningwis. (or a son's expanding question)." **5** But sad he sees it hastening by *IL.* **10–11** To view the bright intellegence / And dawning light of innocense *IL.* **12** *parent*: so fond *IL.*

"Amid the still retreat of Elmwood's shade"

Amid the still retreat of Elmwood's shade,
　　I count the long hours and counting mourn,
My heart with anxious fears is oft dismay'd,
　　And unobserved, I spend those hours forlorn.
　　　　Oft as I glance my eyes around,
　　　　　Fond memory brings him near,
　　　　To him I feel forever bound,
　　　　　　To me, he's more than dear.

[handwritten annotations: "Alone, but can still imagine him", "lonely, sad, unhappy", "more than just a husband?"]

"Amid the still retreat of Elmwood's shade." Text from *LC60*. Untitled. HRS was elected to the Legislative Council of the Territory of Michigan, and in May and June 1828, when he attended a council session in Detroit, JJS kept a journal in Sault Ste. Marie for HRS to read when he returned. The journal, preserved in *LC8* and *LC60*, brims with affection for HRS, and in the course of the entry for May 19, its prose shifts into this poem. In a small way, this poem is unusual for JJS, because—though she seems to have dropped it casually into her journal—she arranges the lines in accord with their meter, indenting tetrameter lines more than she indents the even-numbered pentameter lines in the opening quatrain, and then indenting trimeter lines twice as much as she indents tetrameter lines. For another poem from her journal, see "My heart is gone with him afar" below.

　　Elmwood. The imposing official home for the federal Indian agent in Sault Ste. Marie, at that time being built for and under the direction of HRS and JJS. Moved from its original location, Elmwood now sits next to the surviving portion of the Johnston house (see figure 4).

Resignation [1]

How hard to teach the heart, opprest with grief,
Amid gay, worldly scenes, to find relief;
And the long cherish'd bliss we had in view,
To banish from the mind—where first it grew!
But Faith, in time, can sweetly soothe the soul,
And Resignation hold a mild control;
The mind may then resume a proper tone,
And calmly think on hopes forever flown.

Resignation [1]. There is an eight-line manuscript in *LC70*, a similar eight-line manuscript in *LC64*, and a twelve-line manuscript in *IL*. *LC70* is signed "Jane *Schoolcraft*", while at the end of the poem *LC64* is attributed to "Rosa", one of JJS's pen names. *LC64* and *LC70* differ only in small matters of punctuation. Because *LC64* was probably prepared for readers with JJS's approval, even though it may include changes suggested or imposed by HRS or introduced by the *Literary Voyager* copyist, I have chosen *LC64* for the text. Compare the longer, later version from *IL*, which follows next in this edition. At the bottom of *LC70*, on the left, is written "(3–Dec. 1825.)".

Resignation [2]

How hard to teach the heart, opprest with grief
Amid gay worldly scenes to find relief
  And fix its torn affections and regard
And the long cherish'd bliss we had in view
To banish from the mind, where first it grew
  And clung for succour! oh how hard!
But Faith and time, can sweetly soothe the soul
  Stilling the elements of grief within,
Bid Resignation hold a mild controul
  And calm the troubled passion's noisy din.   10
Then may the mind resume its proper tone,
And meditate on hopes and joys forever flown.

Not as much punctuation C & E

Resignation [2]. Text from *IL*, where it appears under a Roman numeral "II" as the second of two poems grouped under the title "Sonnets." (The first is "Sonnet," which appears below in this edition.) In this context, the term "sonnet" means not the familiar form of fourteen lines, but simply a short poem. Compare the other and presumably earlier version of this poem, above, from *LC70* and *LC64*.

*Sick + depressed all the time

Lines written under affliction

Ah! who, with a sensative mind possest,
  Recalls the swift years that are gone,
Without mingled emotions—both bitter and blest,
  At the good and the ill he has known.

blessed?

Or, how could a beautiful landscape please,
  If it showed us no feature but light?
'Tis the dark shades alone that give pleasure and ease,
  'Tis the union of sombre and bright.

need light & dark to make beauty?

bitter sweet

So wisely has God in his mercy ordain'd,
  That the bitterest cup he has cast,   10
Is mixed with a sweetness which still is retain'd,
  To be drank and enjoyed at the last.

happy & sad
God did this for a reason?

Thus feelings are chasten'd, and life is refin'd,
  By pangs that misfortunes convey,
To minds that have faith, and to bosoms resign'd,
  To bear—to forbear, and obey.

Trying to hold onto last hope

And tho' for a while, he condemns us in strife,
  To languish, and suffer, and die;
Yet the sunshine of promise—of hope and of life,
  Allures us to bliss in the sky.   20

heaven

Lines written under affliction. There are four manuscripts, two in *LC70*, here labeled *LC70-1* and *LC70-2*, another in *LC65*, and another in *IL*. The pattern of revisions suggests a sequence from *LC70-1* to *LC70-2* to *LC65*, and *LC65* is a likely source for HRS's transcription in *IL*. *LC70-1* and *LC70-2* are both unfinished drafts; the first line of *LC70-2*, for example, is metrically shorter and includes a question mark in mid-sentence. Unlike the other drafts, *LC-70-1* has no title, stanza breaks, or indented lines. Because *LC65* appears to complete the revisions in process in *LC70-2* and was probably prepared for readers with JJS's approval, even though it may include changes suggested or imposed by HRS or introduced by the *Literary Voyager* copyist, I have chosen it for the text. Together the various drafts show the gradual process of composition and revision. At the end of the poem, *LC65* is attributed to "Rosa," one of JJS's pen names.

HRS introduces the poem in the *Literary Voyager* with the following remarks: "The opinion we expressed, in our first number, of the poetical accomplishments of 'Rosa,' we have seen no reason to retract. There is a naivetté [*sic*] in her productions which is often the concomitant of taste and genius. The chastness [*sic*] of her images, the lively strain of piety and confiding hope in the dispensations of Providence, and the pensive serenity which marks her favorite morning and evening landscapes, are so many traits which arrest our admiration. When to these positive recommendations of her poetic attempts, we add the limited opportunities of her early life, and the scenes of seclusion [in] which so much of her time had been passed, we think there is still greater cause to appreciate and admire. We think the 'Lines written under affliction,' in the present number highly beautiful, possessing at once both energy and consonance. We solicit a continuation of her efforts."

1 *Ah! who with a sensative*: Who with a feeling *LC70-1*. Who ? with a feeling *LC70-2*. **2** *swift*: not in *LC70-1* or *LC70-2*. lone *IL*. **3** *mingled emotions—both bitter and blest*: feeling sensations of joy *LC70-1*. **4** *he has known*: they have seen *LC70-1*. **4** *he*: it *IL*. **5** *Or,* : Oh! *LC70-2*. **6** *showed us no feature*: exhibited nothing *LC70-1*. **7** *give pleasure and ease*: relieves *LC70-1*. **8** The union of which, gives a zest to delight. *LC70-1*. **10** *has cast*: can give *LC70-1*. **11** *still is retain'd*: no one can taste *LC70-1*. **12** *To be drank and enjoyed at*: By those who patiently drink to *LC70-1*. **13–16** For misfortunes are sanctified / To those who resignedly have—/ Firm faith—on his word to abide / With him ~~everlasting at the last~~ to live—["at the last" is written above "~~everlasting~~"] *LC70-1*. **17** *condemns us in strife*: permits *LC70-1*. permits us in strife *LC70-2*. **18** The dark clouds of affliction to reign; *LC70-1*. **18** *die*: sigh *IL*. **19** *promise—of hope and of life*: hope draws us nearer to him *LC70-1*. **19** *LC70-2* has "glory" crossed out and "promise" written above. **20** Where pure happiness ~~alone~~ can only be found. ["only" is written above the line] *LC70-1*.

Relief

*welcom (?.)
welcom
p welcom.
welcom !*

Thrice welcome, friendly Solitude!
O let no busy fool intrude,
  Nor list'ning ear be nigh
Alone, whilst I my conscious heart,
Its tender sorrow does impart,
  Unseen by mortal eye.
Heave then my breast with painful sighs.
Fast and unstifled may you rise
  Expressing all my grief,—
Trembling the tear drops from my eyes;   10
And on my hand it gently lies
  Giving a slight relief.

Relief. Text from *LC70*. Untitled; title provided by the editor. Above the poem, apparently in HRS's hand, is written "[1824]". HRS's dating implies that he believed JJS wrote the poem. As it happens, she did not write all of it, though she might have written some of it. The first three lines match lines 4–6 of "To Solitude" (1775) by Hester Chapone (1727–1801), a then-famous British writer (Chapone 119–21). Lines 4–5 also echo a couplet from Chapone's "To Solitude": "To thee alone my conscious heart / Its tender sorrow dares impart" (lines 13–14). The two poems follow the same meter and rhyme scheme, rhymed couplets of iambic tetrameter alternating with single lines of iambic trimeter, with the trimeter lines rhymed in pairs (in this poem, "nigh" and "eye," "grief" and "relief"). Their form differs only in that "To Solitude" has a stanza break after each set of six lines. Whether JJS copied all of this poem or wrote some of it herself, it contributes to her characteristic concerns with loneliness and melancholy. Chapone, a proto-feminist member of the "bluestocking" circle, was famous for her letters and essays, which encouraged women to pursue their intellectual interests, and which celebrated marriage for love as opposed to arranged marriages.

A Metrical Jeu d'esprit, designed as an invitation to a whist party

[by John Johnston]

Dear Day, If you will make a party,
You will receive a welcome hearty;
For I am old and sick and lame
And only fit to take a game.

The table shall be spread at six,
Unless some other time you fix;
You'll neither meet with frowns or growls,
We'll leave them to the Bats and Owls.

But to make our party richer,
Be sure you bring down Doctor Pitcher;   10
And worthy King, a steady man,
Who steers his course by honor's plan.

If others you can muster up,
To smoke a pipe and drink a cup,
Bring them all most freely on,
And serve your faithful John Johnston.

Wednesday Evening
21. Feb. 1827

A Metrical Jeu d'esprit, designed as an invitation to a whist party. Text from
LC36. The manuscript is a hurriedly written copy in JJS's hand of a letter-
poem from her father, John Johnston, included here because her own letter-
poem in response follows next in this edition. Both poems are preserved
among HRS's letters. There is another copy of the poem in HRS's hand,
titled "To Mr. Day" but otherwise in the same words, among John Johnston's poems in HRS's papers (*LC70*). JJS refers to a "Mr. Day" in her 1828
journal (*LC60*), but I have not further identified him.

title *Jeu d'esprit*: French for play or sport of the spirit. *whist*: a card game
popular in the eighteenth and nineteenth centuries. **10** Doctor Zina Pitcher,
later a founder of the University of Michigan, mayor of Detroit, candidate

for governor of Michigan, and president of the American Medical Association. He would soon serve at the unexpected death of JJS's and HRS's son William, and—like JJS, HRS, and John Johnston—he would write a poem about that death for the *Literary Voyager*. **11** The manuscript in HRS's hand has a note identifying King as Kingsbury, who would thus be Lieutenant Julius J. B. Kingsbury, who served at Fort Brady in Sault Ste. Marie. **14** *smoke*: editor's emendation of "take smoke", in accord with the manuscript in HRS's hand. "Take smoke" does not fit syntactically or metrically, suggesting an error or unfinished moment in the text or, more likely, an error in JJS's transcription. **16** *faithful*: written above "friend", which is crossed out.

Response

Who rides *this* Pegasus? The Hibernian
On the spur of the moment from Mount Helicon:
Forgetting his gout ache, his age and his colic,
He comes whip in hand, like a youth, full of frolic.

Though he whips and he spurs, not like others makes use
Of a spur at the heel, but the quill of a goose
Gives wings to his steed, with mettle him fires,
While a glass of hot toddy his muse-ship inspires.

A warm welcome doubt me? Let the coward who dares
Miscall his attentions:—by the white of his hairs   10
He shall fight at ten paces—I'll give him the fires,
And I'll part with my life's blood or he with his ires.

Then spread out the table—fill the bowls to the top,
We will drink him long life to the very last drop:
Fetch us in the long candles, set fire to their wicks;
So we'll cut for the deal, play for honours and tricks.

But the cards we'll repack and abandon our play,
As the tapers burn short and the night speeds away;
And we'll moralize thus as they flicker apace,
So fleetly goes time and thus soon ends our race.   20

Wednesday Feb 21. 1827 =

N.B. You will recognize the addition of the colic to your list of maladies as a poetica licentia or as Christopher Caustic would translate it, a specimen of poetical licentiousness.

Response. Text from *LC36*. In this poem JJS responds to the invitation in her father's poem that comes immediately above in this edition.

1 *Pegasus*: a winged horse in ancient Greek mythology, often understood as a figure of poetry. **1** *Hibernian*: Hibernia, typically a poetic term, is the Latin name for Ireland, John Johnston's homeland. **2** *Mount Helicon*: To the ancient Greeks, Mount Helicon in central Greece was the home of the muses, and therefore it is often used to refer to the source of poetic inspiration. **6** *a goose*: editor's emendation of "goose", supposing that an "a", which fits the anapestic rhythm, was left out by mistake. **11–12** "fires" and "ires" are uncertain transcriptions. **16** *honours and tricks*: terms from whist. **20** *our race*: the race that we run through life, not the race of racial identity. **N.B.:** The joke is that the Latin phrase "poetica licentia" should be translated as "poetic license," not "poetic licentiousness." Christopher Caustic was a pseudonym of Thomas Green Fessenden (1771–1837), an American poet known for witty satire and for antagonism to Jefferson and the Democrats. JJS's reference to Caustic matches her wit at the poem's beginning, with its puns about "the spur of the moment" and the goose quill that "gives wings" by writing (lines 2, 6–7). The contrast between the toast to Johnston's long life (line 14) and the somber sense of mortality that comes back in the final line seems all the more poignant when we contrast the frolicsome banter of this poem to the somber mood that would descend on the household—and on its poetry—when young William Henry died three weeks later.

✴ Elegy

On the death of my son William Henry, at St. Mary's

1.

May the winds softly blow
    O'er thy lone place of rest
And the white drifting snow
    Repose light on thy breast.

2.

And when May in her bloom,
    A soft verdure shall bring
I shall deck thy loved tomb
    With the flowrets of Spring

3.

The buds as they swell
    Ere they bloom on the tree   10
I shall gather as emblems
    Of beauty and thee.

4.

And the tears of affection,
    I constantly shed
Like dewdrops those flowrets
    Shall daily o'erspread.

5.

And memory truly,
    Shall still keep in view,
Thy image so lovely,
    So sweet and so true   20

6.

And my sighs shall increase,
    The soft murmurs of spring,
As in thy requiem low,
    I so pensively sing

7.

While in thought I pursue,
    Thy pure spirit on high,
Encircled with blisses,
    That never shall die.

8.

To know thou art blest
     Half assuages the smart,   30
That sorrow inflicts
     On a mother's fond heart
                    9.
That heart where so late
     Thou went pillowed in love
That can ne'er cease to mourn,
     Though it cease to reprove.

[handwritten: Move to Consilation]

Elegy On the death of my son William Henry, at St. Mary's. Text from *IL*. After a sudden, brief illness, William Henry died of croup on 13 Mar. 1827 at the age of two years and eight months. See also the following three poems and the poem in "Dawn" called "on a recent affliction."

   title "death" is written above "grave", which is crossed out. **12** *beauty*: "innocence" is crossed out, and "beauty" is written above it.

[handwritten: Schooled → Should be happy bc they're in heaven → But its hard to be okay w/ the loss]

Sonnet

The voice of reason bids me dry my tears,
 But nature frail, still struggles with that voice;
Back to my mind that placid form appears
 Lifeless,—he seemed to live and to rejoice,
As in the arms of death he meekly lay.
 Oh, Cherub Babe! thy mother mourns thy loss,
Tho' thou hast op'd thine eyes in endless day;
 And nought, on earth, can chase away my grief
But Faith—pleading the merits of the Cross,
 And Him, whose promise gives a sure relief.   10

Sonnet. There are three manuscripts, one each in *LC66*, *LC70*, and *IL*. It is not clear whether either of the versions in *LC66* and *LC70* revises the other or whether other drafts came between. Because *LC70* is a draft in process and *LC66* was probably prepared for readers with JJS's approval, I have chosen *LC66* for the text, even though it may include changes suggested or imposed by HRS or introduced by the *Literary Voyager* copyist. Both *LC66* and *LC70* appear to have been sources for *IL*, which retains different features of each. In *IL*, the poem appears under a Roman numeral "I" as the first of two poems grouped under the title "Sonnets." (The second is "Resignation," which appears above in this edition.) In *LC66*, the poem appears with other poems on the death of William Henry Schoolcraft, including "To my ever beloved and lamented son William Henry" and poems by HRS, John Johnston, and others. At the end of the poem, *LC66* is attributed to "J. S."

 title Here the term "sonnet" means not the familiar form of fourteen lines, but simply a short poem. *LC70* has the title as "Trust." *IL* has it as "on my dead Infant. / 1826." William Henry actually died in 1827. **8** *IL* has "on earth" crossed out and "but faith" written above it. **10** *LC70* has "the promise of Him, who gives" crossed out and "Him, whose promise gives a sure" written above it. **9–10** These two lines become three lines in *IL*: But faith holding up the merits of the Cross, / And Him, whose promise balm to human grief, / Gives hope its crown; and woe a sure relief.

To my ever beloved and lamented Son William Henry

Who was it, nestled on my breast,
"And on my cheek sweet kisses prest"
And in whose smile I felt so blest?
                    Sweet Willy.
Who hail'd my form as home I stept,
And in my arms so eager leapt,
And to my bosom joyous crept?
                    My Willy.
Who was it, wiped my tearful eye,
And kiss'd away the coming sigh,
And smiling bid me say "good boy"?
                    Sweet Willy.
Who was it, looked divinely fair,
Whilst lisping sweet the evening pray'r,
Guileless and free from earthly care?
                    My Willy.
Where is that voice attuned to love,
That bid me say "my darling dove"?
But oh! that soul has flown above,
                    Sweet Willy.
Whither has fled the rose's hue?
The lilly's whiteness blending grew,
Upon thy cheek—so fair to view.
                    My Willy.
Oft have I gaz'd with rapt delight,
Upon those eyes that sparkled bright,
Emitting beams of joy and light!
                    Sweet Willy.
Oft have I kiss'd that forehead high,
Like polished marble to the eye,
And blessing, breathed an anxious sigh.
                    For Willy.
My son! thy coral lips are pale,
Can I believe the heart-sick tale,
That I, thy loss must ever wail?
                    My Willy.

[handwritten: More imagery]

The clouds in darkness seemed to low'r,
The storm has past with awful pow'r,
And nipt my tender, beauteous flow'r!
   Sweet Willy.   40

[handwritten: Sickness has past but has taken him]

But soon my spirit will be free,
And I, my lovely Son shall see,
For God, I know, did this decree!
   My Willy.

[handwritten: mournful before but now sounds determined like this is all she can do to stay okay.]

[handwritten: Talks of losing him but in the end having him again]

To my ever beloved and lamented son William Henry. There are six manuscripts plus one version published in HRS's *Personal Memoirs* (261–62), more versions than for any other of JJS's poems, suggesting a special role for this poem in JJS's emotions and perhaps in her pride as a poet. In his memoirs, HRS calls it "fit to be preserved as a specimen of native composition" (261). The form closely follows the form of Ann Taylor's (1782–1866) once-famous "My Mother" (1804), where the refrain is "My mother" rather than "My Willy." In Taylor's poem, a child addresses its mother, whereas in Schoolcraft's poem, a mother addresses her child. Line 2 quotes line 3 of Taylor's poem verbatim. There are manuscripts in *LC66* and *IL*, and in JJS's hand in *LC7* (among HRS's letters); in a notebook of JJS's younger sister Charlotte Johnston (later Charlotte Johnston McMurray) owned by the Chippewa County Historical Society, of Michigan, and housed in the River of History Museum in Sault Ste. Marie; and another sent to HRS's friend and banker C. C. Trowbridge, preserved among Trowbridge's correspondence in the Burton Historical Collection in the Detroit Public Library. In the Bentley Historical Library at the University of Michigan there is a manuscript in the hand of Charlotte Jane Johnstone (1847–1912 [Weaver 32]), daughter of JJS's youngest sibling, John. For the text, I have chosen the version in Charlotte Johnston McMurray's notebook. Because the notebook seems prepared for diverse readers, and the manuscript is in JJS's hand, that version likely best represents what JJS wanted others to read. Except for a small difference in stanza breaks, it has no significant differences from the version in *LC66*, which was probably also prepared for readers with JJS's approval. All three versions produced by HRS, whether under his supervision (*LC66*), in his hand (*IL*), or printed in his memoirs, have a stanza break after each appearance of the word "Willy," while none of the three versions in JJS's hand has stanza breaks, nor does the version in Charlotte Jane Johnstone's hand. There are no variants of substance except in *IL*, though *LC7* has an exclamation point after each "Willy." In *LC66*, the poem appears with other poems on the death of William Henry Schoolcraft, including "Sonnet" ("The voice of reason") and poems by HRS, John Johnston, and others. At the bottom of the version in Charlotte Johnston McMurray's notebook and of *LC66*, on the right, is written "Jane Schoolcraft," and lower, on the left in *LC66*, "March 23rd 1827."

9–12 not in *IL*. **17–20** Where are those lineaments of grace / And mental promise, clear to trace / In every trait of form and face / Bright Willy. *IL*. **22–24** And lilly's white where mixed they grew / In living tints, so sweet to view / Fair Willy *IL*. **40** *Sweet*: My *IL*. **44** *My*: Sweet *IL*.

Sweet Willy

A hundred moons and more have past,
    Since erst upon this day,
They bore thee from my anguished sight,
    And from my home away
And pensively they carried thee
    And set the burial stone,
And left thy father and myself,
    Forsaken and alone.

A hundred moons and more have past
    And every year have we,   10
With pious steps gone out to sit
    Beneath thy graveyard tree
And often, with remembrance
    Of our darling little boy
Repeated—"they that sow in tears
    "Shall reap again in joy."

Lo! children are a heritage
    A fruit and a reward,
Bestowed in sovreign mercy
    By the fecit of the Lord   20
But he, that giveth gifts to men
    May take away the same
And righteous is the holy act,
    And blessed be his name.

For still it is a mercy,
    And a mercy we can view,
For whom the Lord chastiseth
    He in love regardeth too.
And sweetly in remembrance
    Of our darling little boy   30
Bethink we still, that sorrow's tears
    Shall spring in beds of joy.

And aye, that Word is precious
    As the apple of the eye

[Handwritten annotations in margins: "breaks from the Rhyme", "Because it is quoted", "→ Bringing Religion into it - keeping Faith in God.", "God does things for a Reason", "Re-working of the Psalm", "↳ another note to fruit"]

That looketh up to mansions
    Which are builded in the sky
That palleth with this scene of tears
    And vanities and strife,
And seeketh for that better home
    Where truly there is life. 40
I cling no more to life below,
    It hath no charm for me,
Yet strive to fill my duty here,
    While here below I be.
And often comes the memory
    Of my darling little boy,
For he was sown in bitter tears,
    And shall be reaped in joy.

Sweet Willy. Text from *IL.*

    1 *A hundred moons and more*: These words set the poem over eight years and four months after William Henry Schoolcraft died in March 1827. **15–16** After Psalm 125:5: "They that sow in tears shall reap in joy." **17–18** After Psalm 127:3: "Lo, children are an heritage of the Lord: and the fruit of the womb is his reward." **20** *fecit*: made by (Latin), in effect meaning "doing." **37** *palleth*: covers with a pall (a cloth for covering a coffin).

Lines Written under severe Pain and Sickness

Ah! why should I at fortune's lot repine,
Or fret myself against the will divine?
All men must go to death's deform'd embrace,
When here below they've run their destin'd race;
Oh! then on Thee, my Savior, I will trust,
For thou art good, as merciful and just,—
In Thee, with my whole heart I will confide,
And hope with Thee, forever to abide.
To Thee, my God, my heart and soul I raise,
And still thy holy, holy name I'll praise!   10
O! deign to give me wisdom, virtue, grace,
That I thy heavenly will may ever trace;
Teach me each duty always to fulfil,
And grant me resignation to Thy will,
And when Thy goodness wills that I should die,
This dream of life I'll leave without a sigh.

Lines Written under severe Pain and Sickness. Text from *LC65*. At the end of the poem, *LC65* is attributed to "Rosa," one of JJS's pen names.

On leaving my children John and Jane at School, in the Atlantic states, and preparing to return to the interior

Nyau nin de nain dum
May kow e yaun in
Ain dah nuk ki yaun
Waus sa wa kom eg
Ain dah nuk ki yaun

Ne dau nis ainse e
Ne gwis is ainse e
Ishe nau gun ug wau
Waus sa wa kom eg

She gwau go sha ween   10
Ba sho waud e we
Nin zhe ka we yea
Ishe ez hau jau yaun
Ain dah nuk ke yaun

Ain dah nuk ke yaun
Nin zhe ke we yea
Ishe ke way aun e
Nyau ne gush kain dum

[Free Translation]

Ah! when thought reverts to my country so dear,
My heart fills with pleasure, and throbs with a fear:
My country, my country, my own native land,
So lovely in aspect, in features so grand,
Far, far in the West. What are cities to me,
Oh! land of my mother, compared unto thee?

Fair land of the lakes! thou are blest to my sight,
With thy beaming bright waters, and landscapes of light;
The breeze and the murmur, the dash and the roar,
That summer and autumn cast over the shore,   10
They spring to my thoughts, like the lullaby tongue,
That soothed me to slumber when youthful and young.

One feeling more strongly still binds me to thee,
There roved my forefathers, in liberty free—
There shook they the war lance, and sported the plume,
Ere Europe had cast o'er this country a gloom;
Nor thought they that kingdoms more happy could be,
White lords of a land so resplendent and free.

Yet it is not alone that my country is fair,
And my home and my friends are inviting me there;   20
While they beckon me onward, my heart is still here,
With my sweet lovely daughter, and bonny boy dear:
And oh! what's the joy that a home can impart,
Removed from the dear ones who cling to my heart.

It is learning that calls them; but tell me, can schools
Repay for my love, or give nature new rules?
They may teach them the lore of the wit and the sage,
To be grave in their youth, and be gay in their age;
But ah! my poor heart, what are schools to thy view,
While severed from children thou lovest so true!   30

I return to my country, I haste on my way,
For duty commands me, and duty must sway;
Yet I leave the bright land where my little ones dwell,
With a sober regret, and a bitter farewell;
For there I must leave the dear jewels I love,
The dearest of gifts from my Master above.
New York, *March* 18*th*, 1839.

[New translation]

As I am thinking
When I find you
My land
Far in the west
My land

My little daughter
My little son

I leave them behind
Far away land

[emphatically] But soon   10
It is close however
To my home I shall return
That is the way that I am, my being
My land

My land
To my home I shall return
I begin to make my way home
Ahh but I am sad

On leaving my children John and Jane at School, in the Atlantic states, and preparing to return to the interior. Untitled; text of the Ojibwe poem and free translation from HRS, *Personal Memoirs* (632–33). The new translation was prepared in 2005 for this volume by Dennis Jones, Heidi Stark, and James Vukelich. Title from "Dawn." HRS decided to leave his and JJS's children, Janee (age eleven) and Johnston (age nine), at boarding schools, against JJS's strong preference, though she deferred to his judgment. HRS introduces the poem with the following words in his *Memoirs*: "Mrs. Schoolcraft, having left her children at school, at Philadelphia and Princeton, remained pensive, and wrote the following lines in the Indian tongue, on parting from them, which I thought so just that I made a translation of them." Readers may note that HRS's translation into English, which he acknowledges is "free," is far longer than the Ojibwe original. The date of 18 March may be for the free translation rather than the original. *LC* includes letters about the boarding schools from HRS, JJS, the children, and their teachers, including this letter of 29 Jan. 1839 from JJS to "Mrs. General Patterson," a friend in Philadelphia: "O' dear Mrs. P. you can hardly conceive how ~~hard~~ great a trial it was to part with my poor children as they never were absent from me more than a few days since their birth & not having any others near me to lavish the overflowing of a Mother['] s foolish, fond, heart, I have indeed been at times a sad picture of forlornness, but I know it is for their good & I strive to feel reconciled. My greatest anxiety is about my little boy, he is a mere child & has been accustomed to a Mother's kind love, & going amidst 40 other boys, strangers to him & missing the comforts of home, he must feel sadly, till he gets accustomed to the mode of treatment at school, as to my Janee I feel little anxiety in comparison, as she is among friends, & in the best of schools for a girl of her age—" (*LC16*). Later correspondence confirms that Johnston had trouble adjusting to school, whereas Janee adjusted well.

An answer, to a remonstrance on my being melancholy, by a Gentleman, who, *sometimes* had a *little pleasing* touch of melancholy himself

Still—still! the same—my friend you cry!
Still—still! the same—untill I die!—
Unless *your* friend, and *mine*, soft maid—
I chase away to the darksome shade.
With her, too sure, would *there* repair,
The joys that make, dull life, more fair.
Should I awhile her presence shun,
And join in frolic, laughter, fun—
Yet would my heart, unconquer'd fly,
And woo her back, with many a sigh,   10
Or with her walk the haunted groves,
Where lovely sorceress, Fancy roves,
Such silent joy in her there lies,
'Tis but to taste them once—and prize.
   Since then such bliss you'd have me lose,
Teach me to gain thy pleasing muse.
Enchanted then I'll sing my lays!
And cheerfull spend my happy days.

An answer, to a remonstrance on my being melancholy . . . Text from *LC70*. At the bottom, on the right, the manuscript is signed "Jane—."

Language Divine!

Lines Written in 1816, whilst my Mother was preparing to accompany me on a visit to a family, who had just received distressing news from some of their absent relatives.

Language divine! Thy aid impart
To breathe the feelings of the heart
That burns with sympathetic woe
For those whose tears incessant flow
Those, to whom fortune now doth prove
A tyrant stern, to him they love.
Sweet charity, now points the way
And I the summons must obey
Quickly thy magic flowers impart,
To soothe the broke and bleeding heart   10
To lull dispair into a calm
And make my every word a balm
To cheer the agonized breast
And point to heaven—a place of rest.

    Then, shall I ne'er the time repent,
In service of my neighbour spent.

Language Divine! Text from *IL*. Untitled; title provided by the editor. This is probably the poem that HRS introduces in "Dawn" in the following sobering (and not entirely legible) words: "An event occurred, in 1816, in the remote forests of the north, which caused the case [or care?] of pity and charity "to tingle", and excited a deep sympathy for a poor neighboring family, of French descent, which had lost one of its members, in a season of great want and scarcity, North of lake Superior, by the horrible spirit cannabalism [*sic*]. Not to sympathize, with the distressed mother for a lost son on such an occasion?, would evince? a want of [illegible word] to passing events, and in the forest around, of which the Indian nations, have been unjustly accused. And while she prepared to accompany her mother on the visit of condolence to the bereaved mother she went to her room and committed to paper, the following lines."

"As watchful spirits in the night"

As watchful spirits in the night
O'er Earth pursue their wonted flight,
To guard from ills each saint that sleeps,
Or soothe to rest, where any weeps;
At times they pause to hear a strain,
And swell it back to heaven again;
      Sweetly then
     Joins the choral swell,
"In heaven, on Earth, peace reigns, all's well."

Or when death closes in, at last,   10
On one who ne'er could blessing taste,
Who deem'd her Saviour's visage hid,
His grace to her alone forbid;
E'en then, when friends in anguish stand,
Nor hope to see the lifted hand
      She smiles!
    Those smiles the blessings tell,
"Their God is hers at last, all's well."

"As watchful spirits in the night." Text from *LC70*. Untitled. The focus on spirits seems potentially less Christian than we might expect from JJS, though set in the Christian context of saints. (The saints here refer not to saints in the Catholic sense but instead to the Protestant meaning, which refers to people chosen for salvation in heaven.) The spirits could also fit a typically Ojibwe sense of spirits. Along with the spirits, the diction in the first stanza does not quite seem characteristic of JJS's poetry ("wonted," "swell," "choral"). While I have found no corroboration of her authorship beyond the manuscript in her hand, I have also found no sign that anyone else wrote it, except for the quotation marks around the last line of each stanza. I have not found any source for the lines in quotation marks.

On Meditation

Sweet meditation now be mine—
The sun has sunk—the stars do shine.
Beautifully the moon doth beam;
Its rays rest on the dark deep stream.
The warblers sweet have ceased to raise,
Their customary songs of praise.
The hum of mortals dies away;
And business ends with closing day.
Mild, calm and peaceful is the scene
My soul's disposed to be serene.   10
Come then soft maid, my faithful friend!
And gently teach me to attend,
With list'ning ear, and open heart,
To truths you always do impart.
Teach me to know when reason's voice,
Disproves my acts—or says rejoice—
Teach me to bend to virtue's sway,
And make me better every day.
Then He who makes the sky above
On me, will sure display his love;   20
While I, each duty do fulfil,
And bow submissive to his will.
Then sweet content shall crown each year,
And nought on earth shall make me fear.

On Meditation. Text from *LC70*, which is signed "Jane." There is another manuscript in *IL*, which some readers might prefer. While the two manuscripts are similar, *IL* includes revisions from *LC70*, sometimes with cross-outs directly on the manuscript.

title in *IL*, the title is longer and more descriptive: Poetic Reflections / By LEELINAU, *Grand daughter of Waub Odjeeg. / BUBEESHCOBEE. / On viewing the landscape at St. Mary's Falls at Evening. "at St. Mary's" is added above the line. Leelinau was one of JJS's pen names. The asterisk refers to a note at the bottom of the page that gives JJS's Ojibwe name: "*alias O bah bahm wa wa gee zhick o Kwa." For the sense of wonder evoked by the expression "bubeeshcobee," see HRS's account of a Lake Superior vista, quoted in the introduction. **2** *sunk*—: set, *IL*. **6** *IL* has "customary songs" crossed out and "nugamoons"—an Ojibwe word for songs—written above it. **8** *IL* has "business" crossed out and "tumult" written above it. **10** *soul's disposed to be*: soul's lulled, and all *IL*. **12** *IL* has "And gently" crossed out and "Reflection,—" written after it. **16** Rebukes my acts, or says, rejoice! *IL*. **19** Then, He who Rules the Sky above, *IL*. **24** Compare "Welcome, welcome to my arms" line 16.

[handwritten: To the arms]
[handwritten: D To Death/God?]
[handwritten: of Death/God?]

"Welcome, welcome to my arms"

[handwritten: uniform rhyme]
[handwritten: LD Block Stanza]

Welcome, welcome to my arms,
All that constitutes life's charms;
Welcome day of sweet emotion,
To my heart of deep devotion—
Desponding hours, of grief away,
Upon that happy, happy day;
When faithful hearts in trust shall beat
In joyful unisons—so sweet—
Content shall banish every gloom,
And smiles of love our face illume,   10
Whilst Husband, Wife and Children dear, *[handwritten: 3: Religious Father, son, holy ghost]*
In one strong band of love appear,
To heav'n with one accord we'll raise,
Our voices, in humble, grateful praise;
And spend in peace each coming year,
With naught on earth to make us fear;
Blest in each other's happy smile— *[handwritten: ends w/ death but starts poem very enthusiastic about life]*
Reject the world, with all its guile,
Till summon'd to our rest above,
To live in God's supernal love.   20

"Welcome, welcome to my arms." Text from *LC45*. Untitled. JJS includes this poem in a letter from Mackinac of 13 July 1840 to HRS at Detroit. The letter describes how eager she is for him to return from his travels, "when," she writes, "I can say—" and then she proceeds with the poem. At the bottom of the page, after line 17, she draws a hand pointing to the last three lines in the right margin. The next page then continues: "I had written so far yesterday afternoon, in hopes to have my letter ready for the Boat, when I was interrupted by visitors . . . , & whilst they were in, the Boat passed down, & so my politeness lost me the opportunity of finishing & mailing it in time, & awoke me from poetic fancy's flight, for the night, though I still hope the subject will be realized before long, when I shall *know*, & *feel* it to be *more* than fancy or song." Perhaps she wrote the last three lines after the interruption.

16 Compare "On Meditation," line 24.

A Psalm, or Supplication for mercy, and confession of Sin, addressed to the Author of Life, in the Odjibway-Algonquin tongue

By the late Mrs Henry R Schoolcraft

Gaitche minno pim au diz iy un Gezha Monedo geezhig ong aibey un.

Keen maum auwa ikumig wai oz hemig oy un.

Keen kah ozhi eeyong, keen gaugegaik umig, kai nuhwaunemeong, aikooem au diz eyong.

Keen kainuh wau baimeyong, geeg hik tibbikuk tibishko.

Keen kee ke ozhea an geez hik geezis, tibbik geezis, annung wug gia.

Keen keeg e ozhetoan tshe kimmewung, gia tshe annimik eegkaug; tshe sai sai yung, tshe sogepoog gia.

Keen kau ozhe-eyong tshe senneweeg auboweyaung, kukinnuk kau ozheudjig akeeng.

Kee gemishemin odj echaug wug, wekaukain ebosigoog, ke gemeeshemin ke bahz higo kegwis Jesus Christ, tshe oondj enebood neenowind.

Mo zhug issuh nemudjee inaindumin, kaigat mozhug ne mudje ekidomin; nahwudj nemincoaindumin, tshe mudjee do dumaung.

Kaigate igo me kai oondje izhauy aung ebun mudjee Monedo.   10

Showainemis hinaum, Gezha Monedo,! show ainesmish inaum Jesus Christ. Maishkoodgeto an nemudje odaienaunin; meez his henaum edush oushkee odaiyun.

Apai dush nah saug eig sayun, gia dush to dum aung kau izhee gug eekway un me ozhis sin aun odaiyun tshe min waindumaung tshe annameautog o yun.

Shauwainim neen dun ahwaimaugunenaunig unis henaubaig.

Show ainim kukinn ah meenik paimau dis se djig akeeng.

Shora ain emis henaum kaid o koo pemau diss ey ong, appe dush neeboy ong, show ain emis hon aum neen djeechaugo naunig tshe ghowaud keen.

Kaugeg ai kumig edush tshe, meen ahwaunegoozeyong ozaum ne mudje pemau diz eewin, auno unnahmez auyongin.

Kauween edush kewee piz in dow iss inin, kishpin aitah appainemoyong kegwis Jesus Christ.

Aipetainemud kegwis showainemis heen aun. Kunna gai kunna.

Translation

Merciful spirit, great author of life, abiding above.
Thou hast made, all that is made.
Thou art the greatest and the everlasting preserver of life.
Thou has guarded me by day and by night.
Thou hast made the sun, moon and stars.
Thou hast made the rain and the thunder, hail and snow.
Thou hast, to finish all, made man who stands up erect, and is placed over all that is on the earth.
Thou hast given us souls, that will never die, and hast sent thine only son Jesus Christ, who has died for our bad acts, that we, through faith in him might live.
For our minds are set on evil continuously, and our words are perverted; truly we do, all the day long, think bad thoughts, and do bad acts.
Truly, we deserve to be punished in the place where thou hast prepared thy punishments—even hell.   10
Have mercy upon us, Merciful spirit, have mercy upon us!
Have mercy upon us, Jesus Christ!
Renovate our wicked hearts, and give us new hearts.
May we love thee with our whole hearts, and keep thy commandments, and give us hearts to take a delight in prayer.
Show mercy upon all our kindred and people.
Show mercy to the whole world.
Be our Friend while we live; and when we die, oh take our souls to thine abode, and there, may both soul and body be happy forever.
We are too much abased to ask this in our own name, but beseech thee through Jesus Christ.
In his name, thy Son's have mercy upon us, so be it evermore.

A Psalm. Text from *IL.* The words following "A Psalm" and preceding the first line appear to have been added later. Also added are line numbers in the left margin, which are not included here. There is another version in *Oneota* (126–27). One could choose the *Oneota* text, because HRS completed the process of preparing it for publication, or one could choose the *IL* text, because it *might* be earlier and thus *might* more closely match what JJS wrote. For those who wish to compare the two versions, the *Oneota* version is already available in print, whereas this is the first appearance in print for the *IL* version. *IL* and *Oneota* differ in one Ojibwe word (noted below), in the spelling of Ojibwe words, and especially in the placement of breaks between words. *Oneota* also divides the Psalm into twenty-three lines, compared to nineteen in *IL*. The English versions differ moderately, though they closely paraphrase each other. The English version in *Oneota* strikes me as an effort to make *IL* sound more like biblical English. For example, what *IL* translates as "Truly," *Oneota* translates as "Verily." *Oneota* concludes with the following note: "Those who take an interest in the structure of the Indian languages, may regard the above, as an *improvised* specimen of the capacity of this particular dialect for the expression of scripture truth. The writer, who from early years was a member of the church, had made a translation of the Lords prayer, and, occasionally, as delicate and declining health permitted, some other select pieces from the sacred writings, and hymns, of which, one or two selections may, perhaps, hereafter be made."

Ojibwe original. 7 senneweeg auboweyaung: unnewegauboweyaung *Oneota.*

On reading Miss Hannah Moore's Christian morals and Practical Piety. 1816

These books the truth so plainly shew,
    That none can read but to improve;
And feel the good that they bestow,
    And every Christian moral love.

O that the precepts they impart,
    May ever influence my mind,
And to each virtue form my heart,
    That should adorn all womankind.

In virtue, I could never grow,
    Without the spirit from above
Nor lead a life of bliss below,
    Without my Saviour's tender love.   10

Then may I still what's good pursue,
    And strive to conquer what is ill,
Keep truth forever in my view,
    And God's supreme commands fulfill.

On reading Miss Hannah Moore's Christian morals and Practical Piety. 1816.
Text from *LC70*. There is another manuscript in *IL*. Hannah More (1745–
1833), an eminent English dramatist and poet, later in her life concentrated
on writing about religion and social reform. Her *Practical Piety: or, The Influence of the Religion of the Heart on the Conduct of Life* (1811) and *Christian
Morals* (1813) went through many editions. In his "Notes" for a memoir of
JJS, HRS refers to JJS reading More (98), and in his essay about JJS's poetry,
he says that "She had been early impressed with the writings of Hannah
Moore, whose high moral views of life she ever regarded as entitled to her
highest reflections and study" ("Dawn"). The reformist British writer Harriet
Martineau, who met JJS and HRS on her travels in the United States (H. R.
Schoolcraft, *Personal Memoirs* 541), lamented American reading habits with
witty exaggeration: "I hear no name so often as Mrs. Hannah More's. She is
much better known in the country than Shakespeare. This is, of course, an
indication of the religious taste of the people" (3: 219). The two manuscripts
differ only in punctuation, in that *LC70* is signed "Jane *Johnston*," and in

that *LC70* lacks *IL*'s "tender" at line 12. I have included "tender," which fits the tetrameter pattern and may therefore represent a more accurate rendering or a revision (either by JJS or by HRS). I have also followed *IL* for the title because *LC70* abbreviates Hannah as "H." Otherwise, except as noted, the text comes from *LC70*.

Stanzas

Don't understand the title

Written in 1815 before going to hear my Father read religious services.

First to my God, my heart and thoughts I'll raise,
  Then from my earthly father counsel take
From him I'll learn to sing my Saviour's praise
  Who bids me from the sleep of death awake.

Oh Saviour, deign to make me still thy care
  Do thou my heart with heavenly wisdom fill
Lead me to shun sin's oft close hidden snare
  And make my chiefest joy to do thy will.

Then sweet content, shall crown each coming year,
  With love and gratitude my heart o'erflow,   10
Thy mercies leave me naught on earth to fear
  Whilst on my journey through this vale of woe.

Stanzas. Text from *IL*.

7 *sin's*: editor's emendation of "sin". Someone penciled a mark on the manuscript above "sin", perhaps suspecting a transcription error.

"My heart is gone with him afar"

My heart is gone with him afar,
My home is in his manly breast—
My joy is centred in his smile:
His love is all that makes me blest.

"My heart is gone with him afar." Text from *LC8*. Untitled. While HRS was away in the spring of 1828, JJS kept a journal, partly to show it to him when he returned. She wrote this poem in her entry for 30 April. For another poem from her journal, see *"Amid the still retreat of Elmwood's shade"* above.

Acrostic

A thing of glitter, gleam, and gold,
Loose thoughts, loose verse, unmeaning, old,
Big words that sound a thousand fold;
Unfinished scraps, conceit and cant,
Mad stanzas, and a world of rant.

So its a book?

Acrostic. Text from *LC70*. In an acrostic, a popular form at the time, certain letters in each line, usually the first letters, as in this poem, have a meaning when read together vertically. Sometimes, as in this case, the text of an acrostic offers a riddle that matches the vertical meaning. Albums were popular books that collected a diverse array of writing and pictures, combining the roles of magazine, anthology, and coffee-table book, and often elaborately printed, bound, and decorated with gold.

My Ear-rings

so shis attempting to be whitty

My ear-rings are gone, in the Wars of Fate—
And a pair of red-drops I would not hate. Leelinau

My Ear-rings. Text from *LC45*. Untitled; title provided by the editor. This little poem appears in the margin of a letter of 8 June 1840 from JJS at Mackinac to HRS at Detroit (see figure 7); it is JJS's playful way of asking HRS to buy her new earrings. The same letter also includes the couplet "When the Stormy Winds Do Blow, After Thomas Campbell." Leelinau was one of JJS's pen names.

When the Stormy Winds Do Blow, After Thomas Campbell

'Tis in vain to complain, when the stormy winds do blow
But to trust, in the *love*—of *near* twenty years ago.

When the Stormy Winds Do Blow, After Thomas Campbell. Text from *LC45.* Untitled; title provided by the editor. This little poem appears in a letter of 8 June 1840 from JJS at Mackinac to HRS in Detroit. It plays a variation on the refrain of Thomas Campbell's (1777–1814) famous "Ye Mariners of England," 1801 and 1805: "And the stormy winds do blow" (Campbell 187–89). Perhaps JJS heard a sung version of Campbell's poem or another lyric that included the words "'Tis in vain to complain." HRS remembers "some pieces of . . . Campbell" in John Johnston's library ("Memoir" 64), and JJS may have read or heard of Campbell's then-famous *Gertrude of Wyoming or The Pennsylvanian Cottage* (1809), a long poem partly about Indian people (Campbell 43–94). Below this couplet, she wrote the following, which leads into the signature that closes her letter (aside from some postscripts): "How do you like my additional, last line? O how I long for the day when you & the children will be home again, to cheer my withering frame & heart— There's no place like home after all—'with wife, children & friends' but I must change the word *wife* [meaning, change it to husband?] to suit myself—& perhaps it would suit *you* better too—were the poor wife to be *changed* altogether for a new & better one—having grown old & worn out for any farther pleasure *she can give*, except that her heart, is still, & ever has been, yours affectionately Jane J. Schoolcraft." JJS quotes "wife, children & friends" from the refrain of "Song" ("When the black-letter'd list to the gods was presented"), a once-famous poem by the once-fashionable poet William Robert Spencer (1770–1834; Spencer 103–6 [1811]). The same letter that includes this couplet also includes the couplet "My Ear-rings."

near *twenty years ago:* HRS moved to Sault Ste. Marie in 1822; JJS and HRS first met on his earlier trip through the Sault in 1820.

Elegy on the death of my aunt Mrs Kearny* of Kilgobbin Glebe Dublin, Ireland

And must I—with deep sighs again,
Awake pale sorrow's pensive strain?
For death, has called, with threatened aim,
Another loved and honored name.
One whom, that all that knew her knew,
For faith and fond affection true
That sought, with unofficious air,
To make humanity her care.
A Christian warm without pretence
A ready, kind benevolence   10
That stinted not, by term or line,
The boundary of heaven's design
But wide as open sun light's rays,
E'er felt the wish to mend or raise.

   By reading by reflection taught,
Good will and sense inspired her thought,
Nor was the fire that warmed her breast,
All buried there, or unexprest
Delightful task to her, to praise,
Or prompt, or sing melodious lays   20
But not, to fame's loud trumpet given,
Her aims looked ever up to heaven
That heaven, that all her ardour shared,
And hope now tells—is her reward.

*wife of Rev. Henry Kearney.

Elegy On the death of my aunt Mrs Kearny. Text from *IL.*
   title: The asterisk and note are in the manuscript. **1** This line is written above a crossed-out version of the first line, which reads "Ah once again—ah once again," **2** *Awake*: The uppercase "A" is written over an uppercase "I", which would fit with the crossed-out version of line 1.

Spirit of Peace

Spirit of peace! The precious hour,
Sacred to Wisdom's awful power
And calm reflection's part
A———————————rt.

Spirit of Peace. Text from *LC70.* Untitled fragment; title provided by the editor. The words "power" (especially the "er") and "reflection's" are too faint to transcribe with certainty. The last line, partly faint and perhaps partly crossed out, is mostly illegible. At the bottom on the right, the manuscript is dated "21 Nov."

"Let prayer alone our thoughts engage"

Let prayer alone our thoughts engage.
Let it the standard of our actions be

In prayer let us our time employ   *interesting gramer*

Always let prayer
Let Piety ever
Ever lett Piety be
The rule of our lives here
The Great Church alone
Firmly let us love   *Sounds like
                                       a prayer*

Evile living   10
All, all
Evile living
All let us forsake

"Let prayer alone our thoughts engage." Text from *LC70*. Untitled. This fragment seems to be a set of notes or false starts for a poem, including misspell-
ings that seem uncharacteristic of JJS.

2 *be*: editor's emendation of what looks like "bee". **3** *employ*: an uncertain editor's emendation; there is no "o", and the "m" looks more like "ri"
or perhaps "n".

The Origin of the Robin

An old man had an only son, a fine promising lad, who had come to that age which is thought by the Chippewas to be most proper to make the long and final fast, that is to secure through life a guardian spirit, on whom future prosperity or adversity is to depend, and who forms and establishes the character of the faster to great or ignoble deeds.

This old man was ambitious that his son should surpass all others in whatever was deemed most wise and great amongst his tribe. And to fulfil his wishes, he thought it necessary that his son must fast a much longer time than any of those persons known for their great power or wisdom, whose fame he envied.

He therefore directed his son to prepare with great ceremony, for the important event. After he had been in the sweating lodge and bath several times, he ordered him to lie down upon a clean mat, in the little lodge expressly prepared for him, telling him, at the same time to bear himself like a man, and that at the expiration of *twelve* days, he should receive food, and the blessing of his father.

The lad carefully observed this injunction, laying with his face covered with perfect composure, awaiting those happy visitations which were to seal his good or ill fortune. His father visited him every morning regularly to encourage him to perseverance, expatiating at full length on the renown and honor that would attend him through life, if he accomplished the full term prescribed. To these admonitions the boy never answered, but lay without the least sign of unwillingness till the ninth day, when he addressed his father— "My father, my dreams are ominous of evil! May I break my fast now, and at a more propitious time, make a new fast?" The father answered.—"My son, you know not what you ask! If you get up now, all your glory will depart. Wait patiently a little longer. You have but three days yet to accomplish what I desire. You know, it is for your own good."

The son assented, and covering himself closer, he lay till the eleventh day, when he repeated his request to his father. The same answer was given him, by the old man, adding, that the next day he would himself prepare his first meal, and bring it to him. The boy remained silent, but lay like a skeleton. No one would have known he was living but by the gentle heaving of his breast.

The next morning the father, elate at having gained his end, prepared a repast for his son, and hastened to set it before him. On coming to the door, he was surprized to hear his son talking to himself. He stooped to listen, and looking through a small aperture, was more astonished when he beheld his son painted with vermillion on his breast, and in the act of finishing his work by laying on the paint as far as his hand could reach on his shoulders, saying at the same time:—"My father has ruined me, as a man; he would not listen to my request; he will now be the loser. I shall be forever happy in my new state, for I have been obedient to my parent; he alone will be the sufferer; for the Spirit is a just one, though not propitious to me. He has shown me pity, and now I must go."

At that moment the old man broke in, exclaiming, "My son! my son! do not leave me!" But his son with the quickness of a bird had flown up to the top of the lodge, and perched on the highest pole, a beautiful robin red-breast. He looked down on his father with pity beaming in his eyes, and told him, that he should always love to be near men's dwellings, that he should always be seen happy and contented by the constant cheerfulness and pleasure he would display, that he would still cheer his father by his songs, which would be some consolation to him for the loss of the glory he had expected, and that, although no longer a man, he should ever be the harbinger of peace and joy to the human race.

Leelinau.

In the foregoing story, we recognize the pen of a female correspondent, to whom we have before been indebted. A descendant herself, by European parentage, of the race whose manners and customs, she depicts, in these legends, they derive additional interest from her familiar knowledge of the Indian legendary mind, and the position she occupies between the European and aboriginal races. The tale, she observes illustrates the Indian custom of fasting to procure a personal spirit. The moral to be drawn from it, is perhaps the danger of ambition. We should not seek for unreasonable honors, nor take unusual means to attain them.

The spirit fasted for, by the young man, proving averse to him, he requests his father to exempt him from further fasting; and on being denied, gives a proof of filial obedience, by persevering in abstinence. In reward for this, the spirit, though unfavorable, partly relents, and instead of compelling the son to pass a miserable life in the human form, changes him to a bird, who will take a peculiar delight in lingering around the habitations of men.

The Origin of the Robin. Text from *LC64*. There are four versions: *LC64*, Gilman (1836), Jameson (1838, 3: 114–18), and *AR*. Leelinau was one of JJS's pen names. HRS provided the note after the story. A shorter version of the note appears in Gilman, signed "S——." Perhaps out of a similar concern to explain the story, as an afterthought HRS also appears to have penned in a subtitle and a new sentence before the original first sentence. The added subtitle is "an Oral Allegory." The added opening sentence reads: "Spiritual gifts, are sought by the Chippewas through fasting." Introducing the story, Gilman says "I will give it to you as it was taken down by Mrs. S verbatim, from the lips of an old Chippewa woman. Mrs. S. tells me she has since been assured by very many of the oldest and most intelligent of the tribe that the story of the 'Origin of the Robin-red-breast' has been current in the tribe from their earliest recollections. I know you will agree with me in thinking it a most beautiful fable" (1: 159). Gilman's text is extremely close to *LC64*, whereas Jameson's has minor variations, presumably her own. *AR* drops the note and introduces additional variations, mainly by giving the young man a name, "Iadilla," and by extending the last paragraph and concluding with "Iadilla's Song," presumably written by HRS. HRS mentions hearing the story in his *Personal Memoirs* for 14 April 1823 (170).

Moowis, The Indian Coquette

There was a village full of Indians, and a noted belle or *muh muh daw go qua* was living there. A noted beau or *muh muh daw go, nin nie* was there also. He and another young man went to court this young woman, and laid down beside her, when she scratched the face of the handsome beau. He went home and would not rise till the family prepared to depart, and he would not then arise. They then left him, as he felt ashamed to be seen even by his own relations. It was winter, and the young man, his rival, who was his cousin, tried all he could to persuade him to go with the family, for it was now winter, but to no purpose, till the whole village had decamped and had gone away. He then rose and gathered all the bits of clothing, and ornaments of beads and other things, that had been left. He then made a coat and leggins of the same, nicely trimmed with the beads, and the suit was fine and complete. After making a pair of moccasins, nicely trimmed, he also made a bow and arrows. He then collected the dirt of the village, and filled the garments he had made, so as to appear as a man, and put the bow and arrows in its hands, and it came to life. He then desired the dirt image to follow him to the camp of those who had left him, who thinking him dead by this time, were surprized to see him. One of the neighbors took in the dirt-man and entertained him. The belle saw them come and immediately fell in love with him. The family that took him in made a large fire to warm him, as it was winter. The image said to one of the children, "sit between me and the fire, it is too hot," and the child did so, but all smelt the dirt. Some said, "some one has trod on, and brought in dirt." The master of the family said to the child sitting in front of the guest, "get away from before our guest, you keep the heat from him." The boy answered saying, "he told me to sit between him and the fire." In the meantime, the belle wished the stranger would visit her. The image went to his master, and they went out to different lodges, the image going as directed to the belle[']s. Towards morning, the image said to the young woman (as he had succeeded) "I must now go away," but she said, "I will go with you." He said "it is too far." She answered, "it is not so far but that I can go with you." He first went to the lodge where he was entertained, and then to his master, and told him of all that had happened, and that he was going off with her. The young man thought it a pity she had treated him so, and how sadly she would be punished. They went off, she following behind. He left her a great way behind, but she continued to follow him. When the sun rose high, she found one of his mittens and picked it up, but to her astonishment, found it full of dirt. She, however took it up and wiped it, and going on further, she found the other mitten in the same condition. She thought, "fie!! why does he do so," thinking he dirtied in them. She kept finding different articles of his dress, on the way all day, in the same condition. He kept ahead of her till towards evening, when the snow was like water, having melted by the heat of the day. No signs of her husband appearing, after having collected all the cloth[e]s that held him together, she began to cry, not knowing where to go, as their track was lost, on account of the snow's melting. She kept crying *Moowis* has led me astray, and she kept singing and crying Moowis nin ge won e win ig, ne won e win ig.

Moowis, The Indian Coquette. Text from *LC65*. The name "Leelinau," one of JJS's pen names, appears at the bottom. There are three versions: *LC65*, a version under HRS's name in *The Columbian Lady's and Gentleman's Magazine* (1844), and a version in *Oneota* (381–84). The two later versions soften the suggestions of sex and excrement and are much expanded and Europeanized, presumably by HRS. The later versions differ from each other in many small ways but remain largely similar, except that at the end the *Oneota* version adds a song that the coquette sings in her longing for Moowis. A note with the magazine version suggests something about the origin of the text: "This curious specimen of Indian story-telling . . . was taken down, verbatim, from the lips of an aboriginal narrator, and the translation is as literal as it can be made." We might doubt that note, however, given that it appeared seventeen years after the earlier manuscript, and given that the magazine version considerably embellishes the earlier version. A note in *Oneota* is more expansive: "It is a characteristic of some of the Indian legends, that they convey *a moral* which seems clearly enough to denote, that a part of these legends were invented to convey instruction to the young folks who listen to them. The known absence of all harsh methods among the Indians, in bringing up their children, favours this idea. The following tale addresses itself plainly to girls; to whom it teaches the danger of what we denominate coquetry. It would seem from this, that beauty, and its concomitant, a passion for dress, among the red daughters of Adam and Eve, has the same tendency to create pride, and nourish self-conceit, and self-esteem, and assume a *tyranny over the human heart,* which writers tell us, these qualities have among their white-skinned, auburn-haired, and blue-eyed progeny the world over. . . . The term Moowis is one of the most derogative and offensive possible. It is derived from the Odjibwa substantive, mo, filth, or excrement." While this note reads the tale as critical of feminine vanity, readers might be at least as likely to read either version, and especially the version here, as critical of masculine vanity, especially considering the young man's cruel revenge. In this version, probably closer to what JJS wrote, the coquette scratches her suitor's face, and he is then ashamed to be seen. In the later version, probably revised by HRS, she instead insults him verbally, and he is ashamed because others overhear the insult, not because of anything about his looks. Longfellow retells the story of Moowis in *Evangeline* (part 2, section 4; 1847), well before *The Song of Hiawatha* (1855), and though he would have seen only the later version or versions, which sympathize more with the man, he makes the story sympathize movingly with the woman, even more than the earlier version sympathizes with her. From another perspective, however, the story serves a more concrete purpose, for it is told to bring on warmer weather and the end of winter (see Brittain and MacKenzie),

  nin ge won e win ig, ne won e win ig: *Oneota* translates this as "you have led me astray—you are leading me astray."

Mishösha, or the Magician and his daughters
A Chippewa Tale or Legend

In an early age of the world, when there were fewer inhabitants in the earth than there now are, there lived an Indian, who had a wife and two children, in a remote situation. Buried in the solitude of the forest, it was not often that he saw any one, out of the circle of his own family. Such a situation seemed favorable for his pursuits; and his life passed on in uninterrupted happiness, till he discovered a wanton disposition in his wife.

This woman secretly cherished a passion for a young man whom she accidentally met in the woods, and she lost no opportunity of courting his approaches. She even planned the death of her husband, who, she justly concluded, would put her to death, should he discover her infidelity. But this design was frustrated by the alertness of the husband, who having cause to suspect her, determined to watch narrowly, to ascertain the truth, before he should come to a determination how to act. He followed her silently one day, at a distance, and hid himself behind a tree. He soon beheld a tall, handsome man approach his wife, and lead her away.

He was now convinced of her crime, and thought of killing her, the moment she returned. In the meantime he went home, and pondered on his situation. At last he came to the determination of leaving her forever, thinking that her own conscience would, in the end, punish her sufficiently; and relying on her maternal feelings, to take care of the two boys, whom he determined to leave behind.

When the wife returned, she was disappointed in not finding her husband, having concerted a plan to dispatch him. When she saw that day after day passed, and he did not return, she at last guessed the true cause of his absence. She then returned to her paramour, leaving the two helpless boys behind, telling them that she was going a short distance, and would return; but determined never to see them more.

The children thus abandoned, soon made way with the food that was left in the lodge, and were compelled to quit it, in search of more. The eldest boy possessed much intrepidity, as well as great tenderness for his little brother, frequently carrying him when he became weary, and gathering all the wild fruit he saw. Thus they went deeper into the forest, soon losing all traces of their former habitation, till they were completely lost in the labyrinths of the wilderness.

The elder boy fortunately had a knife, with which he made a
bow and arrows, and was thus enabled to kill a few birds for himself
and brother. In this way they lived some time, still pressing on, they
knew not whither. At last they saw an opening through the woods,
and were shortly after delighted to find themselves on the borders
of a broad lake. Here the elder boy busied himself in picking the
seed pods of the wild rose. In the meanwhile the younger, amused
himself by shooting some arrows into the sand, one of which, happened to fall into the lake. The elder brother, not willing to lose his
time in making another, waded into the water to reach it. Just as he
was about to grasp the arrow, a canoe passed by him with the rapid-
ity of lightning. An old man, sitting in the centre, seized the af-
frighted youth, and placed him in the canoe. In vain the boy
addressed him. "My grandfather" (a term of respect for old people)
"pray take my little brother also. Alone, I cannot go with you; he
will starve if I leave him." The old magician (for such was his real
character) laughed at him. Then giving his canoe a slap, and commanding it to go, it glided through the water with inconceivable
swiftness. In a few minutes they reached the habitation of Mishosha,
standing on an island in the centre of the lake. Here he lived, with
his two daughters, the terror of all the surrounding country.

Leading the young man up to the lodge "Here my eldest daughter," said he, "I have brought a young man who shall become your
husband." The youth saw surprize depicted in the countenance of
the daughter, but she made no reply, seeming thereby to acquiesce
in the commands of her father. In the evening he overheard the
daughters in conversation. "There again": said the elder daughter,
"our father has brought another victim, under the pretence of giving
me a husband. When will his enmity to the human race cease; or
when shall we be spared witnessing such scenes of vice and wickedness, as we are daily compelled to behold."

When the old magician was asleep, the youth told the elder
daughter, how he had been carried off, and compelled to leave his
helpless brother on the shore. She told him to get up and take her
father's canoe, and using the charm he had observed, it would carry
him quickly to his brother. That he could carry him food, prepare a
lodge for him, and return by morning. He did in every thing as he
had been directed, and after providing for the subsistence of his
brother, told him that in a short time he should come for him. Then
returning to the enchanted island, resumed his place in the lodge
before the magician awoke. Once during the night Mishosha awoke,

and not seeing his son in law, asked his eldest daughter what had become of him. She replied that he had merely stepped out, and would be back soon. This satisfied him. In the morning, finding the young man in the lodge, his suspicions were completely lulled. "I see, my daughter, you have told me the truth."

As soon as the sun rose, Mishosha thus addressed the young man. "Come, my son, I have a mind to gather gulls eggs. I am acquainted with an island where there are great quantities; and I wish your aid in gathering them." The young man, saw no reasonable excuse, and getting into the canoe, the magician gave it a slap, and bidding it go, in an instant they were at the island. They found the shore covered with gulls eggs, and the island surrounded with birds of this kind. "Go, my son," said the old man, "and gather them, while I remain in the canoe." But the young man was no sooner ashore than Mishosha pushed his canoe a little from land and exclaimed: "Listen ye gulls: you have long expected something from me. I now give you an offering. Fly down, and devour him." Then striking his canoe, left the young man to his fate.

The birds immediately came in clouds around their victim, darkening all the air with their numbers. But the youth, seizing the first that came near him, and drawing his knife, cut off its head, and immediately skinning the bird, hung the feathers as a trophy on his breast. "Thus," he exclaimed, "will I treat every one of you who approaches me. Forbear, therefore, and listen to my words. It is not for you to eat human food. You have been given by the Great Spirit as food for man. Neither is it in the power of that old magician to do you any good. Take me on your beaks and carry me to his lodge, and you shall see that I am not ungrateful."

The gulls obeyed, collecting in a cloud for him to rest upon, and quickly flew to the lodge, where they arrived before the magician. The daughters were surprized at his return, but Mishosha conducted as if nothing extraordinary had taken place.

On the following day he again addressed the youth. "Come, my son," said he. "I will take you to an island covered with the most beautiful pebbles, looking like silver. I wish you to assist me in gathering some of them. They will make handsome ornaments, and are possessed of great virtues." Entering the canoe, the magician made use of his charm, and they were carried, in a few moments, to a solitary bay in an island, where there was a smooth sandy beach. The young man went ashore as usual. "A little further, a little further," cried the old man. "Up on that rock you will get some finer ones." Then pushing his canoe from land, "Come thou great king of fishes," cried he, "you have long expected an offering from me. Come, and eat the stranger I have put ashore on your island." So saying, he commanded his canoe to return, and was soon out of sight. Immediately a monstrous fish shoved his long snout from the water, moving partially on the beach, and opening wide his jaws to receive his victim.

"When" exclaimed the young man, drawing his knife, and placing himself in a threatening attitude, "when did you ever taste human food. Have a care of yourself. You were given by the Great Spirit to man, and if you, or any of your tribes, taste human flesh, you will fall sick and die. Listen not to the words of that wicked old man, but carry me back to his island, in return for which, I shall present you a piece of red cloth."

The fish complied, raising his back out of water to allow the young man to get on. Then taking his way through the lake, landed his charge safely at the island, before the return of the magician.

The daughters were still more surprized to see him thus escaped a second time, from the arts of their father. But the old man maintained his taciturnity. He could not, however, help saying to himself. "What manner of boy is this, who ever escapes from my power. His spirit shall not however save him. I will entrap him tomorrow. Ha! ha! ha!"

The next day the magician addressed the young man as follows "Come, my son," said he "you must go with me to procure some young eagles. I wish to tame them. I have discovered an island where they exist in great abundance." When they had reached the island, Mishosha led him inland till they came to the foot of a tall pine, upon which the nests were. "Now, my son[,"] said he[, "]climb up this tree, and bring down the birds." The young man obeyed, and when he had with great effort, got up near the nests—"Now," exclaimed the magician, addressing the tree "stretch yourself up, and be very tall." The tree rose up at the command. "Listen ye eagles[,"] continued the old man, "you have long expected a gift from me. I now present you this boy who has had the presumption to molest your young. Stretch forth your claws, and seize him." So saying he left the young man to his fate, and returned.

But the intrepid youth, drawing his knife, and cutting off the head of the first eagle that menaced him, raised his voice and exclaimed—"Thus will I deal with all who come near me. What right have you, ye ravenous birds, to eat living flesh[?] Is it because that old cowardly old magician has bid you do so? He is an old woman. He can neither do you good nor harm. See! I have already slain one of your number[.] Respect my bravery, and carry me back to the lodge of the old man, that I may show you how I shall treat him."

The eagles, pleased with the spirit of the young man, assented, and clustering around him, formed a seat with their backs, and flew towards the enchanted Island. As they crossed the water they passed the magician lying half asleep in his canoe and treated him with great indignity.

The return of the young man was hailed with joy by the daughters, but excited the ire of the magician, who taxed his wits for some new mode of ridding himself of a youth so powerful[ly] aided by his spirit. He therefore invited him to go a hunting. Taking his canoe, they proceeded to an island, and built a lodge to shelter themselves during the night. In the meantime, the magician caused a deep fall of snow and a storm of wind with severe cold.

According to custom the young man pulled off his moccasins and leggons, and hung them before the fire. After he had gone to sleep, the magician, watching his opportunity, got up, and taking one moccasin and one leggon, threw them into the fire. He then went to sleep. In the morning, stretching himself as he arose, and uttering an exclamation of surprize, he exclaimed "My son, what has become of your moccasin and leggon? I believe this is the moon in which fire attracts, and I fear they have been drawn in.["] The young man suspected the true cause of his loss, and rightly attributed it, to a design of the magician to freeze him to death on their march. But he maintained the strictest silence, and drawing his blanket over his head, thus communed with himself. "I have full faith in my spirit, who has preserved me thus far, and I do not fear that he will now forsake me. Great is the power of my Manito; and he shall prevail against this wicked old enemy of mankind."

Then drawing on the remaining moccasin and leggon, he took a coal from the fire and invoking his spirit to give it efficacy, blackened the foot and leg as far as the lost garment usually reached. Then rising announced himself ready for the march. In vain the magician led him through snow and over morasses, hoping to see the lad sink at every moment. But in this he was disappointed, and they, for the first time returned home together.

Taking courage from this the young man now determined to try his own power, having previously consulted with the daughters. They all agreed that the life the old man led was detestable, and that whoever would rid the world of him, would entitle himself to the thanks of the human race. On the following day the young man thus addressed the magician. "My grandfather, I have often gone with you on perilous excursions, and never murmured. I must now request that you will accompany me, I wish to visit my little brother, and to bring him home with me.["] They accordingly went on a visit to the main land and found the little lad in the spot where he had been left. After taking him into the canoe, the young man again addressed the magician "My grandfather, will you go and cut me a few of those red willows on the bank. I wish to prepare some smoking mixture." ["]Certainly, my son," replied the old man "What you wish, is not very hard. Ha! ha! ha! do you think me too old to get up there[?]"

No sooner was the magician ashore, than the young man placing himself in the proper position, struck the canoe and repeated the charm N'*chimaun Pall.* And immediately the canoe flew through the water on its passage to the island. It was evening when the two brothers arrived; but the elder daughter informed the young man, that unless he sat up and watched the canoe and kept his hand upon it, such was the power of their father it would slip off and return to him. The young man watched faithfully till near the dawn of day, when he could no longer resist the drowsiness which oppressed him and suffered himself to nod, for a moment. In an instant the canoe slipped off, and sought its master, who soon returned in high glee; "Ha! ha! ha! my son," said he; "you thought to play me a trick; it was very clever; but you see I am too old for you."

A short time after, the youth again addressed the magician[. "]My grandfather, I wish to try my skill in hunting. It is said there is plenty of game on an island not far off and I have to request that you will take me there in your canoe." They accordingly spent the day in hunting, and night coming on, they put up a temporary lodge. When the magician had sunk into a profound sleep, the young man got up, and taking a moccasin and leggon of Mishosha's from the place where they hung before the fire, threw them in; thus retaliating the artifice before played upon himself. He had discovered by some secret means, that the foot and leg were the only assailable parts of the magician's body; which could not be guarded by the spirits who served him and treated him with great indignity.

The return of the young man was hailed with joy by the daughters[.] He then besought his Manito, to cause a storm of snow, with cold wind and icy sleet, and then laid himself down beside the old man. Consternation was depicted in the countenance of the latter, when he awoke in the morning and found his moccasin and leggon missing. "I believe, my grandfather,["] said the young man, "that this is the moon in which fire attracts, and I fear your clothes have been drawn in." Then rising and bidding the old man follow, he began the morning's hunt, frequently he turned his head to see how Mishosha kept up. He saw him faultering at every step and almost benumbed with cold. But encouraged him to follow, saying we shall soon be through and reach the shore. But still leading him round about ways; to let the frost take complete effect. At length the old man reached the brink of the island, where the woods are succeeded by a border of smooth sand. But he could go no further his legs became stiff; and refused all motion, and he found himself fixed to the spot, but he still kept stretching out his arms and swinging his body to and fro. Every moment he found the numbness creeping higher he felt his legs growing downwards like roots, the feathers on his head turned to leaves, and in a few seconds he stood a tall and stiff sycamore, leaning towards the water.

The young man getting into the canoe, and pronouncing the charm, was soon transported to the island, where he related his victory to the daughters. They applauded the deed, agreed to put on mortal shapes, become wives to the young men, and forever quit the enchanted island. They immediately passed over to the main land, where they lived in happiness and Peace.

Mishōsha, or the Magician and his daughters. There are four versions: *LC65* with JJS's name "Bame-wa-wa-ge-zhik-aquay" in HRS's hand at the bottom; *LC85*, grouped with "The Forsaken Brother" under the heading "Chippewa Tales. Narrated from their traditional lore, By Mrs H. R. Schoolcraft," in William Johnston's hand (hereafter *WJ*); Jameson (1838, 3: 96–113); and *AR*. *LC65* does not include the second half of the story. It probably appeared in the next issue of the *Literary Voyager*, which has not survived, but I follow *LC65* for the first half, because JJS presumably approved *LC65* and probably had the opportunity to correct or revise it. The break between halves, which comes right after the first of Mishosha's several ominously evil laughs ("Ha! ha! ha!"), falls at a moment well chosen for dramatic suspense. I follow *WJ* for the second half, based on an educated guess that it follows JJS's writing more closely than the other versions of the second half. *WJ* is punctuated more casually and lightly than *LC65*, but in the first half it has no substantial differences from *LC65*, suggesting that it provides a reliable text for the second half of the story. At the same time, for the second half of the story, I take an occasional paragraph break from Jameson, because *WJ* does not always indicate where new paragraphs begin, and Jameson's paragraph breaks usually match those in *LC65* and *AR*. Jameson's version is closer to *WJ* than to *LC65*, but it has variants that match each version, suggesting that there was another, slightly different version that Jameson copied and that has not survived. *WJ* probably dates from before *AR*, because after the publication of *AR*, there would be no reason for William to make a copy, and because William broke away from HRS and JJS in 1838.

The Forsaken Brother
A Chippewa Tale

It was a fine summer evening; the sun was scarcely an hour high,—its departing rays beamed through the foliage of the tall, stately elms, that skirted the little green knoll, on which a solitary Indian lodge stood. The deep silence that reigned in this sequestered and romantic spot, seemed to most of the inmates of that lonely hut, like the long sleep of death, that was now evidently fast sealing the eyes of the head of this poor family. His low breathing was answered by the sighs of his disconsolate wife and their children. Two of the latter were almost grown up, one was yet a mere child. These were the only human beings near the dying man. The door of the lodge was thrown open to admit the refreshing breeze of the lake, on the banks of which it stood; and as the cool air fanned the head of the poor man, he felt a momentary return of strength, and raising himself a little, he thus addressed his weeping family. "I leave you— thou, who hast been my partner in life, but you will not stay long behind me—You shall soon join me in the happy land of Spirits. Therefore you have not long to suffer in this world. But oh! my children, my poor children! you have just commenced life, and mark me, unkindness, and ingratitude, and every wickedness is in the scene before you. I left my kindred and my tribe, because I found what I have just warned you of. I have contented myself with the company of your mother and yourselves, for many years, and you will find my motives for separating from the haunts of men, were solicitude and anxiety to preserve you from the bad examples you would inevitably have followed. But I shall die content, if you, my children promise me, to cherish each other, and on no account to forsake your youngest brother; of him I give you both particular charge." The man became exhausted, and taking a hand to each of his eldest children, he continued—"My daughter! never forsake your little brother. My son, never forsake your little brother." "Never, never!" they both exclaimed. "Never—never!" repeated the father and expired.

The poor man died happy, because he thought his commands would be obeyed. The sun sank below the trees, and left a golden sky behind, which the family were wont to admire, but no one heeded it now. The lodge that was so still an hour before, was now filled with low and unavailing lamentations. Time wore heavily away—five long moons had passed and the sixth was nearly full, when the mother also died. In her last moments she pressed the fulfilment of their promise to their departed father. They readily renewed their promise, because they were yet free from any selfish motive. The winter passed away, and the beauties of spring cheered the drooping spirits of the bereft little family. The girl, being the eldest, dictated to her brothers, and seemed to feel a tender and sisterly affection for the youngest, who was rather sickly and delicate. The other boy soon showed symptoms of restlessness, and addressed the sister as follows: "My sister, are we always to live as if there were no other human beings in the world[?] Must I deprive myself the pleasure of associating with my own kind? I shall seek the villages of men; I have determined, and you cannot prevent me." The girl replied. "My brother, I do not say no to what you desire. We were not prohibited the society of our fellow mortals, but we were told to cherish each other, and that we should do nothing independent of each other—that neither pleasure nor pain ought ever to separate us, particularly from our helpless brother. If we follow our separate gratifications, it will surely make us forget *him* whom we are alike bound to support." The young man made no answer, but taking his bow and arrows left the lodge, and never returned.

Many moons had come and gone, after the young man's departure, and still the girl administered to the wants of her younger brother. At length, however, she began to be weary of her solitude, and of her charge. Years, which added to her strength and capability of directing the affairs of the household, also brought with them the desire of society, and made her solitude irksome. But in meditating a change of life, she thought only for herself, and cruelly sought to abandon her little brother, as her elder brother had done before.

One day after she had collected all the provisions she had set apart for emergencies, and brought a quantity of wood to the door, she said to her brother. "My brother, you must not stray far from the lodge. I am going to seek our brother: I shall soon be back." Then taking her bundle, she set off, in search of habitations. She soon found them, and was so much taken up with the pleasures and amusements of society, that all affection for her brother was obliterated. She accepted a proposal of marriage, and after that, never more thought of the helpless relative she had abandoned.

In the meantime the elder brother had also married, and settled on the shores of the same lake, which contained the bones of his parents, and the abode of his forsaken brother.

As soon as the little boy had eaten all the food left by his sister, he was obliged to pick berries and dig up roots. Winter came on, and the poor child was exposed to all its rigors. He was obliged to quit the lodge in search of food, without a shelter. Sometimes he passed the night in the clefts of old trees, and eat the refuse meats of the wolves. The latter soon became his only resource, and he became so fearless of these animals, that he would sit close to them whilst they devoured their prey, and the animals themselves seemed to pity his condition, and would always leave something. Thus he lived, as it were, on the bounty of fierce wolves until spring. As soon as the lake was free from ice, he followed his new found friends and com-panions to the shore. It happened his brother was fishing in his canoe in the lake, a considerable distance out, when he thought he heard the cry of a child, and wondered how any could exist on so bleak a part of the shore. He listened again more attentively, and distinctly heard the cry repeated. He made for shore as quick as possible, and as he approached land, discovered and recognized his little brother, and heard him singing in a plaintive voice—

Neesya, neesya, shyegwuh gushuh!
Ween ne myeengunish!
    ne myeengunish!
My brother, my brother,
I am now turning into a Wolf!—
I am turning into a Wolf.

At the termination of his song, he howled like a Wolf, and the young man was still more astonished, when, on getting nearer shore, he perceived his poor brother half turned into that animal. He how-ever, leapt on shore and strove to catch him in his arms, and sooth-ingly said—"My brother, my brother, come to me." But the boy eluded his grasp, and fled, still singing as he fled—"I am turning into a wolf!—I am turning into a wolf," and howling in the intervals.

The elder brother, conscience struck, and feeling his brotherly affection returning with redoubled force, exclaimed in great anguish, "My brother, my brother, come to me." But the nearer he ap-proached the child, the more rapidly his transformation went on, until he changed into a perfect wolf,—still singing and howling, and naming his brother and sister alternately in his song, as he fled into the woods, until his change was complete. At last he said, "I am a wolf," and bounded out of sight.

The young man felt the bitterness of remorse all his days, and the sister, when she heard of the fate of the little boy whom she had so cruelly left, and whom both she and her brother had solemnly promised to foster and protect, wept bitterly; and never ceased to mourn until she died.

The Forsaken Brother. A Chippewa Tale. Text from *LC65*. The name "Leelinau," one of JJS's pen names, appears at the bottom. There are five versions: *LC65*; *LC85*; grouped with "Mishösha" under the heading "Chippewa Tales. Narrated from their traditionary lore, By Mrs H. R. Schoolcraft," in William Johnston's hand; Gilman (1836); Jameson (1838, 3: 88–95); and *AR*. I follow *LC65* rather than *WJ*, because JJS presumably approved *LC65* and probably had the opportunity to correct or revise it. I use *WJ* as a source for, or as corroboration for, emendations of *LC65*, because the two manuscripts of stories in William's hand, "Mishösha" and "The Forsaken Brother," which appear next to each other in HRS's papers, are close to the versions in *LC65*, suggesting that they are generally accurate copies of the same or similar manuscripts that can help us resolve errors in the transcription of *LC65*. Gilman's text roughly matches *LC65* but has many minor differences that follow no particular pattern. Since the other story in Gilman, "The Origin of the Robin," closely matches the manuscript of the *Literary Voyager*, and since there is no particular pattern to the differences between Gilman's version of "The Forsaken Brother" and the version in the *Literary Voyager* (*LC65*), it seems likely that Gilman copied a manuscript other than *LC65* for "The Forsaken Brother." The *AR* version is heavily rewritten, yet it has several peculiarities in common with Gilman and different from *LC65*, corroborating the impression that the differences between Gilman and *LC65* derive from Gilman's copying a different manuscript, now lost. It is also possible, however, that Gilman made changes that then influenced HRS's choices for *AR*. Below and in Appendix 5 I list the larger variants from *WJ* but not from *AR*, and not from Gilman and Jameson except when they prove useful as corroborations of *WJ*.

   long behind me—You shall soon join me in the happy land of Spirits. Therefore you have not long to suffer: *WJ*; *LC65* reads "long to suffer", accidentally, it appears, skipping the words between the two instances of "long."

Origin of the Miscodeed,* or the Maid of Taquimenon

The daughter of Mongazida, was the pride of her parents, and their only child. Beauty sat upon her lips, and life and animation marked all her motions. Fourteen summers had witnessed the growth of her stature, and the unfolding of her charms, and each spring, as it came around, had beheld her, in her happy simplicity, reveling amid the wild flowers of her native valley. There was no valley so sweet as the valley of Taquiemenon. There, she listened to the earliest notes of the wild birds, who returned from the south, to enliven the forests after the repose of winter; and there, also, she had prepared her bower of branches, and fasted to obtain a guardian spirit, to conduct her through life, according to the belief and customs of her people. Sweet valley of the Taquimenon, thou didst bless her with the charms of thy fragrance, causing the most profound sensations of pleasure. There, she first beheld that little angel, who in the shape of a small white bird, of purest plumage, assumed to be her guardian spirit, in cot and wood, through sun and storm, for the remainder of her days. Happy were her slumbers in this delightful visitation, and happy her awakening, as she hasted back, with fawn-like fleetness, to her parents' lodge, with one more charm—one more pleasing recollection—one more tie to bind her fancy and her heart to the sweet valley of the Taquiemenon. Beautiful valley of soft repose! there, she had first learned to know the sweet face of nature, and seen the river leap and laugh in foam, from the rocks, and then pursue its sylvan course through the green leafed forest. Sweet enthusiast of nature! wild gazer of the woods! There, too, were the sacred graves of her forefathers, and there, she hoped, when the Great Spirit should summon her to depart, her friends would lay her simply bark-enchased [sic] body, under the shady foliage in a spot she loved.

It was early in the Strawberry Moon.* The white coat of winter was remembered for its having lingered on many spots, which were secluded from the sun's influence. But the flowers of the forest were now in bloom, and the birds had re-visited the valley. There was a soft and balmy air, and life and animation seemed to be newly bestowed upon the whole face of the earth. The robin and the ma-maitwa came back to sing, and the murmuring of waters, in the little glens and by-vallies, rose, like pleasing music on the ear, and denoted the time for the opening of buds, and the springing of flowers.

Never, had the scene appeared more attractive to her eye. "Oh," she exclaimed, "that it were ever spring! that I could ever live and revel in the wild beauties of my native valley—the sweet valley of the Taquiemenon."

But while all nature rejoiced, there was a deep gloom gathering over the brows of Mongazida.* Whispers of the sign of an enemy on the lofty shores of the Pictured Rocks, had reached his ears. He thought of the haughty air of the audacious tribe of the Outagamies, who, but a few moons before, invaded the country, and had been baffled in their design. He thought of the bitter feuds of the border bands, yet pleased himself in his own seclusion far from the war path of the enemy, where, for the space of fifteen winters, there had not a hostile foot-print been seen. While he lay on his couch, pondering on these things, sleep ensued, and he fancied himself to be the leader of a hostile band, who broke from the ambush, at the earliest dawn, and carried death and desolation to a slumbering village. Shocked at the catastrophe, he awoke. The dream alarmed him. He remembered that birds of ill omen had crossed his path, the day before.

"Had it been my *enemies*, the Dacotahs," said he to his wife, I should have feared no evil, but to dream of raising the war club against the Outagamies my own blood kindred, and with whom we have been long in peace, bodes me sure disaster. Some hostile foot is, even now, on the track. Some evil bird has flown over my lodge. I will no longer abide here. Had I sons to stand by my side, most freely would I meet the foe; but, single-handed, with no one but thee, to bury me, if I am slain, and my tender Miscodeed to witness my fall, and become their prey, it were madness to abide. And this day, even before the sun is at the zenith, will I quit the peaceful valley I love—the sweet valley of the Taquimenon.["]

In haste, they took their morning's meal, and made their preparations to leave a scene, so loved and cherished, but loved and cherished by none, more than the gentle and enthusiastic Miscodeed. She was indeed a precious wild flower. But while they yet sat around their lodge-fire, the instinctive sagacity of that trusty friend of the Red Hunter, the household dog, betokened approaching evil, at first, by restlessness and low murmurs, and then breaking into a loud bark, as he flew out of the door. It was a daring war party of the treacherous Mendawakantons from the Mississippi. A volley of arrows followed, piercing the thin barks, which hung, like tapestry, around the lodge, and sealing in death at the same instant, the lips of both father and mother. "Oh, bird of my dreams," cried Miscodeed, "my beautiful white wing!—my angel of promise! save me from the hands of my cruel enemies." So saying, she sunk, lifeless to the ground.

With loud yells and rapid footsteps the foe entered. Conspicuous, in front, stood the eldest son of a warrior, who had been killed by the Chippewas in the great battle of the falls of the river St. Croix. His brows were painted red, and his spear poised. But the work of death was soon finished. There lay, motionless, the husband and the wife alike beyond the influence of hope or fear, hate or harm. But no other human form appeared, and the eye of the savage leader rolled in disappointment around, as he viewed the spot where Miscodeed, his meditated victim, had sunk into the earth. A small and beautiful white bird, was seen to fly from the top of the lodge. It was the guardian spirit of Miscodeed. The knife and the tomahawk were cheated of their prey—her guardian angel had saved her from being the slave of her enemy.

But the sanguinary rites of war were quickly performed; the scalps of the hunter and his wife, were torn away, and with hurry and fear, the enemy was soon on his way to his native land. When the friends of the slaughtered family, visited the silent lodge, where welcome had so often greeted them, all they saw on the ground where the maid of Taquimenon had fallen, was a modest little white flower, bordered with pink border which was at once destined to be her emblem.

*Claytonia Virginica
*June
*Means, print of the Loon's Foot.

Origin of the Miscodeed, or the Maid of Taquimenon. Text from *LC66.* The name "Leelina," one of JJS's pen names, appears at the bottom. (Elsewhere, it is usually spelled Leelinau.) There are two versions: *LC66* and *AR.* The story uses two spellings, Taquimenon and Taquiemenon, for the present-day Tahquamenon valley, now part of Tahquamenon Falls State Park. One of the first spring wildflowers, the miscodeed (in Ojibwe), Claytonia Virginica (in Latin), or spring beauty is typically white with pink veins, though sometimes it is all pink. See also JJS's "To the Miscodeed."

mamaitwa: English translation uncertain, possibly mockingbird. *Pictured Rocks*: along Lake Superior, now Pictured Rocks National Lakeshore. *Outagamies:* Meskwakis (see pp. 102–3). *Mendawakantons:* usually spelled Mdewakanton, this refers to a division of the Dakotas.

Corn story (or the origin of corn)

Once upon a time a poor Indian, with his wife and several children lived alone and apart from the tribe. It was on the first indications of spring, that his eldest son, had arrived at that age, when it is thought necessary for youth to fast, to see what kind of spirit would be his guide and guardian through life; accordingly, a little lodge was made for him, as customary on such occasions, some distance from the parents' lodge. The father was a poor man and not very expert, either in hunting or fishing: barely getting enough for the use of his family, day by day; he was contented and happy, and always thankful to the great spirit, for all the comforts, little as they were; he was an humble, peaceable man. His eldest son, of whom we are to speak in particular, had always been a thoughtful, quiet, pensive boy from infancy: he was always ready to assist with his parents, without murmuring—kind and gentle to his brothers and sisters; he was very much beloved by the whole family. The parents felt anxious about the fast and hoped it would be propitious. After the lad had prepared himself and entered the lodge, the few first days of the fast, he amused himself by walking in the woods and on the mountains, examining the early plants and flowers, and as he observed all nature in its progress of re-animation, he sighed and wished to know *all* about how they first came, how they grew without the help of man and every thing else; about their being useful to mankind &c. After a few days he confined himself to his little lodge, thinking how he could be helpful to his poor fellow creatures; he thought how precarious, the exertions of his poor father were, in order to sustain his family, and thought if there could be no other means of support, than that of fishing and hunting; and a great many other ideas came into his xxxxx; such as, who is the author xx maker of all I see? So beautiful, so silent, and yet perceptible in its operations! *"There must be* a Great Spirit" he said to himself "who has made all things and who takes care of all! I must try to find out who it is; perhaps in my visions I shall find out who he is, and he may show me pity and teach me to be like him, bountiful and good—for a good spirit he must be, who bestows such beautiful things for the use of man." On the third day he became weak and faint, and kept his bed and fancied he saw a man come down from the sky, advancing toward him, very gaily and richly dressed, having on a great many blankets of the same color, only slight shades of difference, some were deep green and others lighter; he was very beautiful, having fine waving feathers on his head. When he came near he said, "I am sent to you, my friend by that great spirit who made all things in the sky and on the earth, the same great one you thought *must exist*, from what you observed the other day. He has seen and known your motives in your fasting now. He sees it is to do good to your fellow creatures, and you did not think of yourself. You seek not for grandeur or praise from your fellows, but *their good*, and the great spirit is pleased with your fasting and in consequence I am sent to instruct you, to[?] do your kindred good, as you feel most anxious about that." He thus told the lad to arise and prepare himself to wrestle with him as it would be only by his courage and perseverance, as well as strength, that he could hope to succeed in his wish to do and get good for mankind. The lad knew he was weak in body, but he felt strong in mind and at once rose from his bed determining to die rather than fail in his most ardent wish to do good for mankind and he commenced wrestling with the beautiful stranger and was almost exhausted but he would not give up till the stranger said "My friend it is enough for once; I will come again and try you" and smiling on him encouragingly he ascended, in the same direction he came from. The stranger came the next day at the same hour, and they wrestled as at first and though the lad was weaker from want of food, this day more than the day previous, he would not give way till the stranger again spoke as before and left him, saying in addition "tomorrow will be your last trial; be strong my friend and try to vanquish me, for that is the only way you can do good and get food for yourself and others." The lad felt encouraged from this and determined on the morrow, rather to die than be vanquished. The stranger appeared again at the usual time and said "My friend this is the last struggle between us—three days I have wrestled with you; weak as you are, you have behaved manfully and you seem to struggle more for others, than for yourself and therefore I hope you will prevail" and they continued their combat; the poor youth was very faint in body; but grew stronger in mind determined not to give up the contest but with his life. After the usual time of struggle, the stranger acknowledged himself conquered and the strife ceased and for the first time he entered the lodge of the youth, and sitting down beside him he began to instruct him, in what manner he should take advantage of his having prevailed against him. "Now," said the stranger "tomorrow is the seventh day of your fasting. Your father will give you food to strengthen you and as it is the last day of trial, you will prevail. I know it, and now tell you what you must do for the good of mankind, as well as for your family. Tomorrow" he continued "I shall meet you for the last time, and when you have knocked me down—clean the earth of weeds and roots and make the earth very soft and bury me in the spot, thus prepared, and come occasionally to see where you shall place me. Be careful never to let the grass or weeds grow on the hillock where I am laid and once in the month cover me anew with fresh earth. If you follow my instructions you will do good to your fellow creatures by telling them and teaching them, what I now tell you," and shaking hands with the lad, he disappeared. In the morning the youth's father came with some slight refreshments, saying "My son, you have fasted long enough; if the great spirit *will* do you good, he will do it now. It is seven long days since you tasted any thing and you must not sacrifice your life, as that would be displeasing to the master of life." The youth requested his father to wait till sundown, as he did not wish to break his fast till he had accomplished his vision. "Very well, my son" said the father, I shall wait till you feel inclined to eat. At the usual hour the beautiful stranger appeared and said "You have not availed yourself of earthly strength, but so[?] much the xxx you have strength given you from him you trust in, to enable you to succeed against me"—So[?] saying he continued, "You have already conquered me, and when I fall, bury me as I directed and observe all the directions I gave you and never feel[?] xxxxxx xx xxxx xxxx the weeds and grass from my grave and then you will have your vision[?] and benefit your fellow creatures." Accordingly, they began to wrestle, and the youth felt strengthened more than usual, and prevailed against his adversary. As soon as he found he had slain the stranger, he selected a beautiful spot to bury him. It was a shallow vale[?], where the sun shone daily and the dew[?] descended nightly—and he observed every thing he had been directed to do, about the body, for the stranger had told him not to fear killing him, as he would come to life again, and that it was only through his death for a little while, that any good would come. The youth did all that was directed of him by his friend and felt deeply anxious about the result of his obedience, but determined to watch carefully when his friend would come to life again as he had predicted. He then went home and took sparingly of his father's kind meal, and finished his fast. All spring he attended the grave of his friend, and carefully weeded the spot he was buried in. The lad never told what had occurred, till one day the father followed him, to the place he so often went to. This was after a long absence. To their

mutual surprise, they beheld a strange plant, several feet high and light hair as it were floating in the air at their tops, and large oval clusters on the sides of the stalks. The lad shouted "It is my friend and the friend of all mankind. None need ever depend *alone* upon hunting and fishing, as long as there is *Mondaumin* to live and grow from the ground." He pulled an ear of corn and gave it to his father and said "See Father, this is what I fasted for and the great spirit of all flesh has listened to my wish; henceforth men need not depend alone upon the chase and the produce of the waters, for by careful attention to this plant, they will have plenty to eat, whilst the world lasts." He then told his father what the beautiful stranger had told him before in their conversation, that his blankets must be taken off, and his feathers pulled away, before he could be of any use to man, and when both were done, they returned home, roasted the ear of corn, and felt thankful to the master of life, who so mercifully provides for his creatures. So corn came into the world for the good of mankind and since that time, through the instruction of the little boy, all the Indians have endeavored to get corn for their families——

    Finis—

——————————————————— - | providential. miraculous

Mondaumin—from *mondawwissa* | or fortunate *xxxxxxxxxx*

Corn story (or the origin of corn). Text from *LC72*. X-marks indicate illegible passages, and bracketed question marks indicate uncertain transcriptions. A printed version of this story appears in *AR*, and Longfellow used it as the basis for part V of *The Song of Hiawatha.* Longfellow's friend Bayard Taylor, a writer well known at the time though later mostly forgotten, had already published a poetic version of the story in 1852. "I wrote out the corn story," JJS told HRS in a letter, "& got Francis to copy it for me, which I send you & hope it will please you better than it did him—I was almost tempted to throw it in the fire after I read it to him, from the remarks he made, but I send it to *you*, as it is, he has been accustomed to write out some of the storys [*sic*] William collected so full of magic &c. that he imagines there is [*sic*] no such sentiments among the Indian Tribes as contained in the Corn story—I hope however you will be pleased with it, and correct whatever you find amiss—" (15 Jan. 1838, LC15). "Francis" was Francis W. Shearman, HRS's nephew, who wrote HRS on the same day: "I have just finished copying for Mrs. S. the *corn story*, and have copied it *verbatim* from hers. The story is a good one, but as I remarked to my aunt, I think it is too much anglicised, It strikes me, that the narrator must have been instructed, previously in the english notions to some extent, little though it may have been—or perhaps the idea originates with me, on account of the verbal construction" (LC15). It seems odd that JJS would not make or send her own copy. Shearman's remarks indicate that she translated the story from a narrator who told it in Ojibwe, and JJS's own remarks imply that she wrote it out after she heard the story, rather than as she heard it. Readers are left to speculate which features of the story Shearman objected to as supposedly anglicized. As it turns out, Shearman's copy survives among the manuscripts for *AR*, in *LC72*, and I use Shearman's copy as the text, because I have not found JJS's manuscript. HRS accepted JJS's invitation to "correct" whatever he might "find amiss," though his version of the story repeats enough from her version to have occasionally aided the transcription of Shearman's manuscript. A draft of the revision, in HRS's hand, is also in *LC72*. HRS's version changes a good deal, apparently trying to clarify and smooth out the story, sometimes pruning repetition and other times expanding. By contrast, it appears that even in small details Shearman more or less lived up to his claim that he copied the manuscript verbatim, because the punctuation matches JJS's typical style. As with her manuscript for "The Little Spirit" (below), this manuscript is all one paragraph and roughly, lightly punctuated, noticeably not intended as a final draft. JJS must have expected HRS to take care of paragraphing and punctuation. Indeed, Shearman does not always write punctuation marks clearly, so that in transcribing his manuscript I sometimes defer to what makes sense in context. As in other manuscripts from JJS, the use of quotation marks is haphazard. Sometimes they cannot be distinguished from the writing that bleeds through from the other side of the paper, and sometimes they are missing altogether, or opening quotation marks never lead to closing quotation marks. In this context, I have added a modest number of periods, commas, and quotation marks, while still minimizing such changes and retaining the manuscript's light punctuation, adding only what seems needed for clarity.

only through his death: "through" is added by editorial emendation. *Mondaumin*: corn. The title of the *AR* version is "Mon-daw-min, or the Origin of Indian Corn," and someone, probably Shearman or HRS, has penciled "[Mondäwmin]" in the top left of the first page of Shearman's manuscript.

The Three Cranberries

Three cranberries were living in a lodge together. One was green, one white, and one red. They were sisters. There was snow on the ground, and as the men were absent, they felt afraid and began to say to each other, "what shall we do if the wolf comes." "I," said the green one, "will climb up a shingoup tree." "I," said the white one, "will hide myself in the kettle of boiled hominy." And "I," said the red one, "will conceal myself under the snow." Presently the Wolves came, and each one did as she had said. But only one of the three had judged wisely. The Wolves immediately ran to the kettle and ate up the corn and with it the white Cranberry. The red one was trampled to pieces by their feet, and her blood spotted the snow. But she, who had climbed the thick spruce tree escaped notice, and was saved.

The Three Cranberries. Text from *LC72* in JJS's hand, among the manuscripts for *AR*. There is an almost identical version in *AR*. At the bottom of the manuscript, probably in HRS's hand, appear the words "Short, but sweet," as if jocularly to sugar the tart cranberries with an appreciative pun.

The Little Spirit, or Boy-Man
An Odjibwa Tale

There was once a little boy, remarkable for the smallness of his stature. He was living alone with his sister older than himself. They were orphans, and they lived in a beautiful spot on the Lake shore. Many large rocks were scattered around their habitation. The boy never grew larger as he advanced in years. One day in winter, he asked his sister to make him a ball to play with along shore on the clear ice. She made one for him but cautioned him not to go too far.—Off he went in high glee, throwing his ball before him and running after it at full speed and he went as fast as his ball. At last his ball flew to a great distance. He followed it as fast as he could. After he had run for some time, he saw four dark substances on the ice straight before him. When he came up to the spot he was surprised to see four large, tall men lying on the ice spearing fish. When he went up to them, the nearest looked up and in turn was surprised to see such a diminutive being, and turning to his brothers, he said, "Tia! look, see what a little fellow is here!" After they had all looked a moment, they resumed their position, covered their heads intent in searching for fish. The boy thought to himself, they imagine me too insignificant for common courtesy because they are tall and large. I shall teach them notwithstanding, that I am not to be treated so lightly. After they were covered up the boy saw they had each a large trout lying beside them. He slyly took the one nearest him and placing his fingers in the gills and tossing his ball before him ran off at full speed. When the man to whom the fish belonged looked up, he saw his trout sliding away as if of itself at a great rate, the boy being so small he was not distinguished from the fish. He addressed his brothers and said, "See how that tiny boy has stolen my fish; what a shame it is he should do so"—The boy reached home, and told his sister to go out and get the fish he had brought home. She exclaimed, "Where could you have got it? I hope you have not stolen it." "O! no," he replied, "I found it on the ice." "How," persisted the Sister, "could you have got it there?"—"No matter," said the boy, "go and cook it." He disdained to answer her again, but thought he would one day show her how to appreciate him. She went to the place he left it and there indeed she found a monstrous Trout. She did as she was bid and cooked it for that day's consumption.—Next morning he went off again as at first. When he came near the large men, who fished every day, he threw his ball with such force that it rolled into the ice-hole of the man of whom he had stolen the day before. As he happened to raise himself at the time, the boy said, "Nejee, pray hand me my ball." "No indeed" answered the man, "I shall not," and thrust the ball under the ice. The boy took hold of his arm and broke it in two in a moment and threw him to one side and picked up his ball which had bounded back from under the ice and tossed it as usual before him. Outstripping its speed, he got home and remained within till the next morning. The man whose arm he had broken hallooed out to his brothers and told them his case and deplored his fate. They hurried to their brother, and as loud as they could roar threatened vengeance on the morrow, knowing the boy's speed that they could not overtake him and he was near out of sight, yet he heard their threats and awaited their coming in perfect indifference. The four brothers the next morning prepared to take their revenge. Their old mother begged them not to go. "Better" said she, "one only should suffer, than that all should perish, for he must be a Monedo, or he could not perform such feats," but her sons would not listen and taking their wounded brother along, started for the boy's lodge having learnt that he lived at the place of rocks. The boy's Sister thought she heard the noise of snow-shoes on the crusted snow at a distance. Advancing, she saw the large, tall men coming straight to their lodge, or rather cave for they lived in a large rock. She ran in with great fear and told her brother the fact. He said, "Why do you mind them? Give me something to eat." "How can you think of eating at such a time," she replied—"Do as I request you, and be quick." She then gave him his dish, which was a large *mis-qua-dace* shell and he commenced eating. Just then the men came to the door and were about lifting the curtain placed there when the boy-man turned his dish upside-down and immediately the door was closed with a stone. The men tried hard with their clubs to crack it; at length they succeeded in making a slight opening. When one of them peeped in with one eye, the boy-man shot his arrow into his eye and brain and he dropped down dead. The others not knowing what had happened to their brother did the same, and all fell in like manner. Their curiosity was so great to see what the boy was about so they all shared the same fate. After they were killed the boy-man told his sister to go out and see them; she opened the door but feared they were not dead and entered back again hastily and told her fears to her brother. He went out and hacked them in small pieces saying "Henceforth let no man be larger than you are now," so men became of the present size.

When spring came on the boy-man said to his sister "Make me a new set of arrows and bow." She obeyed, as he never did any thing himself of a nature that required manual labour. Though he provided for their sustenance, after she made them she again cautioned him not to shoot into the lake; but disregardless of all admonition, he on purpose shot his arrow into the Lake, and waded some distance till he got into deep water and paddled about for his arrow so as to attract the attention of his Sister. She came in haste to the shore calling him to return, but instead of minding her he called out, "Ma-mis-quan-ge-gun-a, be-nau-wa-con-zhe-shin," that is, "*You*, of the *red fins* come and swallow me." Immediately that monstrous fish came and swallowed him; and seeing his sister standing on the shore in despair he hallooed out to her, "Me-zush-ke-zin-ance." She wondered what he meant, but on reflection she thought it must be an old mockisin. She accordingly tied the old mockisin to a string and fastened it to a tree. The fish said to the Boy-man, under water, "What is that floating?" The Boy-man, said to the fish "Go, take hold of it, swallow it as fast as you can." The fish darted towards the old shoe and swallowed it. The Boy-man laughed in himself, but said nothing, till the fish was fairly caught. He then took hold of the line and began to pull himself and fish to shore. The Sister, who was watching, was surprised to see so large a fish, and hauling it ashore she took her knife and commenced cutting it open. When she heard her brother's voice inside of the fish, saying, "Make haste and release me from this nasty place," his sister was in such haste that she almost hit his head with her knife but succeeded in making an opening large enough for her Brother to get out. When he was fairly out, he told his sister to cut up the fish and dry it as it would last a long time for their sustenance, and said to her, never, never more to doubt his ability in any way. So ends the Story.———

The Little Spirit, or Boy-Man. Text from *LC74*, in JJS's hand. There are two later versions: *Oneota* (260–63), and H. R. Schoolcraft, ed., *Information Respecting the History, Conditions and Prospects of the Indian Tribes* (1853, 3: 318–20), attributed to Ba-bahm-wa-wa-gezhig-equa (JJS). After the fourth sentence, *Information* has the following additional passage: "There had never been seen a dwarf before, among his people, and they looked on him as a very insignificant being. Some thought him one of those little creations whom they call puk-wud-jinine, or fairies of the hills, who are seen to dance along over the ground, as light as the down of thistle. But the most of them said, 'Nay, we all know this little fellow; he eats and drinks, like one of ourselves, and we knew his father.' But the spirits, seeing him despised, had compassion on him, and determined to give him great power."

As with the manuscript for the "Corn story" (above), this manuscript is all one paragraph and roughly, lightly punctuated, noticeably not intended as a final draft. JJS must have planned for the paragraphing and punctuation to come in later, most likely from HRS, since she seems to have left the final draft of stories to him. He did not include this story in *AR*, perhaps because of its disturbing violence or its abrupt ending, or perhaps because JJS wrote it after the publication of *AR*. In this context, and in accord with the later, printed versions, presumably edited by HRS, I have edited the punctuation for clarity, mostly by adding punctuation, especially periods. The manuscript pays little attention to marking where sentences end, which is typical of JJS's prose. It usually has a comma where we would expect a period and no punctuation where we would expect a comma. I have also changed lowercase letters at the beginnings of sentences to uppercase, and I have followed the printed versions by adding a good many quotation marks. While this adds up to too many changes to list, I have added less punctuation than is added in the printed versions, adding only what seems necessary for clarity while trying to retain a semblance of the manuscript's lightly punctuated, swift pace. The printed versions also introduce a small number of changes in wording, which I have not followed, except once as noted below.

orphans, and they lived: "and" is added by editorial emendation; it also appears in *Oneota*. *sliding away as if of itself*: "itself" is an editor's emendation for "self". *He disdained . . .* : This sentence is added between lines. *Nejee*: translated in *Information* as "Friend". *mis-qua-dace*: translated in *Information* as "turtle". *happened to their brother*: "to" is added by editorial emendation.

Waish-kee, alias Iawba Wadick

A chief of the band of the Sault S*te* Marie. The name is a derivative from the Chippewa animate adjective *oush-kee*, i.e. *young, new*, and, by ellipsis, *first*, having the pronominal form of the word. The meaning here implied is, first, or Eldest. The second name signifies Male Deer.

This chief is the son of the noted War-chief Waub-Ojeeg, or the White Fisher of Lake Superior. He was born at Lapoint about 1782, and is consequently now about 55, years—His father died, while he was still a boy, and his Sister having married an English gentleman, he went to live with the latter at the Falls of Ste Mary, about his 19<u>th</u> year. He still however, pursued hunting, in which he was very expert and successful, untill [*sic*] within a year or two, He was also noted as a great walker, making light, of putting on his snow shoes and going from S*t* Mary to S*t* Joseph, about 45 miles, in a short winter's day. His *Totem* is the *Addick* or American Reindeer. He married a sister of Shingaba W'ossin, by whom he has had 14 children five of whom, have died. He is a most affectionate husband and father, and assiduous, by means of the chase, and other exertions, to provide his family with comfortable clothing and food. And has only been indebted, within these few years, for any aid from his boys, the two elder, now living, are men grown.—Although himself the son of a warrior, he has never made any figure in that character, owing, in a great measure, to his early removal from the frontier lines, and his long residence at a spot without the reach of any alarm from the existing feuds with the Sioux, &c. He was present with the Chippewas at the taking of Michilimackinac during the late War. But did not accompany the subsequent war parties, who repaired to the camp of Proctor and Tecumseh, in 1813–14.

In his domestic character he is mild, affable, and of a peaceful turn of mind. Quiet, modest, and respectful, patient under reverses or bad luck, and disposed to make the best of the little gifts of the season.

Under every afflictive dispensation of Providence, he has manifested a truly submissive and resigned spirit, having professed christianity in 1830, and has since led an exemplary and consistent life as a christian, maintaining constant family worship when at home, and asking a blessing, and returning thanks at every meal.

Since the establishment of a military post at S*t* Mary's, he has been uniformly friendly to our government, and in constant visits at

Figure 11. "Wayishky's Lodge." Mackinac Island. Mrs. (Anna Brownell)
Jameson, 1837. Royal Ontario Museum, Toronto, Ontario.

the agency. He was one of the signers of the treaty of cession obtained by Gov. Cass in 1820. He evinced his interest in the civil
concerns of the Chippewas, by attending the treaties of Prairie du
Chien, Fond du Lac, and Buttes des Morts in the years 1825–6-7. In
stature he is about 6 feet, and slender make.

In the winter of 1836, he went to Washington, as a delegate from
the Northern Chippewas to negotiate for the sale of their lands in
Michigan, and gave his assent to the terms of the treaty of the 28th
March 1836, by which the two nations of Chippewas and Ottawas
cede, upwards of ten millions of acres to the United States. By this
treaty the Indians set apart a portion of the purchase money for the
support of schools and missions—a measure which received his
early acquiescence and support.

Waish-kee, alias Iawba Wadick. Text from *LC84*, in JJS's hand. Waishkey, JJS's
uncle (her mother's half-brother [Cleland, *Place* 14]), was a founding figure
of what is now the Bay Mills Indian Community, just west of Sault Ste.
Marie, near what are now called the Waishkey River and Waishkey Bay. HRS
provides a briefer but similar portrait of Waishkey in his *Personal Memoirs*
for September 1839 (665), and Jameson offers another portrait (3: 186–89).
JJS may have written this biography to help HRS write his portrait, or in
response to HRS's portrait.

Shingaba W'ossin: the leading Ojibwe civil chief at Sault Ste. Marie. *Proc-*

tor and Tecumseh: British General Henry Proctor and Tecumseh, the famous
Shawnee leader; they both fought the Americans in the War of 1812. *treaty of
. . . 1836*: Sault Ojibwe leaders, including Shingaba W'ossin and Shingwauk,
resented the role of Waishkey and HRS in the 1836 treaty (H. R. Schoolcraft,
Personal Memoirs 532–33; Cleland, *Place* 21).

La Renne

Le renne est un animal de l'espèce du cerf, on le trouve dans le pays du nord. Cet quadrupède est le principal bétail de les Lapon. Il à la figure de un cerf, mais est plus grand, et plus ramasse, et les membres sont encore plus delié. La renne donne les Lapon leur lait, et fromage. Les renne sont plus engraisser dans l'automne et dans l'été. La chair de le renne est excellent. La peau de la renne—est aussi tres utile. La renne est plus égal nécessaire à les Lapons, que la vache est à nous.

Jeanne L. H. Schoolcraft.

Decembre vingt-quatre.

New York, Mil-huit-cent-quarante-et-un.

Translation:
The Reindeer

The reindeer is an animal of the stag species, one finds it in the north country. This quadruped is the principal cattle of the Lapps. It has the shape of a stag, but is larger, and bulkier, and its limbs are even slimmer. The reindeer gives the Lapps their milk, and cheese. The reindeer are fatter in the autumn and in the summer. Reindeer meat is excellent. Reindeer skin—is also very useful. The reindeer is more surely necessary to the Lapps, than the cow is to us.

Jane L. H. Schoolcraft.

December twenty fourth.

New York, One thousand eight hundred forty one.

La Renne. This manuscript in French, in JJS's hand, is transcribed here without editorial emendation. The manuscript is labeled "Jane's Christmas Gift / N.2d 25 Dec 1841", in HRS's hand ("N.2d" is an uncertain transcription). It appears among an assortment of poems by various family members in *LC70*. The reindeer was the totem, or clan, of JJS's grandfather Waubojeeg. English translation by the editor.

les Lapon[s]: The Lapps, who call themselves Sami, are an indigenous people in northern Norway, Sweden, Finland, and northwestern Russia who speak a language related to Finnish. *Jeanne L. H. Schoolcraft*: Jeanne is a French version of Jane, and "L" stands for Leelinau, one of JJS's pen names. (The "H" is an uncertain transcription; possibly it is a "J" for Johnston.)

Peboan and Seegwun (Winter and Spring)
A Chippewa Allegory

[Based on a story told by Ozhaguscodaywayquay, Susan Johnston. Probably translated and written by Jane Johnston Schoolcraft, or translated by Johnston family members and written by Henry Rowe Schoolcraft.]

An old man was sitting alone in his lodge, by the side of a frozen stream. It was the close of winter, and his fire was almost out. He appeared very old and very desolate. His locks were white with age, and he trembled at every joint. Day after day passed in solitude, and he heard nothing but the sounds of the tempest, sweeping before it in the new-fallen snow.

One day, as his fire was just dying, a handsome young man approached and entered his dwelling. His cheeks were red with the blood of youth, his eyes sparkled with animation, and a smile played upon his lips. He walked with a light and quick step. His forehead was bound round with a wreath of sweet grass, in the place of a warrior's frontlet, and he carried a bunch of flowers in his hand.

"Ah, my son," said the old man, I am happy to see you. Come in. Come, tell me of your adventures, and what strange lands you have been to see. Let us pass the night together. I will tell you of my prowess and exploits, and what I can perform. You shall do the same. And we will amuse ourselves."

He then drew from his sack a curiously-wrought antique pipe, and having filled it with tobacco, rendered mild by an admixture of certain leaves, handed it to his guest. When this ceremony was concluded, they began to speak.

"I blow my breath," said the old man, "and the streams stand still. The water becomes stiff and hard as clear stone." "I breathe," said the young man, "and flowers spring up all over the plains.["]

"I shake my locks" retorted the old man, "and snow covers the land. The leaves fall from the trees at my command and my breath blows them away. The birds get up from the water, and fly to a distant land. The animals hide themselves from my breath, and the very ground becomes as hard as flint[.]"

"I shake my ringlets," rejoined the young man, "and warm showers of soft rain fall upon the earth, like the eyes of children first opening in the morning. My voice recalls the birds. The warmth of my breath unlocks the streams. Music fills the groves, wherever I walk, and all nature rejoices."

At length the sun began to rise. A gentle warmth came over the place. The tongue of the old man became silent. The robin and bluebird began to sing on the top of the lodge. The stream began to murmur by the door, and the fragrance of growing herbs and flowers came softly on the vernal breeze.

Day light fully revealed to the young man the character of his entertainer. When he looked upon him, he had the white visage of ice of Peboan.† Streams began to flow from his eyes. As the sun increased, he gradually grew less and less in stature, and anon had melted completely away. Nothing remained on the place of his lodge fire but the miskodeed,* a small white flower, with a pink border, which is one of the earliest species in a *northern* Spring.

† Winter.
*The claytonia virginica.]

Peboan and Seegwun (Winter and Spring). Text from *LC64*. There are five versions: in HRS's *Personal Memoirs* for 1 April 1823 (164, a brief summary), McKenney's *Sketches* (303–4), *LC64* (in HRS's hand), Jameson (3: 218–21), and *AR* (1: 84–86). The *LC64* and *AR* versions are almost identical. Longfellow used the *AR* version for part XXI of *The Song of Hiawatha*. Jameson says that the story was "written down from" Ozhaguscodaywayquay's "recitation, and translated by her daughter" (3: 218), which could lead us to suppose that it was translated and perhaps retold and written out by JJS. On the other hand, Jameson's version, which differs considerably from the *LC64* and *AR* versions, closely follows McKenney, which she probably copied, perhaps from the volume owned by JJS and HRS. According to McKenney, Ozhaguscodaywayquay told him the story "with great spirit," and Charlotte Johnston and John Johnston translated it, suggesting that Charlotte is the daughter that Jameson refers to, not JJS. This also tells us that Ozhaguscodaywayquay was an oral source for the story, though it may have come from other storytellers as well. McKenney implies that he himself transcribed the story from memory later that evening, though he could have been given a transcript. JJS or HRS probably wrote the *LC64* and *AR* versions. They are more likely candidates than Charlotte Johnston or John Johnston, because very little of the *Literary Voyager* is attributed to John, and none is attributed to Charlotte. All this puts this story in a different position from the other unattributed stories in the *Literary Voyager* or *AR* that could have come through JJS but that no evidence connects to her, and therefore I include this story, but not the others, in this volume of JJS's writings. Joshua David Bellin, who has looked at three of the five versions—McKenney, Jameson, and *AR*—and who notes that "research on her [JJS] is virtually nonexistent" (246), offers a thoughtful reading of the story (146–48).

The O-jib-way Maid

Original of the O-jib-way Maid.

Aun dush ween do win ane
Gitchy Mocomaun aince
Caw awzhaw woh da modé
      We yea, yea haw ha! &c.

Wah yaw bum maud e
Ojibway quaince un e
We maw jaw need e
      We yea, yea haw ha! &c.

Omow e maun e
We nemoshain yun
We maw jaw need e
      We yea, yea haw ha! &c.

Caw ween gush shá ween
Kin wainzh e we yea
O guh maw e maw seen
      We yea, yea haw ha! &c.

Me gosh shá ween e yea
Ke bish quaw bum maud e
Tehe won ain e maud e
      We yea, yea haw ha! &c.

The Literal Translation of a Young Ojibway Girl's Song

Why! what's the matter with the young American? He crosses the river with tears in his eyes! He sees the young Ojibway Girl preparing to leave the place: he sobs for his sweetheart, because she is going away! but he will not sigh long for her, for as soon as he sees her out of sight, he will forget her.

The O-jib-way Maid. Text from *LC70*, with the score from Jameson. There are four sources and a total of nine versions, as three sources offer more than one version in Ojibwe or English, with or without music. *LC70* includes an Ojibwe version and a literal translation, both in JJS's hand (see figure 12). McKenney (153–56) includes the Ojibwe version and the literal translation,

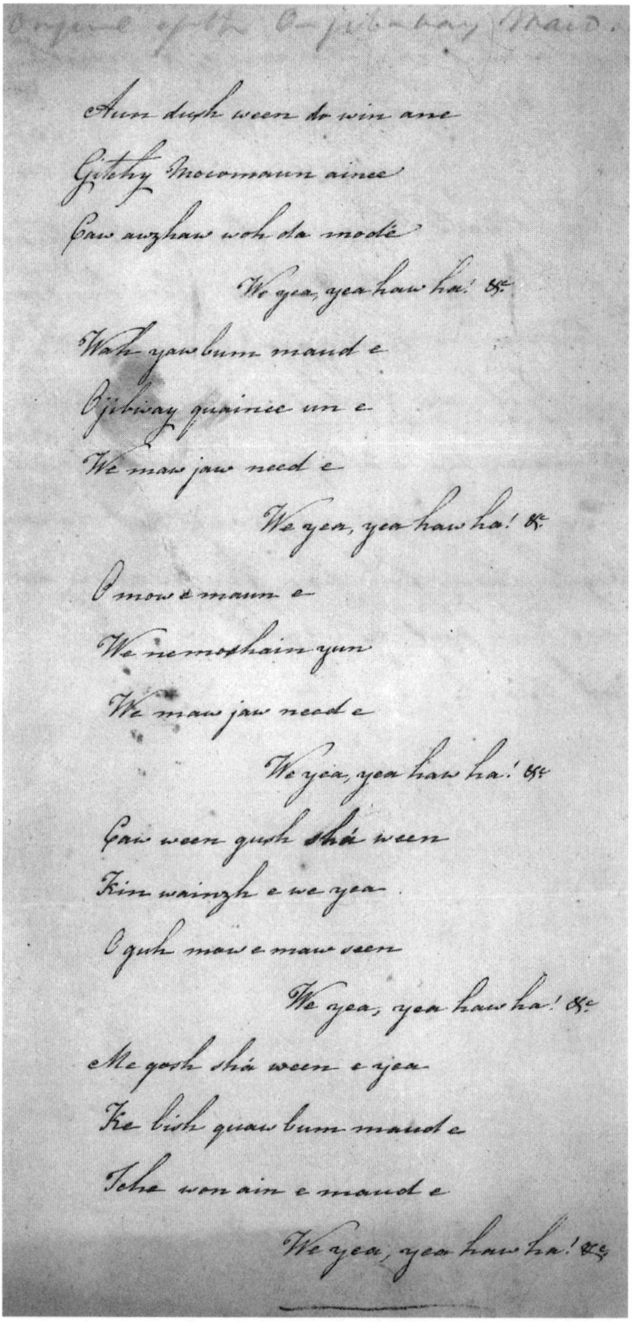

Original of the O-jib-way Maid.

Aun dush ween da win ane
Getchy Mocomaun ainee
Caw auzhaw woh da mode
      We yea, yea haw ha! &c.
Wah yaw bum maud e
Ojibway quiniee un e
We maw jaw need e
      We yea, yea haw ha! &c.
O mow e maun e
We nemoshain yun
We maw jaw need e
      We yea, yea haw ha! &c.
Caw ween gush sha ween
Kin wainzh e we yea
O guh mow e maw seen
      We yea, yea haw ha! &c.
Me gosh sha ween e yea
Ke bish quaw bum maud e
Tohe won ain e maud e
      We yea, yea haw ha! &c.

Figure 12. Manuscript of "The O-jib-way Maid." Henry Rowe Schoolcraft Papers, Manuscript Division, Library of Congress, Washington, D.C.

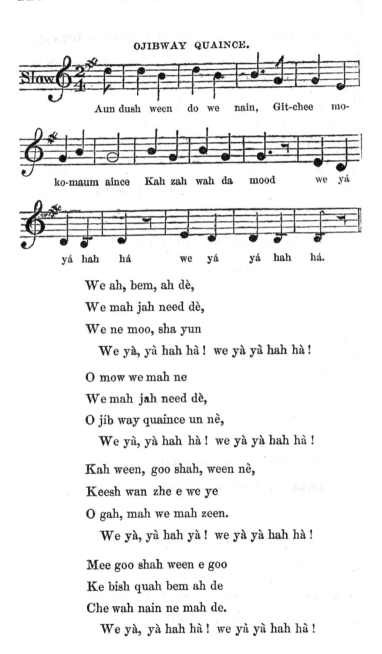

OJIBWAY QUAINCE.

Aun dush ween   do we   nain,   Git-chee   mo-

ko-maum aince   Kah zah wah da   mood   we   yá

yá hah   há   we   yá   yá hah   há.

We ah, bem, ah dè,

We mah jah need dè,

We ne moo, sha yun

    We yà, yà hah hà ! we yà yà hah hà !

O mow we mah ne

We mah jah need dè,

O jib way quaince un nè,

    We yà, yà hah hà ! we yà yà hah hà !

Kah ween, goo shah, ween nè,

Keesh wan zhe e we ye

O gah, mah we mah zeen.

    We yà, yà hah yà ! we yà yà hah hà !

Mee goo shah ween e goo

Ke bish quah bem ah de

Che wah nain ne mah de.

    We yà, yà hah hà ! we yà yà hah hà !

Figure 13. "Ojibwe Quaince," text with score, from Jameson (3, 226). "Quaince" means "girl."

with the following explanation: "I will copy into this letter a beautiful song, which she [JJS's sister Charlotte] sings with the most enchanting effect, called the '*O-jib-way Maid.*' Having prevailed on her to sing this song several times, I have learned the air with a view of having it written out in parts. Mrs. Schoolcraft has obligingly favoured me with the original, and with her *literal* translation of it, in prose; and Charlotte has presented me with a version of it by Major H. S———th, of the United States' army. I have heard this little song sung in both the original and its version. The airs are different; both are plaintive, and both sweet, but that in which the original is sung is the wildest" (153). McKenney's version of the original is close to *LC70*, with minor transcription variants not noted below. Jameson (3: 225–27) includes the literal translation and a score with a version of the Ojibwe text, called the "Ojibway Quaince." (See figure 13. Jameson defines "quaince" as "girl.") The score in Jameson, with Ojibwe text, differs widely from the score for the major's English poetic text in McKenney. Jameson's texts differ as well from those in JJS's hand. Although JJS may still be Jameson's source, Charlotte is a more likely source for Jameson, as indicated in a letter from Jameson to Charlotte, where Jameson expresses confidence, at least, that she has the score correctly, writing that "any more songs or scraps of Chippeway poetry would be invaluable to me—The music of the love song I *cannot* quite re-member & am in despair about it—can you get it noted down for me?—the other the Ojibway maid I have perfectly." Charlotte furnished the text of another song in HRS's papers ("Love Song of an Odjibway Girl," *LC63*), and accounts of Charlotte often describe her pleasure in singing. Except for minor matters of capitalization and punctuation, variants in Jameson for the literal translation are noted below. For yet a ninth version, in not entirely legible English poetry, see "Dawn." HRS calls the "Dawn" version literally rendered, but because it is in verse and differs considerably from the prose translation in JJS's hand, we might wonder how literal it is.

The Literal Translation of a Young Ojibway Girl's Song. Text from *LC70*. *Why!*: Hah! (Jameson). *American*: Long-knife (Jameson).

Song for a Lover Killed in Battle

Oh how can I sing the praise of my love! His spirit still lingers around me. The grass that is growing over his bed of earth is yet too low; its sighs cannot be heard upon the wind.

> Oh he was beautiful!
> Oh he was brave!

I must not break the silence of this still retreat; nor waste the time in song, when his spirit still whispers to mine. I hear it in the sounds of the newly budded leaves. It tells me that he yet lingers near me, and that he loves me the same in death, though the yellow sand lies over him.

> Whisper, spirit,
> Whisper to me.

I shall sing when the grass will answer to my plaint; when its sighs will respond to my moan. There my voice shall be heard in his praise.

> Linger, lover! linger,
> Stay, spirit! stay.

The spirit of my love will soon leave me. He goes to the land of joyful repose, to prepare my bridal bower. Sorrowing must I wait, until he comes to conduct me there.

> Hasten, lover; hasten!
> Come, spirit; come!*

*We are indebted for this fragment, and for the preservation of the two succeeding specimens of Indian poetry, to the polite attainments and literary taste of Miss Jane Johnston, of Johnston Hall, Sault Ste. Marie.

Song for a Lover Killed in Battle. Untitled; title provided by the editor. Text from HRS, *Travels in the Central Portions of the Mississippi Valley* (1825, 425–26). HRS included the song near the end of the story of a young man who dies in battle, trying to impress the father of the young woman he loves. The bereaved woman would "fly to a sequestered spot in the woods, where she would sit under a shady tree, and sing her mournful laments for whole hours together. The following fragment of one of her songs is yet repeated" (425). The note attributing the translation of the "fragment" to "Miss Jane Johnston" is curious, because by the time HRS published this book, Miss

Jane Johnston had been Jane Johnston Schoolcraft for some time, and only seven pages later he refers to her as "Mrs. Jane Schoolcraft." Perhaps HRS wrote out the manuscript of the story and song before their marriage and then inserted it in the larger manuscript for the book, neglecting to update the reference. Mentor L. Williams says that this note "specifically attributes this story to Jane Johnston" (45), but it only attributes the song to her, the "fragment." HRS removed the song from the version of the story that he later published, under the title "The Red Lover," in *AR*. The "two succeeding specimens of Indian poetry" referred to in the note appear immediately below as "Two Songs." All the songs in this section of HRS's *Travels* were reprinted by Jameson, who does not attribute them to *Travels*.

Two Songs

I.

Kaago! Kaago! moweemizhekain,
Neen deekway meedoag neeboyaun:
Keenahwau aatah keedau moweendim;
Keenahwaa kee gideemaugizim:
Eekwaaweeyaig kee gideemaugizim.

II.

Nee nundonaawaug, nee nundonaawaug,
Ainuhwaamungig kau nissindjig:
Nindowee tibbisheemaug,—tibbisheemaug!
Ainuhwaamungig kau nissindjig:

III.

Naudowaasee! naudowaaseewug!
Guyaa weenahwau tibbishko—
Guyaa weenahwau meesugo,
Kaadowee eezhishee mugwau,—eezhisheemug.
                    Kaago, Kaago, &c.

(LITERAL TRANSLATION.)

Do not—do not weep for me
Loved woman, should I die,—
For yourselves alone, should you weep.
Poor are ye all, and to be pitied,
Ye women! ye are to be pitied!

I seek—I seek our fallen relations;
I go to revenge—revenge the slain;
Our relations, fallen and slain.
And our foes—our foes, they shall lie:
I go—I go, to lay them low—to lay them low!   10
                    Do not—do not, &c.

I.

Neezh ogoone, neezh ogoone;
    Kau weesinissee.
                    Neezh, &c.

Aazhee gushkaindumaun;
 Neenemooshain, weeyea!
   Aazhee, &c.

II.

Kee unee bubbeeshkobee;
Kau unee inausheepun;
   Kee unee, &c.

Neenemooshain, weeyea!
Waindjee gushkaindumaun:
   Neenemooshain, &c.

I.

'Tis now two days—two long days,
 Since last I tasted food:
'Tis for you—for you, my love!
 That I grieve—that I grieve,
'Tis for you—for you, that I grieve.

Lot of repitition

II.

The waters flow deep and wide
 On which, love! you have sail'd,—
Dividing you far from me:
 'Tis for you—for you, my love!
'Tis for you—for you, that I grieve.

Two Songs. Untitled, title provided by editor. There are multiple sources: Ojibwe and English texts in HRS, *Travels in the Central Portions of the Mississippi Valley* (1825, 427–29); English texts of both songs in Jameson (3: 223–24), with the first described as "translated literally by Mrs. Schoolcraft"; a slightly different version of the first song, with different Ojibwe spelling, in "Dawn"; and an Ojibwe and English text of the first song in HRS's hand in *LC70*. I take the text from *Travels*, because that version was prepared for publication. Apart from different spelling and punctuation, the Ojibwe texts in *Travels* and *LC70* are the same. Differences in the wording of the English texts are noted below. In *Travels*, HRS introduces the first song as: "the address of a war party to the women on leaving their village." In *LC70* he entitles it "~~Address~~ Chant of a departing War Party addressed to the Women." In *Travels*, he introduces the second song by writing: "The senti-

ments excited by the absence of a person beloved, are expressed in the following lines. They are usually sung in a measured and pensive strain, which
derives much of its effect from the peculiar intonation and pathos, which
render the music an echo of the sense." In *Travels*, he follows these two songs
with a war song from Tsheetsheegwyung, translated by George Johnston, and
then with the dying speech included below.

First song, Ojibwe text. **3** In *LC70*, HRS includes the following note to
this line: "The change in the number of the pronoun, in this line, is literally
followed in the translation. It is not unusual, for them to address a female
individual, in the singular number, and almost immediately refer to them, as
in this instance, in the plural. It is supposed to result from the strong tendency of the language to personification, and the economy of expression, if
I may so say, resulting from it."

First song, English text. **9–10** Our foes—our foes, like them they shall
lie—like them, like them, they shall lie. I go to ~~lay them~~ ~~like~~ give them like
for like—to give them like for like. *LC70.*

A mother's lament for the absence of a child

Naw! nin daun, nin dau niss ance,
Naw! nin daun, nin dau niss ance;
Nin zhick á no goom nin di a,
Waus suh noon goom ke de zhau
Waus suh noon goom ke di zhau
Nin zhick á dush noon goom nin di au

Ne gush kain dum ne zhick a,
Ne gush kain dum ne zhick a;
Nin zhick e ea, can ge ga,
Cau ba ge zhick mow é me non;   10
Can ba ge zhick mow é me non,
Ne gush kain dum, ne zhick a.

Shaw wain dan me tow é shin,
Shaw wain dan me tow é shin;
Nosa gezhick ong a be yun
Caw now wain im, in dau niss
Caw now wain im, in dau niss,
Shaw wain dau me tow é shin.

[handwritten: grammar & age – interesting]

1.

Oh my daughter—my little daughter—oh my daughter my little
daughter! Alone now am I—far far you are gone, and alone now
am I.

[handwritten: Sounds like it could be a song]

[handwritten: A lot of repetition again – No real Rhyme Scheme of structure]

2.

Sorrowful and lone am I—sorrowful and lone am I. Always
alone—all day alone, my tears are shed for you. Sorrowful and
lone am I.

3.

Have pity on me—have pity on me, my Father abiding
above—Take care of my daughter—my little daughter—Have
pity on my love.

A mother's lament for the absence of a child. Text from *LC70*, where it appears
among a group of Ojibwe songs. Except for the Ojibwe text of this song in

JJS's hand, the other song texts and English translations in this group are in HRS's hand. JJS may have played a central or a shared role in the transcription and translation of all or some of these songs, but there is no evidence that she did, except for the song beginning "Kaago! Kaago!" which HRS and Jameson attributed to JJS in print, and which appears above, and the dying speech, which appears below. She probably provided at least an initial draft of the (rather condensed) English translation of this song, perhaps dictating for HRS's transcription, but without more evidence we cannot know for sure. Above the Ojibwe text, the title, which seems more like a descriptive label than a title, appears in HRS's hand.

"My lover is tall and handsome"

[handwritten: + Strong + Wise...]

[handwritten in left margin: a lot of similes w/ lover & natural animals]

My lover is tall and handsome, as the mountain ash,* when red with berries. He is swift in his course as the stately Addick.† His hair is dark and flowing, as the black bird in spring, and his eye, like the eagle's, is piercing and bright.

Bold and fearless is his heart. His arm is strong in the fight, as the hard bow of oak, which he easily bends. His aim is as sure in the battle and chase, as the hawk which ne'er misses his prey.

Then aid me, ye spirits around! while I sing his praise. My voice shall be heard. It shall ring through the sky. And echo, repeating the name of my chief, shall cause it to spread on the winds. His noble deeds shall be praised through the land, and his name shall be known beyond the lakes.

* Sorbus Americana.
† The American species of Reindeer.

"My lover is tall and handsome." Untitled; title provided by the editor. Text from Henry Whiting, *Sannillac, a poem* (1831, 137). A friend of HRS's, Whiting included the song with notes from HRS at the back of *Sannillac*, explaining: "The song translated in the last note, is, we believe, from the pen of Mrs. Schoolcraft, whose perfect knowledge of the Chippewa language, gives assurance that the sentiments and phraseology of the original have been faithfully rendered" (129).

"High heav'd my breast"

High heav'd my breast—fast flow'd
my tears when my lover came to bid
me adieu. Hear my words he said—
weep not but on the good Manito only—
In two moons he will bring me back
    But I spend ~~that in love~~[?]
                          ~~will~~
to you. Perhaps in the battle he'll be slain,
   my love
and ~~him~~ I may never see again.
    But to[?] the Great Manito
        will pray
          I ~~xx xxxx~~ for hat[?] truces[?]
  Two moons he said, will make the
trees look green; & under their shade
you must wait for me—Speak to the
Spirit that my sky may be blue
Then surely
~~And maybe~~ in safety I'll come back to you
He'll meet his foes, like the big Lake's wave
For my love he is brave—he is brave
       And my heart melts away
       When I think on his stay.
The ground was white with snow,
when my lover went away, and now
the trees are white with blossoms
        Many long days beside
the leaves are large—and^two moons
Above[?] now passed heavy away
      long
And still, still each^day his absence I mourn
And my bosom with grief, deep grief is torn.
     Oh why does he stay!
     Great Manito say?
  What shout do I hear! And what do
I see[?]? Great Spirit thou hast heard
heard me—I thank thee![?] for he comes,

he comes, my loves [*sic*]—comes—I see his
    through
plumes wave^the opening of the woods
and a blue sky attend him
The enemy he has again <u>defeated</u>
And his fame is now <u>completed</u>
    Great Spirit I am <u>blest</u>
    On his bosom I'm at rest.

High heav'd my breast. Text from *LC67*. This manuscript appears in HRS's papers among his poems, though it is in JJS's hand. Because the manuscript appears to be a rough draft in process, I have included the revisions from the manuscript, though that requires extra space between printed lines to allow room for added words. Question marks represent uncertain transcriptions; x-marks represent illegible passages. With its many enjambments, caesurae, and unrhymed lines, and with its lowercase beginnings of lines and its extremely irregular meter, this work in progress looks almost like prose, though such rhyme and meter as it has mark it as poetry. It is probably a translation of an Ojibwe song. But JJS's translations of songs usually come paired with an Ojibwe original, suggesting that this might not be a translation. The anapestic rhythm might seem unlikely for a translation, though it could be JJS's effort to find an English approximation for the rhythm of an Ojibwe song. It is also possible that JJS tried to write her own poem in the voice of a more traditional Indian, and she may have based the poem on a story. HRS wrote poems in Indian voices, though there is no other evidence that JJS wrote in a traditional Indian voice, apart from translations. Whether it is a translation or an original poem, the speaker's position as a woman left lonely by her lover's travels echoes a position familiar to JJS.

    Manito: spirit.

Song of the Okogis, or Frog in Spring

See how the white spirit presses us,—
Presses us,—presses us, heavy and long;
Presses us down to the frost-bitten earth.[1]
Alas! you are heavy, ye spirits so white,
Alas! you are cold—you are cold—you are cold.
Ah! cease, shining spirits that fell from the skies,
Ah! cease so to crush us, and keep us in dread;
Ah! when will ye vanish, and Seegwun[2] return?[3]

[1]This is in allusion to the heavy beds of snow which, in the north, often lie late in the spring.
[2]Spring.

[3]Robed in his mantle of snow from the sky,
    See how the white spirit presses our breath;
Heavily, coldly, the masses they lie,—
    Sighing and panting, we struggle for breath.

Spirit, oh! spirit, who first in the air,
    The Great Master Monedo wondrously made;
Cease to be pressing the sons of his care,
    And fly to the blue heights from whence ye have
        strayed.

Then we shall cheerfully, praisingly sing,
    Okógis, Okógis, the heralds of spring.
First to announce to the winter-bound ball,
    Sunshine, and verdure, and gladness, to all!

Song of the Okogis, or Frog in Spring. Text from H. R. Schoolcraft, ed., *Information Respecting the History, Conditions and Prospects of the Indian Tribes* (1853, 3: 329). Under the title, the text reads "By Ba-bahm-wa-wa-gezhig-equa," a variant spelling of JJS's Ojibwe name. The footnotes are in the original. According to JJS's usual pattern, it appears that the text is a literal translation of a song, and that note 3 provides a poetic version, whether by JJS, HRS, both of them collaboratively, or HRS as editor of a version by JJS.

Note 3 *Monedo*: spirit.

"Kaugig ahnahmeauwin/Ever let piety"

<u>1st</u>
Kaugig ahnahmeauwin,
  We tebiagadau,
Gitchy Monedo atau;
    Songee sauge au dau.

<u>2nd</u>
Matche pemaudazewin,
  Kaukinna, kaukinna;
Matche pemaudezewin,
  Kaukinna wabenundau.

———————————

Literal translation.

<u>1st</u>
Ever let piety (or prayer)
Be the rule of our lives.
The great Spirit alone
  Firmly let us love.

<u>2nd</u>
All Evil living of mankind,
  All, all that is bad, or weak
All Evil living—sin enshrined,
  All, let us all forsake.

"Kangig ahnahmeauwin/Ever let piety." Text from *LC67*. This manuscript
appears in HRS's papers among his poems, though it is in JJS's hand.

Character of Aboriginal Historical Tradition

To the Editor of the Muzzinyegun

Sir,

I have learnt from a correspondent of yours, a very distant relation of mine, your intention of publishing a Paper; the utility and
true meaning of which, has been fully explained to me by my friend.
And as you are willing to admit contributors from amongst my
countrymen and women, it has induced me to take the liberty of
addressing you, and by this means I hope you will be able to form a
more correct opinion of the ideas peculiar to the Ojibwas. And at
the same time, my own humble thoughts shall no longer be breathed
out to the moaning of the winds through our dark forests;—sounds
which have formed a lonely response to my plaints, since I became
a poor Orphan.

Alas! no longer does my kind, fond mother braid up my black
hair with ribbons which the good white people gave me, because,
they said, I was always willing and ready in my duties to my dear
father, when he returned weary and thirsty from the chase. And oh!
my father, you can no longer kiss away the starting tear before it
falls from my cheek; nor kindly ask, what grieves your little girl! But
ye, my parents, are now both gone to the pleasant land of spirits!
Still your poor child feels as though you were near, nor will she ever
forget the good advice you have taught her!

I hope Sir, you will forgive this digression. If you had known
my parents personally, I am sure you would have loved them. My
father was descended from one of the most ancient and respected
leaders of the Ojibwa bands—long before the white people had it in
their power to distinguish an Indian by placing a piece of silver, in
the shape of a medal on his breast. However, my father had one of
those marks of distinction given him; but he only estimated it as
being a visible proof of amity between his nation and that of the
whites, and thought himself bound by it, to observe a strict attention
to the duties of friendship; taking care that it should not be his fault,
if it did not continue to be reciprocal. That medal my father used to
wear, and it is the only relic I still retain in memory of him, who
first taught me how to esteem and appreciate white people. He often
told me that you had a right knowledge of every thing, and that you
knew the truth, because you had things past and present written

down in books, and were able to relate, from them, the great and noble actions of your forefathers, without variation.

Now, the stories I have heard related by old persons in my nation, cannot be so true, because they sometimes forget certain parts, and then thinking themselves obliged to fill up the vacancy by their own sensible remarks and experience, but it seems to me, much oftener by their fertile flights of imagination and if one person retains the truth, ten have deviated, and so the history of my country has become almost wholly fabulous?

O Sir, if I could write myself, (and not trouble my generous relation as I now do) I think I should strive to make you acquainted with all our ancient traditions and customs without deceiving you in the least—just as I heard them from my father. Tell me sir, if it is true, that our great father (The President) is going to cause a house to be built, and a man in black to come and instruct us poor Indians, and if we are to dwell in that house. My heart danced with joy, and my eyes filled with tears of gratitude, when I first heard what is before us.

I have often wished to know the reason and source of many things, which have come immediately under my own observation, and not knowing how to account for such curious circumstances, I have said, "it must be a Manito." But you white people say that there is but one true, great, and good God; then I feel a deep sense of regret that I do not know more of that good Spirit, and what I ought to do to please him. But when the man in black comes to teach us poor young ignorant people the right way, I shall know better; and when I can write, I shall not forget to send you all the pretty songs and stories my mother used to teach me—to be put in your paper. Until that time shall arrive Sir, I must wish you health.

Leelinau.

Character of Aboriginal Historical Tradition, To the Editor of the Muzzenyegun. Text from *LC64*. Above the subtitle, the title is added in HRS's hand. "Literary Voyager" is crossed out and "Muzzenyegun," in HRS's hand, written in its place. An introduction from HRS, called "To Our Correspondent Leelinau," precedes this letter: "The letter of our female correspondent 'Leelinau', we have perused with pleasure, and recommend to the attention of our readers. The simplicity and artlessness of her details of Indian life and opinions, do not constitute the exclusive attraction of her letter. It developes [*sic*] truths connected with the investigation of Indian history and traditions. We solicit further communications from the same source, and feel extremely desirous for the promised 'pretty songs and stories.' Her lines under Rosa, possesses [*sic*] chasteness in the selection of her images, united to a pleasing versification." HRS's introduction has caused confusion by conflating JJS and the narrator of the letter that JJS transcribes and translates. The narrator is not JJS but rather a "distant relation" of JJS, whereas "Leelinau" and "Rosa" are pen names for JJS. Because HRS carelessly blends the narrator and the transcriber-translator, one reader has taken his patronizing remarks about the narrator's "simplicity and artlessness" as remarks about JJS's writing (Ruoff 83), which he describes here in more respectful terms, or at least in what he seems to intend as more respectful terms. It may be worth noting that the narrator's self-colonizing abasement before white people may include an element of courtesy or a self-protective desire to tell white people what she thinks they want to hear.

going to cause a house to be built: The 1826 treaty between the U.S. and the "Chippewa," "with a view to the improvement of the Indian youths," called for $1,000 annually to "be appropriated to the support of an establishment for their education, to be located upon some part of the St. Mary's river, and the money to be expended under the direction of the President" ("Treaty" 270).

Dying Speech

Tiiau! gitshee saunahgud ohou aanaindau goozzeeaun, ohomau eezhee nah neenahwuk, maundah nayaushee tshee iiindahnaushee-aun. Weekau gaago bukaun tshee noandahgwusseenoog; meeaatah pimme zheebaaaukwaug tshee bimeh mudwayauneemuk. Appee giieeaa kee pugidaineemeeaig; kukkinnah keegah bozim tshee ee-zhauyeag, giieeaa neen nah kautuzhee neetauwee geeyaun, aindahnu-keeaumbaun, ainaindaugozzeeaun dush neen, weekau meenahwau tshee waubundunzeewaun. Kegah nah guzhim neendinnahway mau-gunedoag, ohomau eezhee nauneenah waindaugwuk, oweeyuh wee-kau oonjee baashooh kaa iiindausig meeaatah gaatshee nodingin tshee bimme mudwayausing mushkoosseewun ogidjiieeee kaa sau-geegingin kaa iiineendauzhishenaun. Auneeshnau nindeezhau giieeaa neen kau unneeizzhauwaud,—Keemisho missenauneeg; nuhkowaa-suh needjeeakkeewaizee edoog, keeguh suginjeeninim tshee bwoh unee maujauyaun.

How hard is my fate, thus to lie on this desolate Point, where no person will bemoan my departure hence; but the winds murmuring whistle along the dark wood. As soon as I'm laid, where my body must lie, you all will embark for that land where I first drew my breath, and which I am doomed never more to behold.

You leave me, my friends, on this bleak uninhabited shore, where nought will be heard but the loud howling winds, which will cause the green grass to wave over my dark place of rest. But I go where my fathers have gone; and, my friends, I must bid you farewell!

Dying Speech. Untitled; title provided by the editor. There are three sources, one in *LC70* in both Ojibwe and English, in HRS's hand and in nonmetrical lines of poetry; a shorter version in "Dawn," which has the English transla-tion only, also in nonmetrical lines of poetry; and another in prose in HRS, *Travels in the Central Portions of the Mississippi Valley* (1825, 433–34). I fol-low the text from *Travels,* because that version was prepared for publication. In *Travels,* HRS introduces this speech by telling the story of "a Chippewa of Lake Superior," who died at White Fish Point in 1821. "The following sen-tences of" his "farewell address were recited at St. Mary's, two days after his decease, by one of his friends. We preserve the original, in which it was noted at the time, and subjoin a translation." He says that the translation is "By Mrs. Jane Schoolcraft." In "Dawn," HRS gives additional details, including the name of the dying man, Akosa. The *LC70* version is titled "Death Song or address of a Dying Indian." I have not used that title for the prose version, because the prose version is not arranged as a song.

Appendix 1

Sources and Editorial Procedures

The hodgepodge array of Jane Johnston Schoolcraft's surviving writings raises challenges that pose a fascinating case study in the history of literary editing. Here, I summarize where I found Schoolcraft's writings and then explain the editorial procedures for this volume in the context of contemporary editorial theory. I have tried to frame this discussion to address readers who have no experience with editorial theory as well as readers already familiar with it. (Those not interested in editorial procedures may simply skip this section.)

Jane Schoolcraft did not write for publication, except for translations included with Henry Schoolcraft's works and stories published under Henry's name, and she left no organized set of manuscripts. Unless more of her writings turn up—and it is my hope that this edition will provoke its readers to find more of her writings—then for the surviving texts of Schoolcraft's writings we depend mostly on manuscripts preserved and materials printed, often after Jane Schoolcraft's death, by her husband Henry Schoolcraft, a sometimes unsavory character known for his corruption as a federal official and his readiness to take credit for other people's work, not least for the work of Indian people. Yet more, while we often have manuscripts in Jane's hand, many other times we depend on manuscripts of Jane's work copied in Henry's hand, and on publications that he edited, and in most of those cases he probably revised her writing, with or without her approval. When she did approve, her approval may have come under varying degrees of implicit or explicit pressure from Henry. We can even document that in some cases she encouraged him to edit her work. Thus the recovery of the writings of this intriguingly early Native woman rely on the mediation, tastes, and habits of an unsavory white male colonialist. Sometimes, that is the way of the world. Still, were it not for the ways that women and Native readers, writers, and critics over the last several decades have changed the questions we ask about American literature, then all Henry's saving would have been for naught, and this project of recovering the writings of Jane Johnston Schoolcraft would never have been imagined, let alone completed.

The analogy to Emily Dickinson has limits, but it is irresistible. Dickinson did not publish her poems, but others published a few of them, and then, when she died, she left a relatively organized body of poems. Others then published her work, and before long it received a good deal of acclaim. Schoolcraft did not publish her poems, though she cooperated with the occasional publishing of her stories and translations by Henry and at least some of the several other people who published them. (She may have thought of her stories predominantly as translations, since they retell tales told earlier in Ojibwe.) After she died in 1842, her husband continued to publish or reprint a poem, translation, or story now and then, through most of his life. At some point, Henry assembled a collection of her poems (mixing in a couple of his own), apparently intending to publish it. Why he did not publish it, we probably will never know. He probably would have had to shoulder the expense of publication, and especially after he was dismissed from his federal office as Indian agent in 1841 Henry was usually short of funds. Then, after his second marriage, in 1847, he probably would have shied away from spending scarce funds to subsidize a book by his first wife.

Aside from the occasional publication of individual items, or the stories that appeared—without attribution to Jane—in Henry's published collections of Native stories, or the rare individual manuscript, I have found manuscripts of her writing in two libraries: the Library of Congress and the Illinois State Historical Library. (The Illinois State Historical Library has since been absorbed by the Abraham Lincoln Presidential Library.) Henry's massive collection of papers in the Library of Congress includes a great many of Jane's manuscripts and offers the largest source of manuscripts and biographical information. Many of her poems and one translated song are stored together in the same container (container 70), whether gathered together by Henry, a librarian, or another intermediary (such as Mary Howard Schoolcraft, Henry's second wife), we may never know. Several songs appear with the manuscripts of Henry's poems, and several stories appear with the manuscripts of Native stories that Henry assembled for publication, two in Jane's hand and another in the hand of Henry's nephew, who copied Jane's manuscript for Henry. Additional poems by Jane appear in her letters to Henry, as part of the letters themselves rather than on separate sheets of paper. One poem appears by itself, among Henry's letters. The papers include a great many of Jane's letters to Henry, which I draw on for the introduction to this volume. But letters did not always reach their destinations. Some were lost or discarded. Few of Jane's letters to people other than Henry have survived. She may have included additional poems in some of those lost letters.

In a remarkable episode of American literary history, Henry helped pass the long, and to him terribly isolated, Sault Ste. Marie winter of 1826–27, far from any printers, by putting together at least fifteen issues of a handwritten magazine, mostly from his own writings but also including writings by Jane Schoolcraft and others. He called it *The Muzzeniegun or Literary Voyager.* (*Muzzeniegun* is Ojibwe for book or magazine.) In 1962, Philip P. Mason published an edition of the surviving issues of the *Literary Voyager* from Henry's papers in the Library of Congress. I have searched many libraries for additional copies, hoping especially to find the issues not saved in Henry's papers, but without success. Still, *The Muzzeniegun* is one of the major sources for this edition. At some much later date, Henry assembled a large collection of diverse manuscripts under the title "The Second Muzzeniegun" (or sometimes just "The Muzzeniegun"), also preserved among his papers in the Library of Congress, and including two of Jane's stories in the hand of her brother, William Miengun (Wolf) Johnston.

After Henry's papers in the Library of Congress, the other major source of Jane Schoolcraft's literary writings comes in a volume of poems that Henry copied out, with an introduction implying that he prepared it with publication in mind. It had been sitting uncataloged in a box in the Illinois State Historical Library until 2002. I cannot help wondering what other uncataloged Schoolcraft items might be sitting unnoticed in or out of libraries. (I have, however, queried many manuscript libraries about their uncataloged holdings.) At the Illinois State Historical Library, librarians had no information about how or when the library acquired the manuscript. Henry's introduction to the Illinois manuscript (included in this volume) refers to "the foregoing songs & chants," as if the volume of poems went together with a companion set of songs and chants. I suspect that he assembled the manuscript after Jane's death, partly because it contains no items in her hand. Even so, he produced the *Literary Voyager* during her lifetime, and none of her work in the *Literary Voyager* appears in her hand. Inside the cover of the Illinois manuscript is a bookplate with the name of the Illinois state librarian (the secretary of state), Henry D. Dement. Dement held office from 1881–89, which tells us that the library received the volume in those years or earlier. Despite extensive research, I have found no other record of this volume or its history. It is not mentioned in the catalog of Schoolcraft items auctioned in 1880 after the death of Mary Howard Schoolcraft (*Catalogue*), but the manuscripts listed in the auction catalog are not itemized, and the date poses the possibility that the manuscript book was sold at that auction and then somehow found its way to Illinois. Or perhaps the auction inspired the owner of the manuscript to sell it.

After Jane's death, Henry published a potpourri of her writings in his own odd assortment of publications: in his journal *Oneota* (1844–45, later collected in book form), in a set of volumes about Indian topics that he published for the Library of Congress from 1851 to 1857, in his *Personal Memoirs* (1851), and in periodicals. During her lifetime, he published Jane's work in his own collection of Native stories, *Algic Researches* (1839), and he published some of her translations in one of his books, *Travels in the Central Portions of the Mississippi Valley* (1825), and in the notes that he provided to a book-length poem by a friend (Whiting, *Sannillac*, 1831). The scholars who have seized on the works attributed to Jane in the *Literary Voyager* manuscripts, published in 1962, have not noticed these various published sources, except for *Algic Researches*, though without examining the manuscripts, they have had no way to tell what Jane may have written for *Algic Researches* beyond the stories in the *Literary Voyager*. Despite my best efforts, however, the scattered array of sources virtually guarantees that there are other sources I have missed.

Finding Jane Schoolcraft's writings has proved a fascinating challenge of detective work. Editing them provides another challenge. To explain the editorial procedures of this volume and the thinking behind them, I would like to review some key principles from the last half century of editorial theory (also called "textual criticism"), a fascinating area of inquiry that shapes a great deal of what we read and has provocative implications for the process of editing Schoolcraft's writings, but that many readers, including many scholars and critics, know little or nothing about.

In the 1950s, a new theory about how to edit literary texts took form under the imaginative instigation of W. W. Greg and, later, Fredson Bowers. For a time their ideas achieved orthodoxy, and other scholars, especially G. Thomas Tanselle, imaginatively built on their approach. At the core of their thinking lay the idea that editors, when faced with multiple versions of a text, should select the version that comes closest to the writer's "final authorial intention," preferably the author's last manuscript or typescript. (Here things get slightly technical, if readers will bear with me briefly.) They called this version the "copy-text," and they made the copy-text the foundation for the edited text. Editors include changes from later versions (such as published texts) or from the editors' educated hunches (called "emendations") when they see evidence that the author made the revision, perhaps while the author looked over the publisher's preliminary mock-up ("page proofs"). Editors also reject changes in the published text when they have no evidence to believe that the author made them. Sometimes they even remove changes approved by the author, if the changes were thought up by someone else (such as an earlier editor or copyeditor). Other times, if the author approved the changes, later editors decide to stick with them. Greg proposed that when "accidentals" (trivial matters like punctuation or formatting) vary, such as between the author's manuscript and the published text, then probably someone besides the author (such as a copyist, editor, or compositor) changed them, whether deliberately or by mistake. The later editor, Greg reasoned, should restore accidentals from the copy-text, if possible the author's manuscript. The newly edited text, based on the copy-text, thus weaves together accidentals from the copy-text with "substantive" changes made by or agreed to by the author and, perhaps, a few editorial emendations, and the result comes as close as possible to the ideal of final authorial intention.

To many scholars and critics, such a procedure seemed like a perfect blend of scholarly ingenuity with common sense. If we edit a text, the thinking went, we should do all that we can to make it match what its author wanted.

As it turns out, it is not that simple, and to many critics and editors, the ingenuity starts to seem overly ingenious. Even if authors have final intentions, their final intentions do not cover everything and often include leaving certain things to the judgment of friends or editors. As James Thorpe and Philip Gaskell argue, authors expect publishers or printers to take care of accidentals, and usually, therefore, their manuscripts do not represent their final intentions, sometimes especially for accidentals. Moreover, if editors construct a text by weaving accidentals from a copy-text with authorially approved changes from later texts, while rejecting changes that do not meet the test of authorial approval, then the result, though advertised as the final authorial intention, may actually be a text produced by the editors, not by the writer, a text that never previously existed and so holds dubious claim to being—as editors in the Greg-Bowers tradition sometimes call it—*the* text or the "correct" text. Schoolcraft's case may seem to differ, since she did not usually write for publication, but sometimes she prepared her manuscripts for Henry's or someone else's recopying, which in this matter is pretty much the same thing, and she expected Henry to publish her stories and translations, especially in *Algic Researches.* Her close proximity to Henry's frequent writing for publication, and her own writing for someone else's recopying, may have influenced her understanding of what was worth her attention in manuscripts, where she seems casual and light-handed about punctuation, especially at the ends of lines of poetry or, in prose, at the ends of what we would usually think of as separate sentences, as if she were happy for someone else to fill in the final details. Her disregard for punctuation suggests a lack of interest rather than ignorance, and it also holds to older traditions of casual punctuation. Thus, when we have a manuscript of her work in Henry's or someone else's hand, it does not automatically follow that it is less reliable than an earlier manuscript in her own hand. We have to use our judgment, which may vary from case to case, as we find reason to prefer one version or multiple versions.

From there, we do not have to travel far to realize that authors do not necessarily have final intentions, and readers do not necessarily agree on how to characterize authors' intentions or agree that they want to see only one version of a text. In many ways, authors cannot have final intentions, because they do not write all by themselves, and there is often no way to sort out what they did and did not write on their own. Authors write within constraints that enable as well as restrict. They write for audiences, and to a degree they try to write for their own interpretations of what audiences desire. They also have to sort out the competing desires of different audiences. Schoolcraft, for example, never writes about Ojibwe ceremonies, which most Ojibwe people would have considered off-limits for general public consumption, though non-Ojibwe readers often wanted to hear about ceremonies, and Henry often wrote about them. Even writers who never plan to publish internalize a sense of a potential audience's response that can influence what the authors choose to say and how they say it. In the process, they write within a numberless variety of preexisting forms and paradigms. To name some examples from Schoolcraft's writing: story, song, poem; iambic hexameter, anapestic tetrameter, blank verse, rhymed couplets; English rules of syntax; cultural (in Schoolcraft's case, sometimes Ojibwe) expectations about kinship relations or religious boundaries; feminine propriety, class pride, racial pride, racial self-doubt, wifely submission, flirting, Christian piety, filial piety, and so on. Authors can influence such forms, even remake them to a degree, but they do not have a free hand. No one does, in writing or in other pursuits. Often, writers even relish their limitations. They enjoy the challenge of working within a given literary form or social expectation. They may even enjoy leaving the final wording to an editor or—disconcerting as it may sound to modern ears—to a husband. If a friend, editor, or spouse suggests a change and the author agrees to it, which version is the "final authorial intention"? The concept of final authorial intention assumes a category that does not always exist.

No edition of Schoolcraft's writings can reasonably match a notion of her final authorial intention. Her children had no children, so that she has no descendants to express opinions about their preferences. While some of her relatives have actively taken pride in her family's story and published or helped with publications about it, they have not paid attention to her writing, and at this distance in time, none of them can have any memories of her. So far as we know, Schoolcraft never expected to publish her poetry, so the very concept of an edition that includes her poetry contradicts the idea of final authorial intention. And if she had published her poems or gathered her writings together, she would have selected only some of the works that she wrote, eschewing the fragments and ephemera (or sometimes completing them) and probably some other pieces, whereas this edition includes all the literary works that I have managed to find. If Schoolcraft had put together a collection of her writings, it would probably have followed the usual pattern for living writers by including only one genre, such as the poems or the stories, and not the poems, translations, stories, and nonfiction prose. She might have included other works that I have not found or that have not survived. She would also have chosen a sequence for the works that would differ from the sequence chosen by a later editor. And of course she would not have included annotations (or only very few).

In recent years theorists of editing have increasingly cast aside the notion of "final authorial intention" (Pizer; Thorpe; Zeller; McGann; Stillinger, *Multiple Authorship* and *Coleridge*). Like anyone else, writers have different intentions at different times and often have competing intentions at the same time. According to Tanselle's classic argument for the notion of final authorial intention, it "would seem clearly to imply that, when an editor has strong reason to attribute a revision to the author, he will accept that revision as 'final' on the grounds that, coming second, it represents the author's considered and more mature judgment" ("Editorial" 29). This principle, developed from Greg, assumes that we desire (or can afford to publish) only one text, only a final text, and only a text that represents the ideological notion of "considered and more mature judgment." But one person's notion of mature judgment—conforming to a particular age, culture, or subculture—may differ from another's. One person's maturity is another person's priggishness or hypercorrection. Similarly, one person's stroke of imaginative inspiration may look, in someone else's eyes, like mere foolishness. And not least, the mature judgment of one person, culture, or age may look, in other eyes, like colonialist or misogynist assumptions hiding, often unwittingly, under the mask of universal standards.

Thus, intentions are not located in the author alone. They are social as well as personal (as Tanselle himself acknowledges in his later work; see especially *Rationale* 73ff.). They come from the history of culture and cultural exchange, including the history of language, literature, and the social conditions that shape literature's writing. They come as well from the history of publishing and marketing, of readers' responses and interpretations, and from the evolving history of a writer's or a work's reputation among readers.

These are social processes. As writers are not utterly isolated, making decisions by themselves, still less are readers isolated as they decide how to read.

For all these reasons, plus literary curiosity and interest, readers sometimes prefer seeing more than one version of an edited literary text, especially when more than one is available. Increasingly, therefore, editors of texts that come in multiple versions cast away the idea of a single "final authorial intention" and offer their readers multiple versions, and in this edition I have followed that strategy. At the same time, the use of multiple versions has practical limits, especially for fiction. Most readers would not want to bother with multiple versions of a long text. For that reason, the developing preference for multiple versions of texts that appear in multiple manuscripts or printings has played a larger role in the editing of poetry, and that is the case for this edition, where I provide multiple texts for poems and songs but not for stories. Nor do readers want multiple versions of every text. Often, it is clear enough that drafts are just drafts, not full-scale "versions."

With all this in mind, then, instead of following the dogma that would ask an editor to produce a text that supposedly equals Schoolcraft's "final authorial intention," or blizzarding readers and cutting down forests to provide full-scale "versions" of a great many drafts, I have, on this issue and throughout, followed the principle of trying to provide what I believe readers would find interesting and useful. I have tried to shape the edition to meet the interests of a wide range of readers, including students, teachers, scholars, and many others. Thus, when texts appear in closely related drafts that do not seem to add up to something so grand as different "versions," I provide only one edited text, while using the annotations to note variants. When they appear in notably thought-over and differing drafts, I provide multiple edited texts. As it happens, and conveniently enough, the stories do not come in drafts or versions so distinct from each other that they call for providing multiple versions. (That would change if we included Henry's identifiable revisions of Jane's stories in *Algic Researches*, published under Henry's name without attribution to Jane.) This makes for a readable edition that provides access to intriguing variations but does not overwhelm readers with minor variations. At the same time, readers interested in the minor variations can still find them in the annotations. Thus, I have not sought an ideal text fit together like puzzle pieces to represent a conjecture about the author's final intention, supposedly produced in her isolated individuality. Instead, I have privileged actually existing texts that come out of Schoolcraft's historical and social world.

An editor of Schoolcraft's work must also face the question of how to choose a sequence for her writings. I chose to put the poetry first, then the prose (mostly stories), then the translations of songs, and finally the translations of nonfiction prose. While some readers might prefer another arrangement, the sequence of genres will not make much difference for reading. The tougher challenge comes in choosing a sequence within the poems, prose, and translated songs. The usual options are to follow the sequence in publications prepared by the writer, or to put things in chronological order. Neither of those options is available for Schoolcraft, who never gathered her work into a sequence, and whose writings are often undated or only roughly datable.

Since most of the translated songs were published, I considered arranging them in the sequence of publication, but that seemed too arbitrary, because there may be little relation between when they were published and when Schoolcraft wrote them, and three were never published. Therefore, I put them in a sequence that I thought might interest readers, beginning with the love songs, a large and diverse group; then following with my favorite, "The Song of Okogis." The volume concludes with the translation of a letter from an unnamed relative of Jane Schoolcraft's, and then—perhaps fittingly for the last item—with the final words of a man at the end of his life.

As responses to the stories might vary less according to their sequence than in the case of the translations or poems, since it is harder to move quickly from one longer text to another, and as the stories appeared in a sequence that bears a likely relation to their sequence of composition, I arranged the stories and other prose chronologically (guessing that "The Little Spirit" was written about the same time as the other stories prepared for *Algic Researches*, though it first appeared in print years later), except that I put the earliest story last, because I could not tell for sure that Jane Schoolcraft wrote it.

The poems present the greatest challenge for sequencing. Since an actual collection of the poems survives in the Illinois manuscript at the Abraham Lincoln Presidential Library—albeit in a sequence that probably owes more to Henry Schoolcraft's taste than to Jane Schoolcraft's—I deferred to that sequence to a degree, but not comprehensively. It offers the view of Jane Schoolcraft's closest literary colleague and, in effect, her literary executor, but it also leaves out many of the poems that appear in this edition. I followed the Illinois manuscript by beginning with "To the Pine Tree" in Ojibwe. It seemed sensible to follow next with the English translation of "To the Pine Tree," though the English version appears far later in the manuscript. It also seemed sensible to divide the poems, roughly, into two groups; first, a main sequence, concluding with the Psalm that closes the Illinois manuscript; and then a sequence of juvenilia, ephemeral poems, and poetic fragments. Since the division between the two groups is not crisp, and I do not want to demean the second group, I have not called attention to the separation between the groups or given them section titles. Indeed, I especially enjoy one of the pieces from the second group, "My Ear-rings." Within both groups, then (though this matters more for the first group), I have sought a sequence that might interest readers. With that aim, I have balanced two competing principles: grouping poems on related topics, and yet arranging them to show variety. When in doubt, I have put earlier poems first, when dates are available. Thus the many poems about melancholy, sadness, mourning, or depression fall mostly together, varied by the joyful wit of "Response," and the poems about Schoolcraft's son Willy go together. I have also grouped the poems about objects or places (the miscodeed, Castle Island, the Doric Rock).

The editing of this volume often depends on the laborious yet fascinating transcribing and editing of manuscripts. Readers interested in following and perhaps critiquing the editing will want to notice whether a given manuscript is in Jane's, Henry's, or someone else's hand, such as that of the unidentified person who copied out most of the *Literary Voyager*. Fortunately, Jane usually wrote neatly and clearly. Many of the manuscripts, however, come in Henry's hand, which ranges widely from the exquisite to the barely legible, perhaps because of intermittent problems with paralysis but sometimes apparently just because he had more, or less, time. Both Henry's and Jane's hands vary as well according to whether the manuscripts are rough or final drafts (so-called "fair copies"). Sometimes the paper has torn, or words are blotted by an ink smear. But considering the possibilities, these are generally readable manuscripts, often fair copies. For the Illinois volume, Henry took care to produce a document of neatness and elegance, sometimes with elaborate calligraphy or with writing crafted to look like an artful imitation of print (as he often did for his own manuscripts).

The reliance on manuscripts in Henry's hand raises intriguing questions. When he copied Jane's manuscripts, he changed some of them. Some readers might suppose that Henry's changes compromise Jane Schoolcraft's writings. I would argue otherwise, however, because for the most part Henry's role only puts Jane in the position of most writers as they see their work through to publication, adapting to editors' preferences and often collaborating with editors rather than clinging to a pristine notion of final authorial intent. Writing from different but complementary perspectives, Jack Stillinger and Jerome McGann, scholars of editorial theory and of British writing from exactly Schoolcraft's era, have urged us to move away from the fanciful stereotype of isolated writers working on their own. That stereotype draws on exaggerated ideologies of individuality, underestimating the social embeddedness of writing, editing, and publishing. As we revise the fantasy of the isolated genius crafting a final authorial intent, we end up not with a compromised view of writers or the writing process but instead with a more accurate, more socially and historically engaged view of the literary imagination. As Stillinger's editing of and writing about John Keats's poetry shows, for example, many hands besides Keats's ended up producing the works that we now call Keats's poems. That has never offered an obstacle to appreciating the poems or even to understanding them as Keats's poems, but it can, and increasingly it has, deepened our readings of Keats's poetry and helped us understand their social world. As for Keats, so for his near contemporary, Jane Johnston Schoolcraft.

Regardless, the collaboration between Jane Schoolcraft and Henry Schoolcraft raises no great obstacle to editing the texts. In some cases, the only manuscripts are in Jane's hand. In others, the only manuscripts are in Henry's hand or in the unidentified hand that wrote out the bulk of the *Literary Voyager*, presumably under Henry's supervision. For still other works, the only sources are the printed texts brought to publication by Henry. Sometimes, however, an editor must choose a manuscript in Jane's hand, Henry's hand, or the *Literary Voyager* hand, or choose to weave the different manuscripts together or to publish multiple versions. Even in such cases, the obstacles are not great. If Jane prepared a fair copy, that makes a difference. (It also makes a difference that she had Henry's nephew make a verbatim copy of her manuscript for the "Corn story.") Though the manuscripts from the *Literary Voyager* do not come in Jane's hand, they must have been prepared with her knowledge, if not concerning each text then at least regarding the general project of copying selections from her work. Implicitly, they were prepared not just with her knowledge but also with her approval, possibly with her participation. And the manuscripts of the *Literary Voyager* closely match Jane's manuscripts when both are available, suggesting that neither Henry nor the copyist did much to rewrite them. Usually, comparing the manuscripts to the published versions shows that Henry did more to rewrite the stories than the poems. In a letter about her "Corn story," Jane encourages Henry to "correct whatever you find amiss." Nevertheless, since this volume collects Jane's writings, not Henry's, I have used the versions of the stories that seem likely to come closest to her own work, as opposed to the later versions that Henry published under his name in *Algic Researches* (1839), his volume of Indian stories, or that he published after Jane's death. Indeed, Henry continued to revise the stories through a bevy of later publications. (For more on Henry's revisions after *Algic Researches*, see Hallowell, "Concordance," and Clements 117–18.)

One particular crux comes up rarely, namely, those instances where we must rely on a manuscript in Henry's hand, and the manuscript includes revisions in Henry's hand. One could argue that the revisions likely represent changes Henry imposes on Jane's writing, and that we should therefore reject such changes. This crux comes up most prominently in a long essay that Henry wrote mostly about Jane's poetry. Called the "Dawn of Literary Composition by Educated Natives of the aboriginal tribes," it has never been published before its appearance in this volume. In the process of quoting Jane's poems for "Dawn," Henry's manuscript revises some of them far more than he does elsewhere. Partly because these texts seem so wayward, I have not chosen them as the source for the texts in this edition, except for one poem and one translated song where "Dawn" is the only source ("on a recent affliction" and "Requiem of an Indian maid"); those appear in this volume as part of "Dawn" but are not grouped with Jane's other poetry and translations (which also avoids the redundancy of printing the same texts twice).

For the Illinois manuscript and for one story ("Peboan and Seegwun," which it is not certain that Jane wrote), the reliance on a manuscript in Henry's hand that includes Henry's revisions poses a more challenging question about the collaboration between Jane and Henry. In such cases, however, there is no way to know for certain that Henry's revisions are outside impositions. When he changes a word, he could be acting on his own initiative, or he could be undoing revisions that he considered on his own initiative, and restoring the words that Jane wrote. He could also be acting on Jane's direction, whether in response to her reading his transcriptions (not possible for the Illinois manuscript, if he prepared it after her death), recollecting her preference expressed at an earlier time, or responding to a record of her preferences, perhaps in a manuscript that includes revisions or considers multiple wordings. Indeed, at least once ("Pensive Hours," 17), Henry writes one thing and then reverts to wording from a manuscript in Jane's hand, underlining that the revisions he makes cannot be counted on as his changes but may instead replace his words with hers or choose among competing versions of her own wording. They may of course also be Henry's own revisions, and probably most of them are. Those that come from Henry probably represent his idea of what is most lyrical, literary, metrical, clear, or proper. In the translations, they might represent his effort to make the texts sound representatively Indian or Ojibwe, and in the poetry they might represent his effort to complete the poems in what he sees as the spirit of Jane's imagination.

If we were to assume that all his revisions come exclusively from him and should be rejected, then we would find ourselves removing those revisions that he left visible as revisions, without removing those that he made silently. In such cases, which could be the majority, he left no trail because he did not change his mind and cross something out. We would thus be producing a text that represents an imaginative construction of the editor, without its ever having existed before. By contrast, leaving in the revisions represents a text that actually exists (Henry's transcript), potentially a hybrid of Jane's writing and Henry's revision. To editorial theorists of the Greg-Bowers school, such a practice would be a travesty of Jane Schoolcraft's so-called final authorial intentions. Moreover, such a practice might be resented not only by those who see writing as the independent labor of the romantically invested individual author (the Greg-Bowers school of editing), but also by those who, supposing themselves more radical, invest romantically in the individual authority of the Indian writer, the female writer, the colonized or subaltern writer, and the Indian female colonized writer. But in practice (as Gayatri Spivak has argued in another context) such would-be radicalism conservatively returns that writer to the in-some-ways stereotypically masculine, European, colonialist models of individuality and selfhood that its advocates supposedly set out to oppose.

By contrast, the method I have chosen, by supplying a record of more substantive variants in the annotations to each poem, allows readers to construct such hybrids as the evidence allows them to imagine, while it presents as a reading text the product of Jane Schoolcraft's authorship in the social environment that she lived in historically. As we have seen, that matches the way that many theorists of editing and of textuality, coming after the Greg-Bowers school, have come to rethink notions of authorship to see it as a collaborative and social process. This social sense of authorship in general and of Jane Schoolcraft's authorship in particular also matches, rather than masks, the social and historical conditions of race, gender, and colonialism that contributed to producing Schoolcraft's writing and that her writing can speak back to. Such conditions were not mere restrictions on her writing, any more than meter is a restriction on poetry. Sometimes deliberately, and sometimes not, she would have taken such conditions into account as she envisioned and crafted her writing. In that sense, the social conditions of her world mediated her writing and even, to a degree, enabled or provoked her writing. That, in turn, made it possible for her to crave a place (as she put it in lines translated from Ojibwe into English, either by her or by Henry) "Far from the haunts of men away," with

>   no sordid fears,
> No crimes, no misery, no tears
> No pride of wealth; the heart to fill,
> No laws to treat my people ill. ("Lines Written at Castle Island, Lake Superior")

But no such place exists, and to imagine that Schoolcraft could produce her writing without the engagement, for better or worse, of other parties is to deny the worldliness in writing that helps attract us to reading literature in the first place.

Technical Notes

For the most part, the notes to individual texts offer information and leave interpretation to readers. Occasionally, however, I have varied from that pattern when it seemed that my experience with the materials offered a vantage point for interpretations that might not otherwise be accessible to readers and that might help readers develop their own approaches. I have tried to let usefulness, clarity, and of course accuracy guide the editing through the tangle of technical decisions that an editor must make. In the interest of readability and access to a wide audience, the notes, as much as possible, do not use the jargon of editorial practice and theory (terms, abbreviations, and signs such as holograph, sigla, ms., ~, and so on). I have corrected spelling errors only when they appear to be a slip, not when they appear to represent a preference. While that distinction depends on educated editorial guessing, in practice it works straightforwardly (and all spelling corrections are recorded in the notes). Titles have been left-justified and rendered in a consistent font, and punctuation at the ends of titles (usually a period, once a dash) has been removed, except for the earliest version of "Pensive Hours," and for "High heav'd my breast," where I have retained those habits of an earlier time to match the feel of a draft that has not been regularized for publication. Occasional horizontal lines dividing a title from the body of a text have not been reproduced. I have refrained from adding or correcting punctuation at the ends of lines of poetry, where both Jane and Henry, like many poets, and without seeming to worry about it, often let a line break do the work of punctuation. Ampersands have been silently expanded, except in quotations from letters and quotations from drafts in the notes. Schoolcraft often leaves out apostrophes in possessives or puts them in the wrong place. I have added or moved them and indicated as much, for the poetry, while elsewhere adding them silently. In accord with routine modern editorial practice, I have not reproduced the now-dated long *s*.

Minor features of some transcriptions must depend on the transcriber's best guess, especially about capitalization and punctuation. Schoolcraft was not much concerned to mark the ends of sentences. She was often casual about the distinctions between commas, periods, and dashes, or casual about whether to use them at all, and she often used a short, low horizontal line that is not clearly a comma, period, or dash. Many manuscripts have stray marks, tears, stains, bleedings from the other side of the page, and so on, making transcription an imperfect process. She was also old-fashioned in her sense of the quotation mark. During her lifetime, the rules for quotation marks were shifting into their current standardized usage, but in the eighteenth-century books that Schoolcraft grew up with, she would have seen many variations in usage (Mylne). Because the irregular, old-style usage would confuse current readers, quotation marks have occasionally been edited, but only where noted.

The poems in the Illinois manuscript book were numbered in pencil, apparently at a time after the manuscript was prepared, and I give no indication of those numbers. The numbers do not quite match the sequence or include every poem, indicating that some numbers may have been changed, or that plans were afoot to rebind the pages. Or perhaps they were bound after they were numbered and mixed with other poems, which would match the irregularity of the handwriting from poem to poem.

Although the poems and stories from the *Literary Voyager* were previously transcribed and published in Mason's 1962 edition of the *Literary Voyager*, I have transcribed them afresh rather than relying on Mason's edition. My transcriptions sometimes differ from Mason's. I have done less to standardize the forms of titles, and there are differences in punctuation, but meaningful differences in the wording are rare and modest. Of course, I have had the benefit of Mason's work. "Peboan and Seegwun" is in Henry's hand, but most of the *Literary Voyager*, including all the other writings from the *Literary Voyager* found in this volume, come in an unidentified hand, perhaps someone recruited to act as copyist because he or she wrote with scrupulous neatness. Occasionally, Henry added something brief to the copyist's transcription, and I have noted those instances in the annotations. Besides the incomplete set of issues preserved among Henry's papers, which run from December 1826 to April 1827, and which Mason transcribes, Henry's memoirs also mention an earlier set of issues begun in December 1825 and not noted by Mason (*Personal Memoirs* 240). No copies of the earlier set seem to have survived.

All the pieces in the *Literary Voyager* signed Rosa or Leelinau were written by Jane Schoolcraft. Some confusion can arise from this reliance on pen names. Jeremy Mumford goes so far as to argue that Rosa and Leelinau each represent different personae for Jane Schoolcraft, Rosa suggesting a mix of the European with the Indian and Leelinau suggesting something more exotically Ojibwe (9–13). I find this distinction appealingly literary, but unconvincing. For one thing, these are overlapping categories. For another, the distinction requires a strained reading of Henry's reference to Rosa and Leelinau as the same person (see the note to her translation of "Character of Aboriginal Historical Tradition"), casting that casual identification of the two as a deliberate effort to make a distinction between them. It also seems unaware of Jane Schoolcraft's habit, later in life, of signing thoroughly unexotic letters to Henry as Jane Leelinau Schoolcraft (and variations thereof, Jane L. Schoolcraft, Jane J. L. Schoolcraft), or signing notes within her letters simply as Leelinau.

In Appendix 5, readers will find a list of "Less Substantive Variants" in the texts. These go at the back to remain available while not interfering with the reading text. Rather than following W. W. Greg's thought-provoking distinction between substantive variants and accidental variants, I am more modestly calling these less substantive, allowing for the possibility that other readers may attribute more weight to them than I do. Sometimes, however, when the less substantive and the more substantive variants come mixed together, they are listed together immediately after the text at hand. Occasionally, the less substantive annotations at the back of the volume indicate illegible words; if such words were legible, then they might seem more substantive.

An Introduction to the Poetry of Jane Johnston Schoolcraft

Henry Rowe Schoolcraft

Most of the following pieces are from the pen of Miss Johnston, or Mrs Schoolcraft. In submitting specimens of versification from the pen of a descendant, in the first degree, from a war chief of the northwest, it is conceived that their claims, as emanations of aboriginal mind, under the influence of education, can hardly be disputed. And it is believed, that as additions to the foregoing songs and chants, taken down from the lips of the natives, they are entitled to the consideration here claimed for them. If the calm resignation, the pious reverence, and the deep and habitual reliance on the Almighty, as exhibited under the character and sufferings of the Saviour, may be deemed a trait foreign to the natural state of the Indian mind, the truth of the engrafting of these principles, upon the native stock, and the feasibility of their extension to the entire tribes, will more than compensate for the deviation ~~from aboriginal sentiment,~~ in this one particular. While the existence of sentiments of a pure theology will be observed, in these little effusions, in connexion with paternal affections, simplicity of expression, and depth of feeling, as true, at least, to the nature, as the civilized state. To draw from the ordinary incidents of domestic life, subjects of poetic interest calculated to please, and worthy of being remembered, is the evidence of no ordinary talent, and has fallen to the lot of but few. And the degree in which the object is supposed to have been attained in these pieces, is not such as would perhaps, justify their exhibition, under other, and ordinary circumstances. It is conceived that public feeling, will regard with a more indulgent eye, the simple impromptings of an Indian girl, wife, and mother.

A few addition[al] facts seem here to be required.

The author is the eldest daughter of Shau gush Co da way quay, and the late John Johnston Esqr. of St. Mary's Falls, Michigan, formerly of the county of Antrim, Ireland. Reared in the vast and remote area, spreading west and north of the Great Lakes, her thoughts have taken a tincture from its scenery. Mr Johnston became himself, the instructor of his little daughter in elementary knowledge, as well as the rules of domestic propriety, and of social intercourse and manners. For the latter, his residence at the interior thoroughfare of St. Mary's, afforded a far better opportunity, than could have been ordinarily expected, in so remote a position. An advantage arising from the acts of hospitality which he was enabled to shew to officers and strangers visiting the country, and particularly, to the gentlemen and partners of the Northwest company, who aimed to make amends for the toils and privations of their annual peregrinations in that region, by living in a kind of baronial splendour at home. And wherever they were received as guests, nothing was spared, to add to their comfort, that a well furnished table, and co[u]rteous attentions, could supply.

From her mother she obtained her native language in its fullest range and fluency, and from her father she derived the English, with the art of both speaking and writing it, in its purity. At a suitable age, he took her with him, to Europe for the purpose of completing her education—an advantage, which his connexions with a polished circle of friends and acquaintances, in the north of Ireland, placed within his reach. On her return to St. Mary's, she naturally came to preside in his household over the department of receiving her father's guests, as her mother, from not speaking the language, felt desirous of being relieved from the embarrassment of her position. And as her younger sisters grew up, she repaid to them, the kind offices of instruction, which her father, and his European friends, had bestowed upon her.

This much was conceived to be necessary, in placing the pieces before the reader. It is only required to add, that they have been selected, ad libitum, from her portfolio, and received a careful and critical revision.

An Introduction to the Poetry of Jane Johnston Schoolcraft. Untitled; title provided by the editor. Henry Schoolcraft's rather grudging introduction to the manuscript of Jane Schoolcraft's poems formerly in the Illinois State Historical Library and now in the Abraham Lincoln Presidential Library raises a number of questions. Each page of the introduction has a big *X* in pencil crossing out the writing on the page. The opening sentence was added later and contrasts with the original first sentence, now the second sentence, which addresses the poems as if they were all by JJS. As it turns out, the manuscript includes two poems from Henry's book *Indian Melodies* (1830), "Sagiahwin" and "Invocation to the Great Spirit," both of them identified as "from Indian 'Melodies,'" though "Sagiahwin" is actually Henry's revision of Jane's poem "The Contrast, a Splenetic Effusion." (See the annotations to the poem in this volume.) The added opening sentence suggests that Henry may have added his poems after he drafted the introduction. His reference to "the foregoing songs and chants" suggests that there was another manuscript, now lost, accompanying this manuscript of poetry. Henry refers to Jane's father—but not to her mother—as "late," indicating that he may have written this introduction while Ozhaguscodaywayquay, who died in 1843, was still alive. But it seems at least equally possible that he deemed John Johnston's death as worth noting without seeing the same magnitude in Ozhaguscodaywayquay's death. Indeed, the feeble praise he bestows on Jane Schoolcraft's writing might make us suspect that he wrote this introduction after his second marriage in 1847. The reference to "the gentlemen and partners of the Northwest company" is to fur traders from what was for many years the leading fur trading company in the region. Henry's remark that he has chosen the poems "ad libitum" (at pleasure) indicates that he chose the poems that he liked the most. The remark that the poems "received a careful and critical revision" raises the question of who provided the revision, Jane Schoolcraft or Henry Schoolcraft. Though she routinely revised her poems, this remark hints that he has given them another layer of revision. Whether or how much such revisions went beyond what any poet would typically encounter from an editor, we cannot know. The manuscript of the introduction itself underwent a modest amount of revision. It contains crossouts and additions, which I have noted only when they seem to hold particular relevance.

Appendix 3

Dawn of Literary Composition by Educated Natives of the aboriginal tribes
Henry Rowe Schoolcraft

[Editor's note: The following excerpt from an invaluable unpublished essay by Henry Rowe Schoolcraft explains the origins of some of Jane Johnston Schoolcraft's writings and provides texts of some of her writings that we would otherwise have in different versions or would not have at all. The excerpt begins about a quarter of the way into the rough draft. Earlier, the essay speculates loosely about the origins of writing and of British poetry, suggesting that it takes a long time for a people to develop a literature. Then it discusses Catharine Brown, a Cherokee who died young and whose letters were published, with diary extracts, in Rufus Anderson's *Memoir of Catharine Brown* (1825). The attention to Brown seems designed partly to make the essay's predominant focus on Jane Schoolcraft seem less like the indulgence of a husband's memories. The excerpt begins at the first mention of Jane Schoolcraft and includes the entire essay from that point, excepting only the passages of her writing referred to but not included in the manuscript.]

During the same year (1800) that marked the birth of Catherine [*sic*] Brown, there was born, at a few degrees more northerly latitude, in the Chippewa nation, a female who, with equal delicacy of mind, and elevation of Christian hope and faith, united a more than equal evidence of poetic impressions, and who was destined, under favourable auspices, after a more extensive career of life, in Europe and America, to leave behind her specimens both in prose and verse, which, as evidence of the intellectual development of the Indian race, are entitled to respect.

Bababauwawägezhigaqua, of Sault Ste. Marie, Michigan, better known as Miss Jane Johnston, and by her Indian soubriquet of Leelinau, was the granddaughter of Wabojeeg, a Chippewa chief of great energy and renowned daring[?], of the region of lake Superior. Born to every advantage of very[?] early instruction in polite letters and religion her mind became deeply imbued, at an early age, with divine truth, and with a taste for English literature. These advantages were further improved by a ~~residence in~~ educational training, at Wexford in Ireland, the country of her father's nativity. Placed there, at the early age of ten, when she was already a fluent reader and elegant penman, she returned from that country, and from a visit to England, with her mind stored, with the perusal of the best works in history and belleslettres, and with manners ennobled by refined examples. She had been early impressed with the writings of Hannah Moore, whose high moral views of life she ever regarded as entitled to her highest reflections and study.

Her mind had in childhood been thoroughly imbued with the lodge-lore and imaginary legends and traditions of her tribe. The Chippewa, or Odjibwa language as the natives term it, was to her, the language of infancy. In it, her first conceptions had been expressed, and she retained a perfect mastery of its rules, and was an adept in the flow of its stately xxxxx syllables.

The legends and verbal traditionary lodge-lore of the forest, had filled her young mind with the fictions of the Indian mythology, which cover the whole aerial sphere of the heavens, and render the doctrines, the existence of gods and spirits familiar to the youthful ear and eye. They were to her, "familiar as household work". She could look, into the heavens, and into the bright tracery of its stars and clouds, and read in them the sublime pictography of the wise men and sages of her forest ancestry.

She spoke the English and Chippewa equally well, with a soft silvery voice; her stature was small, and light, and graceful, her eyes a beaming black, her feet and hands very small, her air mild and benevolent, timid, yet bland and confident in the annunciation of truth. She was a pensive admirer of the grand features of the heavens and xxxxxxx with intense admiration on the evening landscape—the setting sun, the retiring[?] light, the murmuring[?] water of the specter? of great lakes and rivers that mark[?] her native country—the rising moon, the distant stars, and the brilliant auroral phenomena of the northern hemisphere. In these she recognized with passionate intensity the Great author of Creation.

Her letters and occasional compositions, evince great delicacy, propriety and clearness in the use of language; and graphic simplicity of description.

To such a mind, the body of English literature opened up, a new world of thought and reflection, which she poured over with the greatest avidity. And, with a timid hand, she, at an early age committed her thoughts to paper. These memories evince great purity of thought. They indicate an admiration of that mine of new thoughts and wisdom which she observed in the writings of the British essayists, divines, dramatists, poets and moralists. Her heart sympathized deeply with her woodland people whom she viewed as pursuing false objects, through false hopes. The fires of truth that flashed upon her own mind had, as it were, burned out the picturesque tapestry that adorned the temple of her native mythology, and left its frame standing as a collapsed wreck at which she gazed, often with pensive and often with melancholy thoughts. She perceived and regretted their fate, and often became pensive in and sad in view of the many unsuccessful efforts to win them over to civilization and christianity. And after all she had witnessed in Ireland and England she clung with a strong attachment, to the landscape and history of her mother's side of the heritage—her picturesque and wild relations.

One of her earliest attempts in metre was due to a circumstance which happened on her return from Ireland. The journey from Montreal, in those early days, after reaching the Straits of Niagara, led by a rustic road, from Queenstown over the Niagara ridge to Chippewa, and passed near a forest of stately pines. As soon as her eye caught the sight of these well known ergreen [sic] forests, memory reverted to the early prospects of childhood, and with a countenance beaming with pleasure she turned to her father. "Ah![''] cried she, [''in all your boasted and beautiful country I have not seen a tree like that." These sentiments on reaching home she afterwards expressed in the following lines in her native language.

(Insert Nº 1.

The following is a translation of these words[?].

Insert Nº 2.

This feeling of attachment to her native country and her tribe, is evinced, by the following apostrophe, to one of her aboriginal ancestors.

(Insert N° 3.)

Her early and deep tone of piety appears in the ensuing lines, penned after reading Miss Hannah Moore's Christian Morals, and Practical Piety.

(Insert N° 4.)

Of a similar tone, are some Stanzas written before, coming in, to attend family worship.

(Insert N° 5.)

Her sense of the beautiful in nature, and her warm, yet simple appreciation of those beauties, as unfolded by the landscape, is expressed in some lines, addressed to a female friend, who yet coveted the downy pillow of repose, on a summer's morning.

(Insert No 6)

An event occurred, in 1816, in the remote forests of the north, which caused the case [or care?] of pity and charity "to tingle", and excited a deep sympathy for a poor neighboring family, of French descent, which had lost one of its members, in a season of great want and scarcity, North of lake Superior, by the horrible spirit cannabalism [sic]. Not to sympathize, with the distressed mother for ef a lost son on such an occasion[?], would evince[?] a want of xxxxxxxxxx to passing events, and in the forest around, of which the Indian nations, have been unjustly accused. And while she prepared to accompany her mother on the visit of condolence to the bereaved mother she went to her room and committed to paper, the following lines.

(Insert N° 7.)

The scenery at the falls and along the Straits of St. Mary's, which were first[?] regarded[?] by a European face in 1661,* and the picturesque vicinity of lake Superior, has often attracted notice. Its grandeur of outline,—with its widespreading waters and winding shores, are not more remarkable, than the loneliness and silence, which, in years past, and before the influx of population about 1822, often marked the evening xxxxx. It is a scene of this kind, that is brought before the reader[?] in the following evening landscape.

*Rambaultouets[?]

[Editor's note: This seems to refer to Charles Raimbault, whom HRS names in his *Personal Memoirs* (441) as the first (that is, the first European) to visit Sault Ste. Marie, in 1661. Actually, Etienne Brulé reached the Sault much earlier, in 1621–22.]

(Insert N° 8.)

A similar picture of lonely magnificence, is brought before the mind, in the subjoined lines, written under a pensive mood, during the absence of her father in Ireland.

(Insert N° 9.)

Graphic but very simple scenes, in the natural history of the country, were sometimes attempted, as the two following little effusions.

Insert 10 and 11.)

Local attachment, is a very strong and characteristic sentiment in the Indian breast. They cling, as with a death grasp to the places of their birth.

In 1820 a young Chippewa Indian called Akosa, in the last stages of a decline, landed at Whitefish Point, in lake Superior, with his family and friends, on their return from St. Mary's falls to their residence in the interior. He had fondly hoped to see his native place once more, but this desire, he was never destined to realize. It was evident to all, who saw his feebleness, and to himself also, that he had landed, for the last time, on the picturesque and magnificent shores of his favorite lake. He called his family and friends around him and spoke, for some time, on the inevitable fate, that awaited him, and his regret, that he could not return but must leave his body there with them. These words of the dying Indian assumed[?] a tone of pathos and were reported at St. Mary's in the Indian language by a native, who was present, and by their simple effects, so affected Miss Johnston, that she immediately committed the original, to paper, and afterwards made a literal translation of them.

Words of a dying Indian.

(Here insert the Indian words)

How hard is my fate, thus to lie on this desolate
    Point!
Where no person will bemoan my departure hence,
But the winds, murmuring along the dark wood,
And as soon as I'm laid, where my body must lie,
You all, my friends, will embark for that land—
Where I first drew my breath,
But which I am doomed never more to behold.

You leave me, my friend, on this bleak, uninhabited
    and desolate loansome shore,
Where nought will be heard, when I am gone, but
    the loud howling winds,
Sweeping through the branches of the trees,
And the[?] low[?] grass xxxxxxx[?] grave.—But I go,
    where my fathers have gone;
And, my friends, I must bid you farewell.

Another trait which we find recorded in the papers of Miss J. is a strong feeling of attachment for the persons, who [were] left behind, at these forest locations, on the departure of war parties. Such parties have devoted themselves to battles and do not leave the precincts[?] of their families, without letting them know, the sympathy they feel for them, under the probabilities of their never returning.

The mother of Miss Johnston retained in her memory and communicated some of the war songs, and an address[,] which were made by her father, Wabojeeg, during the xxxxxxxx of the war waged by the Chippewas in the latter half of the 18th century against the combined forces[?] of[?] Outagamies and the Sioux. Of the latter Miss J. recorded the words uttered by that chieftain, standing at the head of a war party, and addressed to the women of the village who had assembled on the shores of the lake, to witness their departure. These were recorded by her, an expression of feelings which have not been usually ascribed, as existing in the Indian breast, steeled as it is supposed to be at all times to all sentiments but those of a lazy[?], xxxxxx character.

              Warrior's Address to the women.
       Cago, Cago, moweshecain
       Keen de qua me doag, neboyaun,
       Keen ahwaw atah Ke daw moweendim,

Keen ahwaw Ke gedomawgazim,
Equa mejeeg[?] Ke gedomawgazim

Nee naundonawaug, ne naundonawaug,
Anuhwamaungeg, caw nesinge-eg
Nee duhwe tebishenaug—tebishenaug,
Anuhwamaungeg caw nesinge-eg
Nawdowasee! naudowaseewug!
Gahyea ween awaw tebishco,
Gahyea ween awaw, mesahgo
Ca dah we eg his he mug waw-ezhishemieg.
Cago, Cago, &c.

<u>To the women.</u>

Do not—do not, weep for me
My female ~~friends~~ ~~xxxxxxx~~ ~~villagers~~ relations—should I die
For yourselves alone, should you weep
Poor are ye all, and to be pitied,
Ye women, you are to be pitied.

<u>War-Recitative.</u>
I seek—I seek, our fallen relations,
I go to revenge—revenge the slain
Our relations, fallen and slain
Our own foes, our foes, they shall lie
Like those who are fall[en], they shall lie.
I go to seek revenge ~~their death~~—to seek revenge. ~~their death.~~
[Editor's note: twice, "seek" was added after "their
    death" was crossed out.]
To the women,

Do not—do not, &c.   Xxx.

Those traits in the manners and customs of her kindred tribe,
which evince affection, or elevation of thought, or feeling never escaped her quick attention, in proof of which the metrical data, which
she has collected, from their oral tradition, may be mentioned. The
Indian has a strong capacity for belief in mysterious, or Spiritual
influences. His whole religious character, if we may apply this term
to his forest rites and ceremonies, is based on this trait. Whatever he
seeks, or covets from the invisible world, is based on the meritorious

character of fasting. He believes, that to purify the body, and render it fit for spiritual communication, nothing is so efficacious as abstinence from food. Accordingly, whatever excites elevated feelings in his heart, is sought to be promoted by fasting. It is the common preparative to every rite in religion, war, or even hunting. The guardian spirit, which is selected by every young person, at the age of puberty, is sought through, characteristically, long and severe fasts.

Their powers of endurance, in this respect, are known to be remarkable, from seven to ten days being sometimes reported to be attained in these severe vigils. There is, indeed, no trait of the Indian character, which is more strongly developed and fixed in the mind, than its reliance on fasts. And there is no higher point of meritorious attainment among them, than to say of an individual, that he has stood the test of the most severe fast. That[?] xxxxxx prophets and war captains make their surest expressions on the popular mind by their long and rigid fasts.

That the Indian female, who has seen the great importance attached to this rite, by her nation, in every phase of life, should resort to it, as a proof of her constancy or devotion to one object, in the indulgence of her affections, is in full harmony with the Indian manners and customs. And it will be perceived that it is the first circumstance, and the main[?] merit, named by the native songstress in the following lines, which are closely translated. ~~Both the original, and the translation are given in the precise word spelling.~~

N°. 12 and 13.

The simplicity of the following lines, which are literally rendered from the original, commands them to notice.

Song of an Odjibwa girl ~~xxx~~ her[?] departure for a distant school.

In N° 14.

American, what ails thee now?
A soft remembrance or a vow!
That stream, so often crossed before
With joy thy bark shall cross no more
Tears glisten in thy manly face
Because thou seest th'Ojibwa maid
Run[?] away[?] and depart the place[?]
xxxxx xxxxx a noble breast inviol.
Thou seest her with her trim white sail
Waiting to catch the xxxxxx gale

That bears her off. Nor shall thy[?] sighs,
Long for that forest maid arise
But she, as soon as out of sight,
Shall be by him forgotten quite.

Many of her subsequent pieces, relate to the changes introduced
into that remote region, by exploration and settlement of the country by the Americans, as a part of the great geographical lines of the
definitive treaty of 1783—a treaty, the provisions of which, had lain
dormant in the American mind, for years[?].

In 1820 the American government sent an expedition to explore
that remote portion of the United States, which passed through lake
Superior and created an impression on the Indian mind. The reflections created on her own mind are expressed in these lines:

Progress of the white Man.

N°. 15.

The bustle of commerce, and the introduction of courts of law,
the establishment of an Indian Agency and of missions for the Indian population, the introduction of schools, churches, ~~legislative~~
elections—these filled the once remote and depopulated village, with
new and exciting topics. This period is apparently alluded to, and
forms the date of, the lines entitled

The Contrast.

(Insert N°. 15.)

Still deeper cares, now claimed attention, and received notice from
her pen, ~~and affections~~, which were xxx expressed with a truthfulness and often pathos. The "Happy Valley" of St Mary's was, indeed,
robbed of its seclusion and rural attractions, where the adventurous
traveller and bold Indian trader, with his troubadour boatmen, had
once been the only guests. But this seclusion was forever gone. The
first steamboat entered the peaceful straits of St. Mary's c. 1822. And
the aged Indian prophet, as he sat on his posed and elevated cliff,
beholding the noisy ascent, had his dream fulfilled of the walking
manito of the Lakes, who strode through its deepest channels, driv-
ing[?] before him the xxx xxxxx spirits and demons who had so long
dwelt on and guarded their shores, cried with a loud voice—"away,

away, ye ministers of the Great Spirit, for the destroying of our peace has come." The poetic age of St. Mary's was indeed now past, and that of reality xxxx began. A few years effected a complete revolution in the village, and its inhabitants and its business. The native poetess stood revealed to a new population. Her literary tastes, her modesty and gravity of manners, and her varied accomplishments, the justness of her sentiments, and the dignity and propriety with which she presided over her father's household attracted notice and admiration from many a visitor. She spoke and wrote the English with uncommon purity and elegance. She had also cultivated the Indian language and its grammar, and idioms with great care; and had made herself a proficient in the Indian mythology and forest lore. In a few years she consented to enter the married state; and it is perhaps, from this period, that we are able to trace a deeper tone, and a wider range, in her communications, with the Muse.

The ensuing specimens appear to be of that transitive[?] period.

Sageawin. (Love)
See N°. 18.

Nindawamin. (Knowledge)
See N°. 19.

Lines entitled Keepsake. (Loneliness)
See 20.

The event of her marriage did not interrupt her habit of occasional resort to the haunts of the muses. And these attempts at least and has the force and correctness of moral sentiment.

Neenábame, (a husband's absence)
See 21.
The love of offspring is a natural trait of the female heart.
Ningwis. (or a son's expanding question)
See 22.

In a few years that heart was destined to be deeply xxxxx. The flower was, suddenly, cut down, by the scythe of the destroyer death. But in every situation the muse, was habitually the xxxxxxxxx of religion, and was eagerly resorted to! Rhyme would but seem to transmit thought in the following lines.

on a recent affliction. (1827.)

My son, my son, how wretched am I now!

I saw you in my visions, sinking ~~with~~[?] deep, ~~xxxxx~~,

Xxxxxxxx swift[?] symbolic[?] of that ~~cruel~~ fate,

Which ~~xxxx~~—tore you from my sight, pale, xxxxxx,
    lifeless,

And ~~confined~~[?] swept[?] your tender limbs ~~to~~ in the
    cold ground.
                            The coffin and the grave,

Ah me, my heart[?] is ~~buried~~ dead with that beloved
    form,

Those sparking[?] eyes shall beam on me no more,

That playful smile—that sweet and manly voice,

Those quick and xxxxxxxx gestures

That soul-bespeaking confidence

That oneness[?] of life and love

In every act and motion

All are gone. The black ~~water~~ waves of death

Have covered all. And me, ah me.

What is my portion now but grief,

Deep, bitter, ~~grieving~~ ever-xxxxx, painful grief.
          That rosy cheek
          That diamond eye
          That placid smile
          That voice most musical
          That air and xxxx of life and motion
          Which spoke a mind above its years
          Precocious of intelligence and
   thought
                All, all, has fled
                And all I see is death.

This most afflictive event of the loss of a precocious son, at the early age [of] three is again dwelt on, in the following simple and touching lines.
          ~~Stanza[s] to Resignation~~
    To my ever beloved and lamented son
          William Henry
          See (23.)

A mind reaching[?] after divine supports, is evinced in these
          Stanzas to Resignation
          See Nº 24.

The christian repose of character evinced by these lines and by the following stanzas, shows the habitual, temper of her strains[?].
Lines written under affliction
See Nº. 25.

The death of an esteemed relative, in a foreign land, is thus noticed.
Lines on the death of my aunt Mrs. (Rev. Henry)
Kearney in Ireland
See Nº. 26.

A deeper appeal to maternal affection, is made in the ensuing lines, written in the Algonquin on the occasion of separation from her children in[?] placing[?] them[?] at xxxxxxxxx xxx.

On leaving my children John and Jane at School,
in the
Atlantic states, and preparing to return to the
interior.
1839.
Nº. 28. See Personal Memoirs.
In 1828 it was evident that her health was fast sinking and a boat voyage on lake Superior was resorted [to]. Its inspiring views were moving and invigorating. And the habit of her life, of resorting to her pen, did not forsake her.
On visiting a volcanic little island called Nebiquon
in the
entrance of lake Superior, 1828.
Here, in my native inland sea
Where wild magnificence extends,
From pain and sickness I would flee
And make these glorious all[?] my friends.
Here, for its xxxxxx island bright,
Where storms are[?] gone to sleep
Gladly I gather fresh delight,
Of stones[?] a shining heap

Lone island of the deep blue sea,
How vast is all, how grand how free!
Waves, water, rocks of xx xxxxxx,
Are bathed in one, broad beam of light.

And summer with the balmy heath[?]
Whisper the reign of peace
I am myself an atom here
And look into the blue profound
With fearful glance—for if a storm arise
The[?] storm[?] xxxx with his horrid cries
      And tempest breath,
Xxxxxx ready with xx xxxxxxx xx xxxxx
      To herald death:
How beautifully, the big waves roll, oh sea! oh sea!
Thus may not sins o'erwhelm and swallow me.

Requiem of an Indian maid sitting near the grave of
    her lover*

I heard a rustling in the leaves,
      I raised my eyes in fear,
I thought Thinking on him whose absence grieves
      And I heard[?] his footsteps near,
But no, it was a beauteous bird,
      A little bird of blue
That feasted near, whose wings I heard
      It was his spirit true
             It was a[?] this[?] bird—a bird of blue
             I saw my lover's xxxxxx spirit true.
That beauteous little bird of blue
      Began its little song.
"Grieve not fair maid, for I am true
      And shall not leave you long
For you, like me, shall shortly go
      To those enc[h]anted plains
Where joy there shall xxx xxxxxxxx xxxx xx be no further[?] woe
      And only pleasure reigns"
             It came in this bird—a bird of blue
             I saw my lover's spirit true.

*vide[?] Algic Researches [Editor's note: this song does not appear
in *Algic Researches*.]

    The Indians from the selection[?] of their village and burial sites,
have not been thought to want a true perception of the beautiful

and poetical in nature. The same inference is to be made from their pertinance and beauty of their names for places. Had, the Algonquins, indeed lacked all of the proof of this taste for the beautiful but that arising from the poetic attempts of the granddaughter of Wabojeeg, these would certainly attest their xxxxxxxess on this point. And if their history shall ever be written it would appear to be injustice or neglect to omit her name. It may be said that her blood judged[?] by a moiety[?] xxxxxx its[?] greater[?] enthusiasm[?] from the green isle of Erin—That once[?] The argument of xx xxxxxxx of xxxxxx of[?] a[?] similar ancestry, may[?] be urged, against the aborigine, the world[?] xxxx and it is questionable whether the whole history of poetry could ever dispense with it. War songs and choruses are were[?] the rough material of the[?] poetry[?] of ancients; music is a higher element of civilization and comes in to xxxx and soften the man into plastic strains.

[Note. The writer of the preceding extracts being the first wife [of] the author of these volumes, expired, suddenly, at Dundas, Canada West[?], while on a visit to her sister, Mrs (Revd[?] Wm) McMurray, in 1842, during the absence of her husband on a tour to England and the Continent.]

Dawn of Literary Composition by Educated Natives of the aboriginal tribes.
Text from *LC62*. Since the essay refers to HRS's *Personal Memoirs,* published in 1851, it must have been written in 1851 or later. The closing note makes it sound as if HRS intended the essay for the six-volume anthology of materials about Native America that he edited for the U.S. Congress, which was published from 1851–57.

By that time, HRS's paralysis often affected his handwriting, and perhaps for that reason, and because it is a rough draft, the manuscript is hard to read and transcribe. Through haste or slips of the pen, it often condenses words into something like abbreviations, leaving out one or more letters, especially at the ends of words, and it includes many crossouts and squeezed-in additions as well as revisions or additions on smaller pieces of paper (about a quarter of a page) pasted in to cover or to fold over and add to earlier passages. In this edited version, x-marks indicate illegible passages, and bracketed question marks indicate uncertain transcriptions. There may be transcription errors even on words without question marks, but the gist of the piece comes through. It did not seem worthwhile to include legible crossed out words, mainly because, in this manuscript, they do not make much difference, and also because readers of this particular document would probably prefer a readable text. Partly for that reason, I have usually spelled out abbreviated words, but also because in a manuscript with so many illegible or uncertainly legible letters, trying to represent spellings as they appear in the manuscript would introduce a misleading arbitrariness. Often, instead of copying JJS's writings, the manuscript refers to them by number with directions to insert them. The numbers usually but do not always match the numbers penciled onto the corresponding poems in *IL*. Perhaps they refer to a similar but different manuscript, or perhaps at some point the numbers in *IL* were changed.

Appendix 4

Misattributions and Potential Misattributions

This appendix lists writings that have been attributed to Jane Johnston Schoolcraft inaccurately and writings that could understandably be mistaken for her work. The list begins with misattributions centering on *The Literary Voyager* and then moves on to misattributions and potential misattributions that appear elsewhere. Because scholars have relied on Philip P. Mason's edition of *The Literary Voyager*, the small number of misattributions or unclear attributions in that volume have led to confusions. Page numbers for *The Literary Voyager* are for the Mason edition; the *Literary Voyager* manuscripts are in LC64, LC65, and LC66.

• "Character of Aboriginal Historical Tradition," unsigned (5-7): This letter is translated but not written by Jane Schoolcraft. See the annotations to the letter in this edition.

• "Native Comity," signed "R. A. Native" (48): Mason's annotation says: "This statement may have been made by Mrs. John Johnston or one of her daughters" (176). From there, Jeremy Mumford has concluded: "The author is not identified but is probably Jane writing as Rosa, since no other name beginning with "R" appears in the magazine" (9). On the contrary, this letter was surely not written by Jane Schoolcraft or by any other members of the Johnston family. There were many other Natives around besides the Johnstons, to say the least. There are also many names that begin with R, regardless whether they appear elsewhere in the magazine, but there is no reason to suppose that this particular Native person's name begins with R, for "R. A. Native" is only a weakly punning pseudonym. The letter opens with these words: "I am an Indian, and although I do not pretend to the knowledge of politeness, I mean that sort which regards domestic manners, yet I believe there is a native politeness . . . in every human breast; and that an Indian feels it, and exercises it." None of the Johnstons could have written or spoken such disclaimers about their own proud fluency in European politeness or domestic manners. Such a statement would have been inconceivable for them.

• "Algonac, a Chippewa Lament on Hearing the Reveille at the Post of St. Mary's" (87-89): Mason says: "The author of this poem is not known. It was probably one of the Johnstons, perhaps George" (178). The actual author is Henry Schoolcraft. The issue of *The Literary Voyager* with this poem appeared in early February 1827. A manuscript of the poem appears in LC69 among Henry's poems and in Henry's hand, dated February 1. At that time, George Johnston was far away in LaPointe. Henry also included the poem in one of his books of poetry, *Indian Melodies* (13-15). (Attributed to "Daoemtas," a version of—or misprint for—one of Henry's pseudonyms, Damoetas, it also appears in the *American Eagle Magazine,* 1847, edited by Jane and Henry's son, John Johnston Schoolcraft.)

• "The Otagamiad" (138-42): This poem, which Mason attributes to Jane Schoolcraft (182-83), appears instead to be by Henry Schoolcraft. Based on the Mason edition of *The Literary Voyager,* it has attracted a fair amount of attention as Jane Schoolcraft's work and has been reprinted in anthologies of writing by women. Mason's attribution to Jane looks suspect even within the context of his edition. Although it is about her grandfather, it is otherwise the only poem that he attributes to Jane Schoolcraft without offering evidence that she wrote it. It also looks conspicuously incomplete, ending in the middle of the story, as if the rest of the poem were planned for a later issue and then displaced by the focus, especially in the next issue, on William Henry Schoolcraft's death. As it happens, a manuscript draft of the poem appears among Henry's poems and in Henry's hand in LC69, confirming that the version in *The Literary Voyager* is only the first half of the poem. The poem is much more in Henry's style than in Jane's. Like many of Henry's (mostly unpublished) poems on Indian and other topics, and like no other poem attributable to Jane, it aspires to an epic sound. (The title, "The Otagamiad," echoes Homer's *Iliad* and Virgil's *Aeneid.*) It also focuses on political debate in a way that fits Henry's interests and poetic habits but differs from Jane's. More subjectively, I would suggest that it sounds too "Indian" for a poem by Jane Schoolcraft, in the sense that it fits the high-adventure romance that the Henry Schoolcrafts of the world wanted and still want to see in Indian people, in contrast to Jane Schoolcraft's poetic preoccupations with the profoundly ordinary events of daily life. Even in her address to "the republic" in "The Contrast," she speaks to how the domestic and personal figure the geographically larger entities not as a way to grant the domestic and personal greater authority, but—in a more soft-spoken tone—as a way to understanding the greater authority that the domestic and personal already hold.

• "Woman's Tears" (159): This poem, which *The Literary Voyager* attributes to "J. J.," Mason correctly attributes to John Johnston (184). One scholar has assumed, probably by accident, that the J. J. stands for Jane Johnston (Ruoff 84), but as Mason notes, the poem appears among John Johnston's poems in Henry Schoolcraft's papers (LC70). By this date, 1827, Jane Schoolcraft—married and living under the name Schoolcraft since 1823—would never sign herself J. J.

• Devotional songs and poems. The Henry Rowe Schoolcraft Papers in the Library of Congress include a bound volume of what might appear to be religious poems by Jane Schoolcraft (LC70). The volume is in her hand, carefully transcribed with a table of contents listing 68 poems. (The last three items in the table of contents are missing from the back of the volume.) I believe, however, that Schoolcraft copied these materials rather than writing them herself. Her other manuscripts never include materials from this volume or any similar materials. If she had she written them herself, then other manuscripts of some of them would probably survive among her other papers or among other people's copies of her writings. Many of the texts in this volume begin by identifying a familiar tune that the words then fit, revealing that they are song lyrics rather than poems. Many of the tunes are recognizable as popular airs of the day, and some of the texts come with dates. Several of the dates follow a two-digit system for indicating the year (20, 18, 17) that is not clear but probably means 1820, 1818, and 1817, and those that are clear include one from 1811, two from 1815, one from 1816, and two from 1820. One is dated "Delgany July 9th 1816." Schoolcraft could not have been in Delgany, Ireland in 1816, when she lived at Sault Ste. Marie. While she could perhaps have written poems or lyrics such as these in 1820, at the age of twenty, she certainly could not have written them in 1811, and it seems highly unlikely that she could have written them in 1815 or 1816. All this suggests that she made a copy of someone else's song book. I have tried to identify the song book, or even a similar song book, without success.

• Among Jane Schoolcraft's poems in LC70 appear two manuscripts of an "Epitaph on Miss Jane Martin," in Jane Schoolcraft's hand, which could lead readers to suppose that she wrote it. But another manuscript of the poem appears in Henry's hand among Henry's transcriptions of John Johnston's poems, also in LC70, which suggests that it was written by John Johnston rather than by Jane Schoolcraft.

• Mentor L. Williams remarks that the story "The Red Lover," from *AR*, first "appeared as 'Love and War' in [Henry] Schoolcraft's *Travels in the Central Mississippi Valley*," where, Williams says, Henry "specifically attributes this story to Jane Johnston, p. 426" (45). Actually, the attribution is for the song at the end of the story, not for the story. The song appears in this volume under the title "Song for a Lover Killed in Battle." Because Henry specifically attributes the song and not the story to Jane, it would appear that she did not write the story, though she may still have translated or helped translate it.

• The guide to the Henry Rowe Schoolcraft Papers in the Library of Congress mistakenly attributes a set of John Johnston's poems in LC70 to Jane Johnston (*Henry Rowe Schoolcraft: A Register*). The latest revision of the guide corrects this error.

• In a letter from Melancthon C. Woolsey to JJS, 3 July 1831, quoted in the annotations to "On the Doric Rock, Lake Superior," Woolsey writes that "The forest resounded with 'the sweet notes of the summer birds [#]", and then below, at the bottom of the page, he adds the following note "[# Mrs. Schoolcraft, I suspect, published in the Detroit Journal]". I have not found this item in the *Detroit Journal* or anywhere else.

• "Lament," a poem by Amelia Opie, appears without attribution in a manuscript in Jane Schoolcraft's hand (LC19), which has led to the inaccurate conclusion that it was written by Jane Schoolcraft. (See the "Introduction," note 36.)

• The Illinois manuscript of Jane Schoolcraft's poems (described in Appendix 1) includes two poems from Henry Schoolcraft's *Indian Melodies* (1830), which could therefore easily be misattributed to Jane Schoolcraft. See the editorial note at the end of Henry's introduction to the Illinois manuscript.

Appendix 5

List of Less Substantive Variants

The annotations below are included for any use they might provide, though they are likely to carry less interest than the annotations in the body of the text.

To the Pine Tree. Ojibwe text: **1** Faint quotation marks are penciled in before the first and after the second "Shing wauk!" **17** *ait*: editor's emendation of "Ait," supposing that the upper-case "A" is accidentally left over from before the addition of "Ween."

To the Miscodeed. **10** The manuscript has a period after the dash, perhaps by accident.

Lines written at Castle Island, Lake Superior. Beneath the title, *IL* has the year "1838." "Dawn" gives the date twice. The first appears to be 1828, with the 2 written over a 3; the second is 1828, which must be an error.

Invocation To my Maternal Grandfather, Wabojeeg, *on hearing his descent misrepresented. Shorter draft.* **19** *child's*: editor's emendation of "childs." *Longer draft.* **11** *band*: written above "ranks", which is crossed out. **22** *loud*: it appears that "loved" has been written over to say "loud."

Lines to a Friend Asleep. **3** In the right margin, *LC70-2* has "a beautiful ing" ("ing" is an uncertain transcription). **12** *figured*: above the "e" is an apostrophe, either accidental or meant to replace the "e," with the "e" retained by accident. **14** Before this line, *LC70-2* has crossed out "All nature se" ("se" is an uncertain transcription). **16** *pleasing*: charming *LC70-1* and *LC70-2*. **17** indented *IL*. **18** *forth*: forth now ("forth" might be crossed out) *LC70-2*. **22** *Am*: the upper case A is written on top of a lower case a.

By an Ojibwa Female *Pen, Invitation to sisters to a walk in the Garden, after a shower.* **9** *whisp'ring*: whispery *LC70*. **12** *sorrow's*: editor's emendation of "sorrows".

Pensive Hours. **15** *IL* begins a new stanza here. **16** *and*: of *IL*. **17** *slowing*: slowly *IL*. **19** *—and*: Soon *IL*. **27** *IL* begins a new stanza here. **29** *Till*: When *IL*. **30** "breath of" is crossed out between "soft" and "balmy." **31** *breeze*: wind *IL*. **33** *Softer*: As softer *IL*. **38** *and*: written above "with", which is crossed out just before "mankind"; *IL* has "with". **39** *that*: editor's emendation of "that that". **42** *should*: might *IL*. **44** *sublime*: editor's emendation of "sumblime"; *IL* has "sublime."

The Contrast, a Splenetic Effusion. **4** In pleasures sweet my hours then flew— *LC70-1*. **9** *been*: *LC35* has "felt" crossed out and "been" written above it. **9** *one*: a *LC70-1*. **22** The source—from which, flow'd all my ease *LC70-1*. The source from which, sprang all my ease! *LC35*. **26** *love's*: editor's emendation of "loves". **34** *fancy's*: Fancy's *LC70-1* and *LC35*.

On Henry's Birthday. **2** The end-line punctuation is not clear and might be a semicolon or exclamation point. **5** *gave*: added above the line.

Absence. Nindahwaymau. **9** *woody*: the "d" is an uncertain transcription. *Neezhicka.* **8** *I am*: am I *IL*. **12** *To heav'n I breathe*: I breathe to heaven *IL*. *Neenawbame.* **10** The question mark looks more like an exclamation mark or a colon, but is probably meant as a question mark. **11** *in stillness*: in the stillness *LC70*. **13** *pray'r*: editor's emendation of praye'r. *Ningwisis.* **1** *spies*: aspies *IL*. **3** *crys*: cries *IL*. **3** *Papa*: papa *IL*. **3** closing quotation mark included by editor's emendation.

Resignation [1]. **1** *opprest*: oppressed *LC70*. **2** *LC70* has no commas after "gay" and "scenes". **3** *cherish'd*: cherished *LC70*. **4** *mind—*: mind *LC70*. **4** *exclamation point*: period *LC70*. **5** *Faith,*: Faith *LC70*. **6** *Resignation*: resignation *LC70*. **6** *semicolon*: colon *LC70*.

A Metrical Jeu d'esprit, designed as an invitation to a whist party. title the "i" and "c" of "Metrical" are written together and look more like a dotted "c". **15** An open parenthesis comes before "most," but there is no closing parenthesis. The manuscript in HRS's hand has no parentheses here.

Elegy on the death of my son William Henry, at St. Mary's. On the first page (stanzas 1–6), stanza numbers are fit tightly in what would ordinarily be stanza breaks, as if the numbers were an afterthought. The manuscript has no period after the stanza numbers for stanzas 1, 5, 7, and 8. **12** *thee*: theee *IL*. **23** *in*: the manuscript is faint here, so that "in" might not be the correct reading. **24** *so*: in faint pencil, replacing "do," which is crossed out.

Sonnet. **4** *he*: it *LC70, IL*. **5** *he*: it *LC70, IL*. **8** *can*: could *LC70*. **8** *my*: that *LC70*.

To my ever beloved and lamented son William Henry. **2** *cheek*: cheeks *Bentley*. **6** *in*: to *IL*. **36** The period is added by editorial emendation. **38** *has*: hath *IL*. **39** *tender, beauteous*: beautious, tender *IL*.

Sweet Willy. At the bottom, on the left, is written "1826", which is crossed out. **7** The word "left" is added above the line.

Language Divine! **10** *soothe*: editor's emendation of "sooth".

"As watchful spirits in the night." **12** *Saviour's*: editor's emendation of "Saviours".**18** The apostrophe and period are not in the manuscript but are added to match line 9.

On Meditation. **1** indented *IL*. **1** *dash*: exclamation mark *IL*. **2** *period*: no end-line punctuation *IL*. **3** *Beautifully the*: Beautifully, the *IL* **3** no end-line punctuation *IL*. **5** no end-line punctuation *IL*. **7** no end-line punctuation *IL*. **9** new stanza with indentation *IL*. **9** *scene*: scene, *IL*. **11** *then*: then, *IL*. **13** *ear, and*: ear and *IL*. **13** no end-line punctuation *IL*. **14** *To truths you always*: The truths you ever *IL*. **15** *reason's*: editor's emendation of "reasons", in accord with *IL*. **17** *me*: me, *IL*. **18** no end-line punctuation *IL*. **20** *will sure display his*: will pour a father's *IL*. **21** *While I*: As I, *IL*. **22** no end-line punctuation *IL*. **23** *content*: content, *IL*. **23** *year;*: year, *IL*. **24** *nought*: naught *IL*.

"Welcome, welcome to my arms." **2** *life's*: editor's emendation of "lifes". **4** end-line punctuation not clear. **8** *unisons*: editor's emendation of "unisions".

A Psalm. English translation. **2** Before "made" are two hard-to-read, crossed-out words, perhaps "presented us". **4** The first "by" is added above the line. **6** Before "hail", "snow and" is crossed out. **7** "erect" appears above "up," and a caret appears faintly beneath "up," as if "erect" were being considered as an option for "up." **8** *for*: editor's emendation of "four". **8** "faith in" is added above the line. **11** The first "us" is added above the line. **12** "us" is added above the line. **19** "thy Son's" and "so be it" are added above the line.

On reading Miss Hannah Moore's Christian morals and Practical Piety. 1816. title **1** *shew:* show *IL.* **6** *comma:* editor's emendation of a period. **12** *my:* a *IL.* **16** *fulfill:* fulfil *IL.*

Stanzas. The punctuation at the ends of lines is not clear. Lines 2, 5, 6, and 10 might end with a period.

Elegy On the death of my aunt Mrs Kearny. title the words "my aunt" and "Kilgobbin Glebe" are added above the line. "Ireland" is abbreviated as "I." **11** "a" is crossed out between "by" and "term." **14** *E'er felt:* written above a crossed-out, illegible word or words, perhaps "Expands." **15** "and" is crossed out between "reading" and "by"; perhaps HRS meant instead to cross out "by." **16** "and" (as an ampersand) is crossed out and another word is written above it, but "and" is retained here because the other word is illegible.

The Origin of the Robin. painted with vermillion: the word "painted" appears twice in succession in the manuscript. *dwellings:* editor's emendation of dwelling's.

Moowis, The Indian Coquette. and that he was going: "that" is written above "told him", which is crossed out.

Mishösha, or the Magician and his daughters. title The umlaut in "Mishösha" appears in the title but not in the text. As an afterthought HRS appears to have added "or Legend" after "A Chippewa Tale." "A Chippewa Tale" appears in brackets, with the first bracket crossed out. In *WJ* it is in parentheses. Under the title, "No. 1" is crossed out; presumably it indicated the first of two installments.

The Forsaken Brother. A Chippewa Tale. "Never, never'": WJ and Jameson; *LC65* reads "'Never, never'!" *below the trees:* WJ reads "behind the trees"; Jameson reads "down behind the trees." *no to:* WJ, Gilman, and Jameson; *LC65* reads "no: to". *were not prohibited:* WJ reads "are not prohibited". *do nothing:* WJ; *LC65* reads "no nothing." *myeengunish!:* all other texts have a "w" where *LC65* has an "s."

Origin of the Miscodeed. or the Maid of Taquimenon. reveling: editor's emendation of revelling. *bless:* written in HRS's hand above a crossed-out word.

leap and: written, possibly in HRS's hand, above the line. *hate*: written in HRS's hand above "good", which is crossed out. *enemy*: written in HRS's hand above "captor", which is crossed out. *hurry and fear*: in the manuscript, "which"—crossed out—comes before "fear", and another crossed out word, perhaps "executed", comes after "fear". *When the friends*: "When" is written—in a hand that could be either the copyist's or HRS's—above the line after "And", which is crossed out. *border*: written in HRS's hand above the line. *destined*: (not a certain transcription) is written in HRS's hand above another hard-to-read word, perhaps "supposed", which is crossed out.

The Three Cranberries. were sisters: "three" is added and then crossed out between "were" and "sisters." While quotation marks surround each cranberry's use of "I," the quotation marks are left out in the remainder of each sentence beginning with "I." They have been added silently both here and in *AR*. *shingoup*: spruce (as noted in *AR*). *hominy*: editor's emendation of "hommony." *Presently the Wolves*: editor's emendation of "Presently the Wolfes."

The Little Spirit, or Boy-Man. imagine: editor's emendation for immagine. *The boy's Sister*: editor's emendation for "They boy's Sister".

*The Literal Translation of a Young Ojibway Girl's Song. title immediately to the right of the title, in another hand, appears ", by Mrs. S." and then an illegible word. *Ojibway Girl*: Chippewa girl (Jameson). *long for her, for as soon as he sees her out of her sight*: for her long: as soon as she is out of sight (Jameson).

A mother's lament for the absence of a child. Ojibwe text. **5** *goom*: editor's emendation of "goon". **18** *period*: added by editor's emendation. *English text.* *1.*: period added by editor's emendation.

WORKS CITED

A Note on Sources

Citations to LC refer to the Henry Rowe Schoolcraft Papers, Manuscript Division, Library of Congress, Washington, D.C., which I have accessed on microfilm. Materials from these papers that are not included elsewhere in this volume are cited by storage container; LC66, for example, refers to container 66.

Abrams, M. H. "The Correspondent Breeze: A Romantic Metaphor." *The Correspondent Breeze: Essays on English Romanticism*. New York: Norton, 1984. 25–43.

Allen, James. "Journal of Lieutenant James Allen. 1833–34. In Mason, *Schoolcraft's Expedition*. 164–231.

Anderson, Rufus. *Memoir of Catharine Brown, a Christian Indian of the Cherokee Nation*. Boston: S.T. Armstrong, and Crocker and Brewster; New York: J.P. Haven, 1825.

Apess, William. *On Our Own Ground: The Complete Writings of William Apess, a Pequot*. Ed. and intro. Barry O'Connell. Amherst: University of Massachusetts Press, 1992.

Audrain, François [Frances]. Letter to George Johnston. 27 Mar. 1827. George Johnston Papers, Burton Historical Collection, Detroit Public Library.

Ball, John. *Autobiography of John Ball*. Glendale, Calif.: Arthur H. Clark, 1925.

Baraga, Frederic. *A Dictionary of the Ojibway Language*. 2nd ed., 1878-80. Rpt. with foreword by John D. Nichols. St. Paul: Minnesota Historical Society Press, 1992.

Barnouw, Victor. *Wisconsin Chippewa Myths & Tales and Their Relation to Chippewa Life*. Madison: University of Wisconsin Press, 1977.

Bauman, Richard. "The Nationalization and Internationalization of Folklore: The Case of Schoolcraft's 'Gitshee Gauzinee.'" *Western Folklore* 52 (April 1992): 247–69.

Bellin, Joshua David. *The Demon of the Continent: Indians and the Shaping of American Literature.* Philadelphia: University of Pennsylvania Press, 2001.

Bennett, Paula Bernat. *Poets in the Public Sphere: The Emancipatory Project of American Women's Poetry, 1800–1900.* Princeton, N.J.: Princeton University Press, 2003.

Bieder, Robert E. *Science Encounters the Indian, 1820–1880: The Early Years of American Ethnology.* Norman: University of Oklahoma Press, 1986.

Bigsby, John J. *The Shoe and Canoe or Pictures of Travel in the Canadas.* 2 vols. London: Chapman and Hall, 1850.

Bingham, Abel. "Journal Concerning My Labours at Sault Ste. Marie." Ms. Clarke Historical Library, Central Michigan University, Mount Pleasant.

Birk, Douglas A. "John Sayer and the Fond du Lac Trade: The North West Company in Minnesota and Wisconsin." In *Rendezvous: Selected Papers of the Fourth North American Fur Trade Conference, 1981,* ed. Thomas C. Buckley. St. Paul, Minn.: North American Fur Trade Conference, 1984. 51–61.

Bowers, Fredson. "Some Principles for Scholarly Editions of Nineteenth-Century American Authors." *Studies in Bibliography* 17 (1964): 223–38.

Brazer, Marjorie Cahn. *Harps upon the Willows: The Johnston Family of the Old Northwest.* Ed. Historical Society of Michigan. Ann Arbor: Historical Society of Michigan, 1993.

Bremer, Richard G. *Indian Agent and Wilderness Scholar: The Life of Henry Rowe Schoolcraft.* Mount Pleasant: Clarke Historical Library, Central Michigan University, 1987.

Brittain, Julie, and Marguerite MacKenzie. Introduction to Umayichis, *Voices from Four Directions.* Ed. Brian Swann. Lincoln: University of Nebraska Press, 2004. 572-79.

Brooks, Joanna. *American Lazarus: Religion and the Rise of African-American and Native American Literatures.* New York: Oxford University Press, 2003.

———. "Six Hymns by Samson Occom." *Early American Literature* 38, 1 (2003): 67–87.

Brown, Jennifer S. H. *Strangers in Blood: Fur Trade Company Families in Indian Country.* Vancouver: University of British Columbia Press, 1980.

Buffalohead, Priscilla K. "Farmers, Warriors, Traders: A Fresh Look at Ojibway Women." *Minnesota History* 48 (Summer 1983): 236–44.

Burton, Frederick R. *American Primitive Music, with Especial Attention to the Songs of the Ojibways.* New York: Moffat, 1909.

Campbell, Thomas. *The Complete Poetical Works of Thomas Campbell.* Ed. J. Logie Robertson. London: Oxford University Press, 1907.

Cass, Lewis. Letter to John C. Calhoun, Secretary of War, 17 June 1820. *The Territorial Papers of the United States.* Vol. 11, *The Territory of Michigan, 1820–1829.* Ed. Clarence Edwin Carter. Washington, D.C.: GPO, 1943. 36–37.

Catalogue of the Books, Pamphlets, Autograph Letters, Original Manuscripts, Documents, &c., Belonging to the Late Henry R. Schoolcraft: the Indian Historian, and to Mrs. Schoolcraft, Lately Deceased. New York: Bangs, 1880.

Chapman, C. H. "The Historic Johnston Family of the Soo." *Michigan Pioneer and Historical Collections* (title listed in multiple ways) 23 (1903): 305–53.

Chapone, Mrs. [Hester]. *Miscellanies in Prose and Verse, by Mrs. Chapone.* Dublin: J. Williams, W. Wilson, and R. Moncrieffe, 1775.

Charvat, William. *The Profession of Authorship in America, 1800–1870.* 1968. New York: Columbia University Press, 1992.

Chute, Janet E. *The Legacy of Shingwaukonse: A Century of Native Leadership.* Toronto: University of Toronto Press, 1998.

———. "Shingwaukonse: A Nineteenth-Century Innovative Ojibwa Leader." *Ethnohistory* 45, 1 (Winter 1998): 65–101.

Cleland, Charles C. [E.]. "Cass, Sassaba and Ozhaw-guscoday-wa-g[q]uay: History, Ethnohistory and Historical Reality." In *Entering the 90s: The North American Experience,* ed. Thomas E. Schirer. Sault Ste. Marie, Mich.: Lake Superior State University Press, 1991. 74–81.

Cleland, Charles E. *The Place of the Pike (Gnoozhekaaning): A History of the Bay Mills Indian Community.* Ann Arbor: University of Michigan Press, 2001.

Clements, William M. *Native American Verbal Art: Texts and Contexts.* Tuscon: University of Arizona Press, 1996.

Coleridge, Samuel Taylor. "Dejection: An Ode." *The Complete Poems.* Ed. William Keach. London: Penguin, 1997. 307–11.

———. "The Eolian Harp." *The Complete Poems.* Ed. William Keach. London: Penguin, 1997. 87–88.

Colton, C[alvin]. *Tour of the American Lakes and among the Indians of the North-West Territory, in 1830: Disclosing the Character and Prospects of the Indian Race.* London: Frederick Westley and A.H. Davis, 1833.

Cornell, George L. "The Imposition of Western Definitions of Literature on Indian Oral Traditions." In *The Native in Literature,* ed. Thomas King, Cheryl Calver, and Helen Hoy. Oakville, Ont.: ECW Press, 1987.

Cox, Ross. *Adventures on the Columbia River including the Narrative of a Residence of Six Years on the Western Side of the Rocky Mountains, among the Various Tribes of Indians Hitherto Unknown: Together with a Journey across the American Continent.* London: Henry Colburn and Richard Bentley, 1831.

Daoemtas [Henry Rowe Schoolcraft]. "Algonac. A Chippewa Lament: On Hearing the Reveille at the Post on St. Mary's." *American Eagle Magazine: A Journal, Dedicated to Science, Art, and Literature* (June 1847): 5–7.

Darnell, Regna. *And Along Came Boas: Continuity and Revolution in Americanist Anthropology.* Amsterdam: John Benjamins, 1998.

Delafield, Joseph. *The Unfortified Boundary: A Diary of the First Survey of the Canadian Boundary Line from St. Regis to the Lake of the Woods by Major Joseph Delafield.* Ed. Robert McElroy and Thomas Riggs. New York: privately printed, 1943.

Densmore, Frances. *Chippewa Music.* Bureau of American Ethnology. Bulletins 45 and 53. Washington: GPO, 1910, vol. 1; 1913, vol. 2.

Doty, James Duane. "Papers of James Duane Doty. Official Journal, 1820. Expedition with Cass and Schoolcraft." *Collections of the State Historical Society of Wisconsin* 13 (1895): 163–246.

Dougherty, Peter. "Diaries of Peter Dougherty, Volume I." Intro. Charles A. Anderson. *Journal of the Presbyterian Historical Society* 30, 2 (June 1952): 95–114.

Franchère, G. *Relation d'un voyage à la côte du nord-ouest de l'Amérique Septentrionale.* . . . Montreal: C.B. Pasteur, 1820.

Franchère, Gabriel. *Narrative of a Voyage to the Northwest Coast of America.* . . . 1854. Trans. and ed. J. V. Huntington. Chicago: Lakeside Press, 1954.

Freeman, John Finley. "Religion and Personality in the Anthropology of Henry Schoolcraft." *Journal of the History of the Behavioral Sciences* 1, 4 (Oct. 1965): 301–11.

Fuller, Margaret. *Summer on the Lakes, in 1843.* 1844. Urbana: University of Illinois Press, 1991.

Gaskell, Philip. *A New Introduction to Bibliography*. New York: Oxford University Press, 1972.

Gilbert, Angie Bingham. "A Basket of Fragments, Being a collection of sketches and incidents of half a century ago, drawn from personal recollection, or as given me in early childhood." *Reminiscences & Sketches, Old Sault*. Book Second. Ms. Abel Bingham Papers, Clarke Historical Library, Central Michigan University, Mount Pleasant.

———. "Synopsis of paper read at Mrs. Hamilton's Missionary meeting." *Reminiscences & Sketches, Old Sault*. Book No. 3. Ms. Abel Bingham Papers, Clarke Historical Library, Central Michigan University, Mount Pleasant.

———. "A Tale of Two Cities." *Michigan Pioneer and Historical Collections* 29 (1901): 322–37.

Gilbert, Mrs. Thomas B. (Angie Bingham Gilbert). "Memories of the 'Soo.'" *Grand Rapids Sunday Herald*, 8 October 1899. *Michigan Pioneer and Historical Collections* 30 (1903): 623–33.

Gilman, Chandler Robbins. Letter to Henry Rowe Schoolcraft, 14 April 1839. LC17.

———. *Life on the Lakes: Being Tales and Sketches Collected During a Trip to the Pictured Rocks of Lake Superior*. 2 vols. New York: Goorse Dearborn, 1836.

Goldstein, Laurence. *Ruins and Empire: The Evolution of a Theme in Augustan and Romantic Literature*. Pittsburgh: University of Pittsburgh Press, 1977.

Gray, Janet. *Race and Time: American Women's Poetics from Antislavery to Racial Modernity*. Iowa City: University of Iowa Press, 2004.

Greg, W. W. "The Rationale of Copy-Text." *Studies in Bibliography* 3 (1950–51): 19–36. Rpt. in Greg, *The Collected Papers*, J. C. Maxwell. Oxford: Oxford University Press, 1966. 374–91.

Grimm's Household Tales. With the Author's Notes. Trans. and ed. Margaret Hunt. 2 vols. London: George Bell, 1884.

Hallowell, A. Irving. "The Beginnings of Anthropology in America." In *Selected Papers from the American Anthropologist 1888–1920*, ed. Frederica de Laguna. Evanston, Ill.: Row, Peterson, 1960. 1–90.

———. "Concordance of Ojibwa Narratives in the Published Works of Henry R. Schoolcraft." *Journal of American Folklore* 59, 242 (April–June 1946): 136–53.

———. "Myth, Culture, and Personality." *American Anthropologist* n.s. 29, 4, 1 (October–December 1947): 544–56.

Hambleton, Elizabeth. "John Johnston and Oshauguscodaywayquay." In Hambleton and Stoutamire, 1–24.

Hambleton, Elizabeth, and Elizabeth Warren Stoutamire, eds. *The John Johnston Family of Sault Ste. Marie.* N.p.: John Johnston Family Association, 1992.

Helbig, Alethea K., ed. *Nanabozhoo: Giver of Life.* Brighton, Mich.: Green Oak Press, 1987.

Henry Rowe Schoolcraft: A Register of His Papers in the Library of Congress. Prep. Edwin A. Thompson and others. Rev. Harry G. Heiss. Rev. ed. Washington, D.C.: Manuscript Division, Library of Congress, 1999.

Hochbruck, Wolfgang and Beatrix Dudensing-Reichel. "'Honoratissimi Benefactores': Native American Students and Two Seventeenth-Century Texts in the University Tradition." *Studies in American Indian Literatures* n.s. 4, 2–3 (Summer–Fall 1992): 35–47.

Houghton, Douglass. Letter to Richard Houghton, 15 June 1831, "Trip to Sault Ste[.] Marie, 1831." Ed. and intro. Philip P. Mason. *Michigan History* 39, 4 (December 1955): 474–80.

Huddleston, David. "Saurin, William (1757–1839)." *Oxford Dictionary of National Biography.* Oxford: Oxford University Press, 2004. 11 May 2005.

Hymes, Dell. *"In vain I tried to tell you": Essays in Native American Ethnopoetics.* Philadelphia: University of Pennsylvania Press, 1981.

"Indian Ladies." *Cherokee Phoenix,* 21 July 1828: 3.

Irigaray, Luce. "Commodities Among Themselves." In *This Sex Which Is Not One.* 1977. Trans. Carolyn Burke. Ithaca, N.Y.: Cornell University Press, 1985. 192–97.

Jameson, (Anna Brownell). *Winter Studies and Summer Rambles in Canada.* 3 vols. London: Saunders and Otley, 1838.

———. Letter to Charlotte [Johnston] McMurray, 26 August 1837. Ms. Col. 47 (Henry Sproatt Collection), Box 3, Thomas Fisher Rare Book Library, Toronto.

Johnson, Joseph. *To Do Good to My Indian Brethren: The Writings of Joseph Johnson, 1751–1776.* Ed. Laura J. Murray. Amherst: University of Massachusetts Press, 1998.

Johnston, Anna Maria. Letter to Jane Johnston Schoolcraft, 16 October 1833. LC38.

Johnston, Basil. *Ojibway Heritage.* New York: Columbia University Press, 1976.

Johnston, George. Letter "To the public of the state of Michigan," 16 July 1844. Bentley Historical Library, University of Michigan, Ann Arbor.

——, trans. *The Morning and Evening Prayer, Translated from the Book of Common Prayer of the Protestant Episcopal Church in the United States of America, Together with a Selection of Hymns.* Detroit: Geiger & Christian, 1844.

——. Notebooks. Ms. Bayliss Public Library, Sault Ste. Marie, Michigan.

——. "Reminiscences by Geo. Johnston, of Sault Ste. Marie." 2nd ed. *Michigan Pioneer and Historical Collections* 12 (1908): 605–11.

Johnston, John. "An Account of Lake Superior." In *Les Bourgeois de la Compagnie du Nord-Ouest: Récits de Voyages, Lettres, et Rapports Inédits Relatifs au Nord-Ouest Canadien*, ed. L. R. Masson. Québec: Imprimerie Générale Coté et Cie, 1890. 2: 143–74.

——. "Autobiographical Letters of the Late John Johnston, Esq., of the Falls of St. Mary's, Michigan." Introductory Remarks by Henry R. Schoolcraft, 1844. *Michigan Pioneer and Historical Collections* 32 (1903): 328–53.

——. Letter [to Sir George Drummond], 7 March 1816. Record Group 8, I: 91. Library and Archives Canada.

——. Letter to George Johnston, 8 August 1814. George Johnston Papers, Burton Historical Collection, Detroit Public Library.

——. Letter to George Johnston, 15 June 1817. George Johnston Papers, Burton Historical Collection, Detroit Public Library.

——. Letter to George Johnston. 30 October 1818. George Johnston Papers, Burton Historical Collection, Detroit Public Library.

——. Letter to David Trimble, 24 January 1822. LC84.

——. "Memorial of John Johnston to the Lords Commissioners." *Michigan Pioneer and Historical Collections* 25 (1896): 663.

——. *Poetic Remains of John Johnston Esqr.* LC70.

Johnston, Susan. "John Johnston's Administratrix." 24th Cong., 1st Sess., House of Representatives, Doc. 47, 7 Jan. 1836.

Johnstone, Anna M. "Recollections of One of the Old Houses of the Soo." Carbon ts. Johnston Family Papers, Bentley Historical Library, University of Michigan, Ann Arbor.

Kawbawgam, Charles, Charlotte Kawbawgam, and Jacques LePique. *Ojibwa Narratives of Charles and Charlotte Kawbawgam and Jacques LePique.* Ed.

Arthur P. Bourgeois. Recorded with notes by Homer H. Kidder. Detroit: Wayne State University Press, 1994.

Kinietz, Vernon. "Schoolcraft's Manuscript Magazines." *Papers of the Bibliographical Society of America* 35 (1941): 151–54.

Kinzie, Juliette M. *Wau-Bun: The "Early Day" in the North-West.* 1856. Urbana: University of Illinois Press, 1992.

Kroeber, Karl, ed. *Traditional Literatures of the American Indian: Texts and Interpretation.* Lincoln: University of Nebraska Press, 1981.

Landes, Ruth. *The Ojibwa Woman.* 1938. Lincoln: University of Nebraska Press, 1997.

Lavender, David. *The Fist in the Wilderness.* New York: Doubleday, 1964.

Lewis, Janet. *The Invasion: A Narrative of Events Concerning the Johnston Family of St. Mary's.* 1932. East Lansing: Michigan State University Press, 2000.

———. Libretto. *The Legend: The Story of Neengay, an Ojibway War Chief's Daughter, and the Irishman John Johnston.* Music by Bain Murray. Santa Barbara, Calif.: John Daniel, 1987.

Loeffelholz, Mary. *From School to Salon: Reading Nineteenth-Century American Women's Poetry.* Princeton, N.J.: Princeton University Press, 2004.

Longfellow, Henry Wadsworth. *Evangeline.* 1847. *Poems and Other Writings.* Ed. J. D. McClatchy. New York: Library of America, 2000. 57–115, 829–30.

———. *The Song of Hiawatha.* 1855. *Poems and Other Writings.* Ed. J. D. McClatchy. New York: Library of America, 2000. 141–279, 831–38.

Love, Harold. *The Culture and Commerce of Texts: Scribal Publication in Seventeenth-Century England.* 1993. Amherst: University of Massachusetts Press, 1998.

Love, W. DeLoss. *Samson Occom and the Christian Indians of New England.* 1899. Syracuse, N.Y.: Syracuse University Press, 2000.

Marryat, Captain Frederick. *Diary in America.* Ed. Jules Zanger. Bloomington: Indiana University Press, 1960.

Marsden, Michael T. "Henry Rowe Schoolcraft: A Reappraisal." *Old Northwest* 2, 2 (June 1976): 153–82.

Martineau, Harriet. *Society in America.* 3 vols. London: Saunders and Otley, 1837.

Mason, Philip P., ed. *Schoolcraft: The Literary Voyager or Muzzeniegun.* East Lansing: Michigan State University Press, 1962.

————, ed. *Schoolcraft's Expedition to Lake Itasca: The Discovery of the Source of the Mississippi.* East Lansing: Michigan State University Press, 1958.

[Mathews, Cornelius.] Preface. *The Indian Fairy Book: From the Original Legends.* By [Henry Rowe Schoolcraft.] New York: Mason Brothers, 1856.

McDonall, Robert. "Certificate of Lieut. Col. Robt. McDonall." *Michigan Pioneer and Historical Collections* 25 (1896): 664.

McDouall, Robert. Letter to Sir Gordon Drummond. 8 Mar. 1816. Record Group 8, I: 91, Library and Archives Canada.

McGann, Jerome J. *A Critique of Modern Textual Criticism.* Chicago: University of Chicago Press, 1983.

McKenney, Thomas L. *Sketches of a Tour to the Lakes, of the Character and Customs of the Chippewa Indians, and of Incidents Connected with the Treaty of Fond du Lac.* 1827. Barre, Mass.: Imprint Society, 1972.

McMurray, Charlotte Johnston. Notebooks. Ms. Owned by the Chippewa County Historical Society, Sault Ste. Marie, Michigan. Currently housed in River of History Museum, Sault Ste. Marie, Michigan.

McMurray, William. Letter to Jane Johnston Schoolcraft, 21 January 1838. LC43.

Medicine, Beatrice. *Learning to Be an Anthropologist and Remaining "Native": Selected Writings.* Urbana: University of Illinois Press, 2001.

Morton, W. L. "Sayer, Pierre-Guillaume." *Dictionary of Canadian Biography,* vol. 7. Toronto: University of Toronto Press, 1988.

Mumford, Jeremy. "Mixed-Race Identity in a Nineteenth-Century Family: The Schoolcrafts of Sault Ste. Marie, 1824–27." *Michigan Historical Review* 25, 1 (Spring 1999): 1–23.

Murphy, Lucy Eldersveld. *A Gathering of Rivers: Indians, Métis, and Mining in the Western Great Lakes, 1737–1832.* Lincoln: University of Nebraska Press, 2000.

Mylne, Vivienne. "The Punctuation of Dialogue in Eighteenth-Century French and British Fiction." *The Library* 6th ser. 1 (1979): 43–61.

Oneota, or The Red Race of America. Ed. Henry R. Schoolcraft. New York: Burgess Stringer, 1844–45.

Opie, Amelia. *Lamp for the Dead.* 2nd ed. London: Longman, Rees, Orme, Brown, Green, & Longman, 1840.

————. "Stanzas Written under Aeolus's Harp." *Poems by Mrs. Opie.* London: T. N. Longman and O. Rees, 1802. 131–24.

Osborn, Chase S. and Stellanova Osborn. *Schoolcraft—Longfellow—Hiawatha.* Lancaster, Pa.: Jaques Cattell Press, 1942.

Peastitute, John. "Umayichis." Trans. Julie Brittain, Alma Chemaganish, Marguerite MacKenzie, and Silas Nabinicaboo. In *Voices from Four Directions,* ed. Brian Swann. Lincoln: University of Nebraska Press, 2004. 580-90.

Perdue, Theda. "Native Women in the Early Republic: Old World Perceptions, New World Realities." In *Native Americans and the Early Republic,* ed. Frederick F. Hoxie, Ronald Hoffman, and Peter J. Albert. Charlottesville: University Press of Virginia, 1999. 85–122.

Peters, Bernard C. "John Johnston's 1822 Description of the Lake Superior Chippewa." *Michigan Historical Review* 20, 2 (Fall 1994): 25–46.

————. *Lake Superior Place Names: From Bawating to the Montreal.* Marquette: Northern Michigan University Press, 1996.

Petrino, Elizabeth A. *Emily Dickinson and Her Contemporaries: Women's Verse in America, 1820–1885.* Hanover, N.H.: University Press of New England, 1998.

Pizer, Donald. "On the Editing of Modern American Texts." *Bulletin of the New York Public Library* 75 (1971): 147–53.

Pope, Alexander. *The Poems of Alexander Pope.* Ed. John Butt. London: Methuen, 1963.

Porter, Jeremiah. Journal. Ms. Box 294, Chicago Historical Society Library.

Prevost, Sir George. Letter to John Johnston. 12 May 1814. Registrar General. Record Group 68, vol. 100, p. 100, Library and Archives Canada.

Radin, Paul. *The Trickster: A Study in American Indian Mythology.* 1956. New York: Schocken, 1972.

Radisson, Peter Esprit. *Voyages of Peter Esprit Radisson: Being an Account of His Travels and Experiences among the North American Indians, from 1652 to 1684.* Ed. Gideon D. Scull. Boston: Prince Society, 1885.

Ramsey, Jarold. *Reading the Fire: The Traditional Indian Literatures of America.* Rev. ed. Lincoln: University of Nebraska Press, 1999.

Ranta, Judith A. *The Life and Writings of Betsey Chamberlain: Native American Mill Worker.* Boston: Northeastern University Press, 2003.

"Religion Tames the Savage." *Cherokee Phoenix,* 5 Nov. 1828: 1.

Richards, Eliza. *Gender and the Poetics of Reception in Poe's Circle.* Cambridge: Cambridge University Press, 2004.

Rose, Wendy. "Just What's All This Fuss About White Shamanism Anyway?" In *Coyote Was Here: Essays on Contemporary Native American Literary and Political Mobilization*, ed. Bo Schöler. Special issue of *The Dolphin* 9 (1984): 13–24.

Rubin, Gayle. "The Traffic in Women: Notes on 'The Political Economy' of Sex." In *Toward an Anthropology of Women*, ed. Rayna R. Reiter. New York: Monthly Review Press, 1975. 157–210.

Ruoff, A. LaVonne Brown. "Early Native American Women Authors: Jane Johnston Schoolcraft, Sarah Winnemucca, S. Alice Callahan, E. Pauline Johnson, and Zitkala-Sa." In *Nineteenth-Century American Women Writers: A Critical Reader*, ed. Karen L. Kilcup. Oxford: Blackwell, 1998.

Sarris, Greg. *Keeping Slug Woman Alive: A Holistic Approach to American Indian Texts*. Berkeley: University of California Press, 1993.

Schoolcraft, Henry Rowe. *Algic Researches, Comprising Inquiries Respecting the Mental Characteristics of the North American Indians, First Series: Indian Tales and Legends*. 2 vols. New York: Harper & Brothers, 1839.

———. "Biographical Sketches of the Late John Johnston, Esq." Part 5. *Oneota*. 444–47.

———. "Castle Island." Ms. LC62.

———. "Dawn of Literary Composition by Educated Natives of the aboriginal tribes." Ms. LC62.

[———.] *The Enchanted Moccasins, and Other Legends of the Americans* [*sic*] *Indians*. [Ed.] Cornelius Mathews. New York: Putnam's, 1877.

[———.] *The Indian Fairy Book, from the Original Legends*. [Ed. Cornelius Mathews.] New York: Mason Brothers, 1856.

[———.] *Indian Melodies*. New York: Elam Bliss, 1830.

———. *Information Respecting the History, Conditions and Prospects of the Indian Tribes of the United States: Collected and Prepared Under the Direction of the Bureau of Indian Affairs*. Part 3. Philadelphia: Lippincott, Grambo, 1853.

———. Letter to C. C. Trowbridge. 5 Mar. 1827. C. C. Trowbridge Papers. Burton Historical Collection. Detroit Public Library.

———. "Memoir of John Johnston." Ed. J. Sharpless Fox. *Michigan Pioneer and Historical Collections* (title listed in multiple ways) 36 (1908): 53–90. Ms. LC63.

———. "Moowis, or the Indian Coquette." *Columbia Lady's and Gentleman's Magazine* 1 (1844), 90–91.

————. *The Myth of Hiawatha, and Other Oral Legends, Mythologic and Allegoric, of the North American Indians.* Philadelphia: J.B. Lippincott, 1856.

————. "Mythology, Superstition and Languages of the North American Indians." *Literary and Theological Review* 2 (March 1835): 96–121.

————. *Narrative Journal of Travels, through the Northwestern Regions of the United States Extending from Detroit through the Great Chain of American Lakes, to the Sources of the Mississippi River.* Albany, N.Y.: E. and E. Hosford, 1821.

————. *Narrative of an Expedition through the Upper Mississippi to Itasca Lake, the Actual Source of This River; Embracing an Exploratory Trip through the St. Croix and Burntwood (or Brule) Rivers; in 1832.* New York: Harper, 1834.

————. "Notes intended to be used in drawing up a biographical notice, or memoir of Mrs. Henry Rowe Schoolcraft." Ms. published as "Notes for Memoir of Mrs. Henry Rowe Schoolcraft by Henry Rowe Schoolcraft." Ed. J. Sharpless Fox. *Michigan Pioneer and Historical Collections* (title listed in multiple ways) 36 (1908): 95–100.

————, ed. *Oneóta, or The Red Race of America.* New York: Burgess, Stringer, 1844–45.

————. "Peboan und Siegwun, oder Winter und Frühling." *Magazin für die Literatur des Auslandes* 43 (1844): 172.

————. *Personal Memoirs of a Residence of Thirty Years with the Indian Tribes on the American Frontiers.* Philadelphia: Lippincott, Grambo, 1851.

————. "Private Journal of Henry Rowe Schoolcraft kept during his voyage from Prairie du Chien to Phil[adelphi]a 1825." [Philadelphia is an error for Sault Ste. Marie.] Ms. Rosenbach Museum and Library, Philadelphia, Pennsylvania.

————. "Pud-Wudschi-Inini, oder die Entstehung des Morgensterns." *Magazin für die Literatur des Auslandes* 45 (1844): 183–84.

————. "Der Roibe Schwan." *Magazin für die Literatur des Auslandes* 89 (1844): 353–54.

————. "Sketches of the Upper Peninsula. No. 5." Ms. LC63.

————. *Summary Narrative of an Exploratory Expedition to the Sources of the Mississippi River, in 1820: Resumed and Completed, by the Discovery of Its Origin in Itasca Lake, in 1832.* Philadelphia: Lippincott, Grambo, 1855.

————. *Travels in the Central Portions of the Mississippi Valley: Comprising Observations on Its Mineral Geography, Internal Resources, and Aboriginal Population.* New-York: Collins and Hannay, 1825.

————. "Waub Ojeeg or the Tradition of the Outagami and Chippewa History." Ms. LC64–65. Published in Mason, *Schoolcraft: The Literary Voyager* 23–26, 39–43, 50–56.

Schoolcraft, Jane Johnston. [As "the late Mrs. Henry R. Schoolcraft."] "Invocation to my Maternal Grand-father on hearing his descent from Chippewa ancestors misrepresented." *Southern Literary Messenger* (Jan. 1860): 31.

————. *Poetry, 1815–1836.* Ms. Illinois State Historical Library. Springfield.

[Schoolcraft, Henry Rowe and the Johnston family.] *A Vocabulary of the Ojibwa Language, 1822 & 1823.* Ms. LC61.

Schoolcraft, Mary E. Howard. [As "Mrs. Henry R. Schoolcraft."] *The Black Gauntlet: A Tale of Plantation Life in South Carolina.* Philadelphia: J. B. Lippincott, 1860.

Sanjek, Roger. "Anthropology's Hidden Colonialism: Assistants and Their Ethnographers." *Anthropology Today* 9,2 (Apr. 1993): 13–18.

Sedgwick, Eve Kosofsky. *Between Men: English Literature and Male Homosocial Desire.* New York: Columbia University Press, 1985.

Shaw, Robert. "Samson Occom (1723–1792): His Life and Work as a Hymnist." Master's Thesis, New Orleans Baptist Theological Seminary, 1986.

Sherbrooke, John Coape. Letter revoking commissions of the peace. 28 Oct. 1816. Registrar General. Record Group 68. Vol. 100, p. 325. Library and Archives Canada.

Silko, Leslie Marmon. *Yellow Woman and a Beauty of the Spirit.* New York: Simon, 1996.

Sleeper-Smith, Susan. *Indian Women and French Men: Rethinking Cultural Encounter in the Western Great Lakes.* Amherst, Mass.: University of Massachusetts Press, 2001.

Smith, Elizabeth Oakes. Letter to Jane L. [Johnston] Schoolcraft. 25 Apr. 1842. LC46.

Soetebier, Virginia. *Woman of the Green Glade: The Story of an Ojibway Woman on the Great Lakes Frontier.* Blacksburg, Va.: McDonald & Woodward, 2000.

Spencer, William Robert. *Poems.* London: T. Cadell and W. Davies, 1811.

Spivak, Gayatri Chakravorty. "Can the Subaltern Speak? Speculations on Widow-Sacrifice." *Wedge* 7/8 (Winter/Spring 1985): 120–30.

————. "Three Women's Texts and a Critique of Imperialism." *Critical Inquiry* 12 (Autumn 1985): 243–61.

Steele, Eliza R. Stansbury. Letter from Eliza R. Steele. 2 July 1840. *Summer Journey in the West.* New York: John S. Taylor, 1841.

[Steele, Richard.] *The Spectator.* No. 11, 13 Mar. 1711. Ed. Donald F. Bond. Vol. 1. Oxford: Oxford University Press, 1965. 47–51.

Stevens, Wallace. *The Collected Poems of Wallace Stevens.* New York: Knopf, 1954.

Stevenson, Robert. "The First Native American (American Indian) Published Composer." *Inter-American Music Review* 4, 2 (Spring–Summer 1982): 79–84.

Stillinger, Jack. *Coleridge and Textual Instability: The Multiple Versions of the Major Poems.* New York: Oxford University Press, 1994.

———. *Multiple Authorship and the Myth of Solitary Genius.* New York: Oxford University Press, 1991.

———, ed. *The Poems of John Keats.* Cambridge, Mass.: Harvard University Press, 1978.

———. *The Texts of Keats's Poems.* Cambridge, Mass.: Harvard University Press, 1974.

Stocking, George W., Jr. "The Ethnographer's Magic: Fieldwork in British Anthropology from Tylor to Malinowski." In *The Ethnographer's Magic and Other Essays in the History of Anthropology.* Madison: University of Wisconsin Press, 1992. 12–59.

Stone-Gordon, Tammrah. "Woman of the Sound the Stars Make Rushing Through the Sky: A Literary Biography of Jane Johnston Schoolcraft." Master's Thesis, Michigan State University, 1993.

Stoutamire, Elizabeth Warren. "Jane Johnston Schoolcraft." In Hambleton and Stoutamire, 41–46.

Swann, Brian, ed. *On the Translation of Native American Literatures.* Washington, D.C.: Smithsonian Institution Press, 1992.

———, ed. *Smoothing the Ground: Essays on Native American Oral Literature.* Berkeley: University of California Press, 1983.

Swann, Brian, and Arnold Krupat, eds. *Recovering the Word: Essays on Native American Literature.* Berkeley: University of California Press, 1987.

Tanselle, G. Thomas. "The Editorial Problem of Final Authorial Intention." 1976. In *Textual Criticism and Scholarly Editing.* Charlottesville: University of Virginia Press, 1990. 27–71.

———. "Greg's Theory of Copy-Text and the Editing of American Literature." 1975. In *Selected Studies in Bibliography.* Charlottesville: University of Virginia Press, 1979. 245–307.

———. *A Rationale of Textual Criticism.* Philadelphia: University of Pennsylvania Press, 1989.

Taylor, Ann. "My Mother." *Original Poems for Infant Minds. By Several Young Persons.* 1804. New York: Garland, 1976. 76–78.

Taylor, Bayard. "Mon-da-min; or, the Romance of Maize." *A Book of Romances, Lyrics, and Songs. Boston: Ticknor, Reed and Fields,* 1852. 3–19, 253.

Tedlock, Dennis. *The Spoken Word and the Work of Interpretation.* Philadelphia: University of Pennsylvania Press, 1983.

Thorpe, James. *Principles of Textual Criticism.* San Marino, Calif.: Huntington Library, 1972.

Thwaites, Reuben Gold, ed. *Collections of the State Historical Society of Wisconsin* 19 (1910).

Toelken, Barre. "Life and Death in the Navajo Coyote Tales." Swann and Krupat 388–401.

Toelken, Barre, and Tacheeni Scott. "Poetic Retranslation and the 'Pretty Languages' of Yellowman." In Kroeber, 65–116.

Tomaszewski, Deidre Stevens. *The Johnstons of Sault Ste. Marie.* [Sault Ste. Marie, Mi.?]: n.p., [1992?].

"Treaty with the Chippewa, 1826." In *Indian Affairs: Laws and Treaties*, ed. Charles Kappler. Vol. 2. Washington, D.C.: GPO, 1904. 268–73.

Trowbridge, C. C. Letter to Henry Rowe Schoolcraft. 11 May 1827. LC7.

———. Letter to Henry Rowe Schoolcraft. 6 November 1827. LC38.

———. "With Cass in the Northwest in 1820: The Journal of Charles C. Trowbridge." Ed. Ralph H. Brown. *Minnesota History* 23, 2 (June 1942): 126–48.

Trowbridge, C. C., and anonymous. "Gen. Cass at St. Marie in 1820." *Report and Collections of the State Historical Society of Wisconsin* 5 (1868): 410–16.

Van Kirk, Sylvia. *Many Tender Ties: Women in Fur-Trade Society, 1670–1870.* 1980. Norman: University of Oklahoma Press, 1983.

Walker, Cheryl. *The Nightingale's Burden: Women Poets and American Culture Before 1900.* Bloomington: Indiana University Press, 1982.

Warren, William W. *History of the Ojibway People.* 1885. Rpt., intro. W. Roger Buffalohead. St. Paul: Minnesota Historical Society Press, 1984.

Warrior, Robert. *The People and the Word: Reading Native Nonfiction.* Minneapolis: University of Minnesota Press, 2006.

Wasagunackank, "Dung-Warm Weather." *Ojibwa Texts. Publications of the American Ethnological Society* Vol. 7, part II. Collected by William Jones. Edited by Truman Michelson. New York: G. E. Stechert, 1919. 414-27.

Washburn, Wilcomb E. "Symbol, Utility, and Aesthetics in the Indian Fur Trade." In *Aspects of the Fur Trade: Selected Papers of the 1965 North American Fur Trade Conference.* St. Paul: Minnesota Historical Society, 1967. 50–54.

Weaver, Margaret Curtiss. *The Descendants of John Johnston and Oshaugusco-daywayquay of Sault Ste. Marie, Michigan.* N.p.: n.d. [1991?]

Welter, Barbara. "The Cult of True Womanhood, 1820–1860." *American Quarterly* 18 (Summer 1966): 151–74. Rpt. in *Dimity Convictions: The American Woman in the Nineteenth Century.* Athens: Ohio University Press, 1976. 21–41.

White, Bruce M. "'Give Us a Little Milk': The Social and Cultural Significance of Gift Giving in the Lake Superior Fur Trade." In *Rendezvous: Selected Papers of the Fourth North American Fur Trade Conference, 1981,* ed. Thomas C. Buckley. St. Paul, Minn.: North American Fur Trade Conference, 1984: 185–97.

———. "The Woman Who Married a Beaver: Trade Patterns and Gender Roles in the Ojibwa Fur Trade." *Ethnohistory* 46,1 (Winter 1999): 109–47.

White, Richard. *The Middle Ground: Indians, Empires, and Republics in the Great Lakes Region, 1650–1815.* Cambridge: Cambridge University Press, 1991.

Whiting, Henry. Letter to Henry R. Schoolcraft. 2 June 1829. In *The Territorial Papers of the United States,* vol. 12, *The Territory of Michigan, 1829–1837,* ed. Clarence Edwin Carter. Washington, D.C.: GPO, 1945. 36–37.

———. *Sannillac, a poem.* Notes by Lewis Cass and Henry R. Schoolcraft. Boston: Carter and Babcock, 1831.

Williams, Mentor L., ed. *Schoolcraft's Indian Legends.* East Lansing: Michigan State University Press, 1956.

Woolsey, Melancthon L. Letter to Henry Rowe Schoolcraft. 29 September 1831. LC37.

———. Letter to Jane Johnston Schoolcraft. 5 July 1831. Published in "Sketches of Lake Superior." [By Henry Rowe Schoolcraft.] *Southern Literary Messenger* 2, 3 (February 1836): 166–71.

Zanger, Jules. Introduction. Captain Frederick Marryat. *Diary in America.* Ed. Zanger. Bloomington: Indiana University Press, 1960.

Zeller, Hans. "A New Approach to the Critical Constitution of Literary Texts." *Studies in Bibliography* 28 (1975): 231–64.

Zumwalt, Rosemary. "Henry Rowe Schoolcraft (1793–1864): His Collection and Analysis of the Oral Narratives of American Indians." *Kroeber Anthropological Society Papers* 53–54 (1976): 44–57.

Index

Acknowledgments

I am fortunate in having many people to thank for their encouragement or help with this project. While a few of them may not remember the conversations or assistance that I am grateful for, many of them have gone far out of their way to help. No one named here, of course, is responsible for my oversights and errors.

Among the many people who have helped as I prepared this book, I take great pleasure in thanking and naming Nina Baym, Matti Bunzl, Paula Carrick, Leon Chai, George Cornell, Kathryn Danner and the other patient and helpful people at the Interlibrary Borrowing Office at the University of Illinois at Urbana-Champaign (UIUC) Library, Randy Dills, Alma J. Gottlieb, Janice N. Harrington, Ann Haugo, LeAnne Howe, Frederick Hoxie, Susan E. James of the Bayliss Public Library in Sault Ste. Marie and the Chippewa County Historical Society (who repeatedly went beyond the call of duty to provide expert help), Jenny Marie Johnson of the UIUC Map and Geography Library, Dennis Jones, Suvir Kaul, Jo Kibbee of the UIUC Library Reference Department, Kathleen Kluegel of the UIUC English Library, Donald W. Krummel, Katharine Kyes Leab, Kerry C. Larson, Zachary Lesser, Daniel F. Littlefield, Jr., of the Native American Press Archives in the Sequoyah Research Center at the University of Arkansas, Little Rock, Mary Loeffelholz, Tim Long of the Chicago Historical Society, Trish Loughran, Scott Lyons, Sharon MacLaren of the Chippewa County Historical Society, Mary Mallory of the UIUC Government Documents Library, Robert Markley, Carol P. McConnell, Brian McHale, Peter Mortensen, John D. Nichols, Brian O'Broin, Roberta J. M. Olson of the New-York Historical Society, Anthony Pollock, Isabel Quintana-Wulf, Carter Revard, David B. Ruderman, Siobhan Senier, Siobhan Somerville, Cristina Stanciu, Heidi Stark, Mark Steinberg, Nancy Steinhaus of the Bayliss Public Library in Sault Ste. Marie and the Chippewa County Historical Society, Jack Stillinger, Mary Stuart of the UIUC History, Philosophy, and Newspaper Library, Brook Thomas, David Treuer, Joseph P. Valente, James Vukelich, and David Wright.

D. Anthony Tyeeme Clark, William J. Maxwell, Jr., John McKinn, Naomi Reed, Debbie Reese, Michael Rothberg, and Julia A. Walker read one or another draft of the introduction and made invaluable suggestions; I am deeply grateful for their insight, good sense, and collegiality, and for the collegiality that extends across the Department of English and the Program in American Indian Studies at the UIUC. Marlie P. Wasserman was a continuous source of wisdom and encouragement. Virginia Jackson read the manuscript and offered keen suggestions and encouragement. Arnold Krupat, whom I barely knew before he took an interest in this project, generously read multiple drafts of the manuscript. I am deeply grateful for his feedback and encouragement. Jerome Singerman has been a terrific editor. Dennis E. Baron, former Head of the Department of English at the UIUC, provided extra research funding, and Richard P. Wheeler, also a former Head of the Department of English, with his usual good grace made possible the bulk of the research funds that played a large role in preparing this book and in making it possible to imagine the book in the first place.

Apart from thanking individuals, I also want to thank a general class: librarians. These include librarians and staff at the UIUC Library, the Abraham Lincoln Presidential Library, the Bentley Historical Library at the University of Michigan, the unusually helpful librarians at the Burton Historical Collection at the Detroit Public Library, the Chicago Historical Society, the Clarke Historical Library at Central Michigan University, the Thomas Fisher Rare Book Library at the University of Toronto, Library and Archives Canada, the Library of Congress, the J. M. Longyear Research Library of the Marquette County History Museum, the Minnesota Historical Society Library, the Petersen Center Library at Mackinac State Historic Parks, the River of History Museum in Sault Ste. Marie, the Rosenbach Museum and Library, the Royal Ontario Museum, the Sequoyah Research Center at the University of Arkansas, Little Rock, the U.S. National Archives and Records Administration, and the many other libraries that have assisted through interlibrary loan and correspondence. I have depended immeasurably on the imagination, dedication, perseverance, foresight, professionalism, skill, and just plain smarts of librarians.

Most of all, this book, like all my work that I care about most, is dedicated to Janice N. Harrington, who enlivens everything that this book cherishes and honors.